EQUAL TIME

THE HISTORY OF COMMUNICATION

Robert W. McChesney
and John C. Nerone, editors

*A list of books in the series appears
at the end of this book.*

Equal Time

*Television and the
Civil Rights Movement*

ANIKO BODROGHKOZY

UNIVERSITY OF ILLINOIS PRESS

URBANA, CHICAGO, AND SPRINGFIELD

First Illinois paperback, 2013
© 2012 by the Board of Trustees
of the University of Illinois

∞ This book is printed on acid-free paper.

The author and the publisher would like to acknowledge the generous
publication subsidy provided by the Dean of the College of Arts and
Sciences and the Vice President for Research and Graduate Studies at
the University of Virginia.

Chapter 6 originally appeared in a different version as "Negotiating
Civil Rights in Prime Time: A Production and Reception History
of *East Side/West Side*," in the journal *Television and New Media* 3
(August 2003). An earlier version of chapter 7 was published as "Is
This What You Mean by Color TV: Race, Gender, and Contested
Meanings in NBC's *Julia*," in *Private Screenings: Television and the
Female Consumer,* edited by Lynn Spigel and Denise Mann
(Minneapolis: University of Minnesota Press, 1992). Chapter 8
appeared somewhat differently as "Good Times in Race Relations?
CBS's *Good Times*
and the Legacy of the Civil Rights Movement in 1970s Prime-Time
Television," in the journal *Screen* 44, no. 4 (Winter 2003).

The Library of Congress cataloged the cloth edition as follows:
Bodroghkozy, Aniko
Equal time : television and the civil rights movement / Aniko
Bodroghkozy.
p.   cm. — (The history of communication)
Includes bibliographical references and index.
ISBN 978-0-252-03668-2 (hardcover : alk. paper) —
ISBN 978-0-252-09378-4 (e-book)
1. Television broadcasting—Political aspects—United States.
2. Television broadcasting of news—Political aspects—United States.
3. African Americans on television.
4. Race relations on television.
5. African Americans in television broadcasting—History—20th century.
6. Civil rights movement—United States—History—20th century.
7. Television broadcasting—United States—Influence. I. Title.
PN1992.6.B58   2012
302.23089'96073—dc23   2011032471

PAPERBACK ISBN 978-0-252-07970-2

For Elliot and Aviva

CONTENTS

ACKNOWLEDGMENTS

This book has had a rather long gestation. Its origins date to the early 1990s when, as a graduate student at the University of Wisconsin–Madison, I found myself in the Wisconsin State Historical Society archives foraging through the papers of TV writer-producer Hal Kanter and not finding what I had hoped to find. I was looking for network memos and production files about the creation of *Julia* so that I could write a production history on the development of the series. What I found instead were scripts and audience letters—lots and lots of audience letters. I was not interested in audiences, and I would have abandoned the project had my advisor Lynn Spigel not urged me to go back to the archive and take a look at those letters. I took her advice. What resulted was a published article that got reprinted a number of times and eventually formed the nucleus for this book. So, first of all, a big thanks to Lynn Spigel for urging me on and helping to set me on my scholarly path.

I thank the many archivists and archives that made this work possible. Maxine Fleckner Ducey of the Center for Film and Theater Research and all the other archivists at Madison have made my numerous trips gratifying as well as productive. Thanks also to the staff of the Division of Motion Pictures, Broadcasting and Recorded Sound at the Library of Congress. There is no more congenial place to spend hours and hours in front of a Steenbeck machine. I am also grateful to the staff of the American Heritage Center at the University of Wyoming for sending me papers from the Allan Manings Collection so that I would not have to travel to Laramie to see them. Finally, many thanks to CBS News for graciously letting me into their archive and treating me so well. Wyatt Andrews, a CBS senior correspondent (but more important, a University of Virginia alum), made it all possible for this UVa faculty member. Wahoowa! Head of the CBS News Archive, Dan DiPierro, opened the doors for me, and Tony Mordente and Roy Carubio made my time on West 57th Street very pleasant. But most of all, I want to thank Laura Galli who did research for me and took time away from her real job assisting CBS producers and reporters to ferret out materials for me from the archive's idiosyncratic cataloging system.

Friends and colleagues have been enormously encouraging over the long years this book has been in process and have provided much-needed support when I encountered complications. I particularly want to acknowledge my friend and cheerleader of many years, Henry Jenkins, who read a revision of this work and provided just the feedback I needed at a difficult time.

Thanks also to the following friends and colleagues who have helped over the years: Horace Newcomb, Michele Hilmes, Susan J. Douglas, Jan Levine Thal, Moya Luckett, Steven Classen, Norma Coates, Sasha Torres, Jan Hadlaw, and numerous colleagues and listeners who have provided feedback when I presented portions of this work at conferences, symposia, and panels over the years.

Particular thanks go to the "Becoming Alabama" symposium organizers at Auburn University, Jay Lamar and Mary Helen Brown, as well as Susan Brinson, for bringing me to the cradle of the civil rights movement to talk about Alabamians' response to television coverage of the Selma campaign. They made it possible for me to make my pilgrimage to Selma and to drive down Highway 80. I will never forget how moving it was to put my own feet on the Edmund Pettus Bridge. Thanks to the National Voting Rights Museum at the foot of the bridge and especially to Selma campaign veteran, Annie Pearl Avery, who guided me through the museum and made it all come alive.

At the University of Virginia I have been blessed with the most collegial and wonderful colleagues in the Department of Media Studies. I feel very lucky to be part of this intellectual community of supportive, warm, and nurturing fellow scholars. Grateful thanks to my chair, Andrea Press, and my comrades in arms, Bruce Williams, Siva Vaidhyanathan, Hector Amaya, and Jennifer Petersen. But it is our fabulous Media Studies majors who make the work most fulfilling. I have learned so much from them, and their insights have helped inform my own work throughout this project.

The University of Virginia has also been generous in supporting the travel and research costs of a project that requires so much archival investigation. The Office of the Dean for Arts and Sciences has provided me with a number of grants over the years, for which I am very thankful.

I also want to thank Robert McChesney for recommending this book for the History of Communication series at the University of Illinois Press. It has been a great experience for me working with UIP and in particular having Willis Goth Regier shepherd my book through the publication process. Thanks also to Tad Ringo and Julie Gay for their help in the production process.

Finally, my greatest debt of gratitude goes to my husband, Elliot Majerczyk, who has lived with this book for many years, and to my daughter Aviva. She does not remember a time when I was not working on this book. Elliot put all the illustrations together on an insanely tight deadline and also helped me to untangle needlessly convoluted sentences. For all they have put up with over the years, this book is dedicated to Elliot and Aviva, with love.

Introduction

Montgomery, Alabama, March 17, 1965. The black voting rights campaign led by Dr. Martin Luther King Jr. was into its third month of marches and protest fifty miles east in the small city of Selma. On this day a group of black and white college students accompanied by priests and rabbis had decided to bring the movement's demands to the state capitol. Perhaps because there were so many white youths in the demonstration, television news reporters were out in force.

Suddenly, the peaceful march filled with "freedom songs" turned ugly. Out of nowhere a sheriff's posse on horseback and brandishing canes, whips, clubs, and lariats charged into the group of marchers, trampling students under horses' hooves, leaving marchers beaten, dazed, and bloody. On the TV news that night, audiences saw a poignant shot of a young black man in bib overalls and a rabbi cradling a limp young black woman. The man in the bib overalls pleaded, "Hey, can we get a doctor!"[1]

The glaring light of television: beating of student marchers by sheriff's posse makes for poignant TV images.

The next day, King declared before marchers protesting the students' beating—and to the assembled crush of news media: "We are here to say to the white men that we no longer will let them use clubs on us in the dark corners. We're going to make them do it in the glaring light of television."[2]

Television magazine, a broadcast industry journal, excerpted the speech, alongside a column by the *New York Times*' James Reston extolling the significance of modern communication such as television to the Selma story and to politics more generally. According to Reston, "We are told by our philosophers and sociologists that our machines are enslaving and debasing us, but in this historical battle over voting rights, these very machines are proving to be powerful instruments for equality and justice."[3]

The journal and its industry readers must have been pleased to find voices like this acknowledging the important role the medium played in the ongoing movement for black enfranchisement, desegregation, and equality. Here was King, the man television and other media organs had long since anointed as *the* movement spokesman, openly crediting television's role. It was a rare admission. King and other civil rights organizers seldom acknowledged their own self-conscious use of the mass media, especially the new, highly visual medium of television, with its penchant for dramatic imagery of opposing forces and narratives of melodramatic good-versus-evil clarity.[4]

Civil Rights in the "Glaring Light of Television"

What did it mean for the civil rights movement when its activities, goals, and concerns were captured in the "glaring light of television"? What did it mean for television, still a novel form of news and entertainment during key years of this social change struggle? How would this new form of broadcast journalism handle a largely unprecedented grassroots movement for black social and political empowerment? For television news, the civil rights issue was its first major ongoing domestic story, second only to the Cold War. For the entertainment part of the industry (certainly the most important aspect of the business), how would prime time handle questions of race relations in its comedies and dramas when those questions could no longer be ignored? In a business all about delivering up the larger share of national audiences to advertisers and offending as few as possible, how would prime-time entertainment represent a rapidly shifting consensus on what "blackness" and "whiteness" meant and how they now fit together—or did not? How to provide representations that acknowledged what was happening on the streets and in the halls of Congress without offending or angering audiences whose sensibilities might not be keeping up with all the change blowin' in the wind?

And what about those audiences? Television during the civil rights era was the "massest" of mass media; by the early 1960s, 92 percent of the U.S. households had at least one television set.[5] Network television by the 1960s may have been a national medium that constructed audiences as undifferentiated bulk units, but perhaps not surprisingly, those audiences tended to respond with localized reactions based on social factors such as geographical place as well as race, class, gender, and age. News and entertainment programming in the 1960s on race issues encouraged audiences to engage self-reflexively with "Northern" and "Southern" categories of regional identity, as well as categories of "blackness" and "whiteness." For many Americans, television became a key site on which they grappled with the changes fomented by the civil rights movement. Television brought the nonviolent campaigns of the Jim Crow South to viewers in all parts of the country. Television challenged viewers on ideals of color-blindness. Television brought black people, imaginatively at least, into white people's living rooms. The people in those living rooms, whether they lived in the urban North or the more rural South, had to come to terms with these television images. And what about television executives, producers, and creative personnel? As decision makers and gatekeepers, how did they determine what their industry could and could not do in responding to the revolution in race relations?

Equal Time explores the crucial role American network television played during the civil rights revolution in reconfiguring a new "common sense" about race relations. Conventional wisdom has it that network television, at least in its news divisions, functioned as an "instrument of the revolution" wielded by civil rights activists to broadcast their messages, demands, and actions to a sympathetic, nationwide audience.[6] Civil rights histories often note the crucial presence of television cameras with the assumption that the resulting news reports carried unmediated discourses and imagery serving the political goals of the movement. An accompanying assumption is that TV viewers received and decoded the televised material in the appropriate way, leading the American public to embrace those movement goals.[7] Memoirs by television news personnel tend to amplify this conventional wisdom for all the obvious self-serving and aggrandizing reasons.[8] A more nuanced argument along these lines suggests that the networks and the movement made "common cause" because both shared a desire for a national consensus on race, if not for the same reasons (the networks needed a more ideologically unified audience to efficiently sell those audiences to advertisers).[9] In entertainment television, the assumption is that viewers had the choice of either no images at all of blacks or minstrelsy throwbacks or, for a short period during a "golden age" in the 1960s, a moment of non-stereotyped, respectable, middle-class blacks showing the networks' provisional alliance with the goals of the integrationist civil rights movement.[10]

Equal Time does not set out to demolish these assumptions and pieces of conventional wisdom but rather to complicate the picture of the relationship among the civil rights movement, television, audiences, and partisans on either side of the black empowerment struggle. By closely examining key news and entertainment texts of the era that grappled with questions of race relations, their production contexts, and, crucially, their reception among various audience segments, we can begin to chart with more precision how television producers, audiences, and activists mediated and made sense of what was going on while that "glaring light" shone so intensely. What we find is a more ambivalent place for television in the civil rights revolution. Network television provisionally embraced integrationist civil rights, as long as whiteness and white people (at least non-Southern and nonrural) were neither marginalized nor discomforted, and as long as white political elites in Washington remained supportive.

Weaving through the stories told both by news coverage and prime time entertainment, *Equal Time* explores the recurring theme that America's racial story was one of color-blind equality grounded on a vision of "black and white together." African Americans may have been the key drivers of the revolution in race politics, but network television insisted on situating whites, if not at the very center of the narrative, then right alongside worthy black "civil rights subjects." Herman Gray coined this term to argue that television in the United States, in its cultural work of reconstructing and remembering the civil rights era, produced as a "necessary, cultural trope," a very particular representation of blackness—middle class, hard working, successful, willing to sacrifice, individualized—as the worthy beneficiary of the civil rights movement. This "civil rights subject" contrasted favorably in televisual discourse with the poor, disenfranchised segments of the black community who did not fit with the civil rights narrative of achieved equality.[11] Gray developed this concept to make sense of post-1970s black representations on television, particularly within the context of the Reagan-Bush era, such as *The Cosby Show*'s Huxtable family. However, this trope was very much in evidence on network television in the civil rights years as well. In envisioning equality, news and entertainment television gave viewers a representation of blackness that at one point went by the label "white Negro"—a particularly pointed trope signifying "black and white together." Network television premised equality on a largely white definition whereby African Americans were ready for equal time to the extent that their representations conformed to whitened standards of middle-class and professional respectability.

So, news documentaries gave viewers a black Mississippian deemed illiterate and thus ineligible to vote but who happened to be a member of the National Science Foundation and a master's candidate at Cornell University.[12] Viewers met James Meredith as he attempted to integrate the University of Mississippi, himself a Korean War veteran who emphatically was not an activist with the NAACP or any other "militant" organization.[13] More generally, TV viewers typically saw civil rights marchers as mute but dignified and orderly figures in crisp business attire as they petitioned for integration and voting rights.[14] In entertainment programming, viewers saw the same respectable and middle-class figures effortlessly integrating into white milieus, held back only by residual white prejudice:

a well-spoken and educated black family attempting to integrate an all-white Long Island suburb, an elegant black nurse and her precocious young son living a largely color-blind lifestyle in Los Angeles.[15] Network television tried to make it as easy as possible to embrace these "civil rights subjects."

But while the proliferation of these representations on network television served the interests of a particular race politics around civil rights and voting rights legislation at the federal level, and while activists attempted to influence how their media images were broadcast to the nation, their ability to bend the medium to their needs was constrained by the medium's preoccupation with satisfying its predominant white audiences, affiliated stations, and national advertisers. Television's embrace of the civil rights movement was provisional. Even the most "moderate" and camera-ready black activist groups and individuals sometimes lost the battle over televisual representation.

And in the struggle over entertainment imagery, the situation became particularly fraught once the networks, by the mid-1960s, began to experiment with "integrating" prime time. Black and white advocates for black advancement clashed heatedly over the politics of black representation. Phillip Brian Harper maps out the conflict as one between "mimetic" versus "simulacral" realism: should popular-culture imagery of African Americans reflect the social realities that large numbers of black people experienced, thus providing seemingly "relevant" and "authentic" representations that may be devoid of uplift, or should such imagery emphasize more aspirational images of exemplary "Super Negroes" whose accomplishments and successes could serve to uplift the race?[16] In an era of rapid change and social turbulence, these questions generated heated intensity.

Civil rights activists and supporters were not the only viewers passionately engaged with the politics of media representation; Southern white segregationists were also keenly aware of the glaring light of television. In fact, these Southerners were notably media-savvy about how television functioned when the medium trained its lenses on them and their communities.[17] And although network television would never show outright sympathy to the segregationist cause, in the medium's perpetual attempt to place whiteness at the center, news programming would go out of its way to search for Southern white "moderates" to celebrate.[18]

Both civil rights activists and Southern segregationists understood the political power of television, and both were interested in using this new instrument to speak to national (read: non-Southern) audiences. The former were clearly more successful in negotiating with the medium, but network television was not interested in doing the bidding of even the most moderate of civil rights groups, nor was television bent on always demonizing and dismissing the segregationist position. If a civil rights group could be labeled "militant"—and we will see NBC's Chet Huntley so label the NAACP in 1959—then that group could be delegitimated as a political player as segregationists cheered and welcomed Huntley in as potentially one of their own.

Ultimately, television news wanted to tell a story of progress through moderation and the legislative and legal process, even though a celebration of moderation deprived the medium of its very oxygen: images of conflict, violent clashes,
dramatic narratives of opposing passions.[19] In entertainment programming, prime
time typically celebrated racial moderation achieved.

The civil rights movement, more often than not, managed to negotiate the
"moderate" frame that network television news wanted to use in figuring its "civil
rights subjects." Martin Luther King's Southern Christian Leadership Conference
(SCLC), in particular, understood the semiotics of the medium. However, some
segregationists did as well. Sheriff Laurie Pritchett managed to defeat King and
the SCLC's attempt to desegregate his town of Albany, Georgia, by presenting
himself to TV cameras as a nonviolent white moderate—which, in fact, he was
not. More generally, however, white segregationists had a tough time occupying
the position of "moderate," and over and over again they railed at television's
representation of civil rights demonstrators and leaders, King in particular, as
"moderate." Southern segregationists knew that King and the movement were
not "moderates," and they distrusted television profoundly for what they saw
as fundamental misrepresentations of the racial situation in the South: for the
medium's lack of "equal time" for their side, for being little more than electronic
modern carpetbaggers publicizing and propagandizing a second Reconstruction
on a beleaguered and misunderstood region.[20]

Conventional wisdom has it that the modern civil rights movement would have
been impossible without the presence of network television and its ability to bring
the images of Southern racial brutality almost instantly and with its vivid pictures
to a nationwide—and almost as important—a worldwide audience. While this
is undoubtedly true, mixed into this truism at times is a mystification of television as a medium that tends to reify the technology *as* technology: television as
medium created social change.

For instance, in her exploration of how the "culture of segregation" evolved,
historian Grace Hale explores the challenge to segregation in the 1950s, particularly with the Emmett Till lynching case, by arguing that television was "less
mediated" than other forms of mass communication, such as film, in making
"visible [the] civil rights activists' sense of the difference between the South and
the rest of the nation."[21] She suggests that "television shaped a new collective out
of many of its viewers."[22] This technological determinism separates the medium
from the larger field of forces that shapes it, the professionals who work within
it, the diversified audiences who engage with it, and the texts that are produced
and received within specific social contexts. Television was, indeed, a significant
player in the civil rights era, but exalting it as a unique instrument of truth and
light, as do some observers of the civil rights era, does not really help us understand how television functioned as a meaning-making apparatus.

Hale's work, however, does provide a useful way to fit television into a larger
history of modernity and consumer culture and their challenges to a Southern

race relations formerly grounded on agricultural economies and on slavery-based relations of power. Hale shows how the post-Reconstruction development of national commercial markets, advertising, chain-store shopping—and, in particular, railroads—broke down and crossed what had been "personalized local relations of class and racial authority."[23] De jure segregation arose, in part, as a means to insist on the marking of racialized spaces "for white" and "for colored" in an increasingly modern and urbanizing geography of anonymity. De jure segregation insisted on marking "for colored" spaces as inferior in the face of a rapidly developing black middle class eager to partake of national consumer culture with its threat of fostering social equality based on access to material goods produced for an undifferentiated national market. Train travel served as a key site of struggle over race and region as the trains carried not only people to and from the urban North to the rural South but also transported consumer culture, which "spread a new world of goods, a revolution in representation, and an associated proliferation of identities across the nation."[24] Interstate travel became a central site of struggle because this institution of modernity created a national market; it threatened regional sensibilities, power structures, and sense making if they conflicted with those in the national market.

Network television, as the newest manifestation of modernity and consumer culture extending its lines into the deepest reaches of the South fifty-some years after the railroads, did much the same thing. Network television both created national audiences and needed to appeal to such audiences in order to sell their attention to national advertisers. Southern segregationists had developed tactics to deal with the nationalizing and standardizing of interstate travel by trying to build geographies of racial difference that communicated local assumptions about whiteness and blackness. Television, in its representations of race and race struggle, presented Southerners with a new technology of modernism that came from "outside," and it too would become a central terrain of struggle over assumptions about whiteness and blackness. Television, therefore, was not unique. It did not suddenly penetrate a South that had previously been walled off from "Northern" images, ideas, and ideology. Network television functioned as a component in a longer history of the South's fraught engagement with mass culture, market capitalism, and urban modernity.

An Overview

Equal Time is divided into two sections, the first on network news coverage in the period between 1957 and 1965 and a second section on prime-time entertainment programming. The latter explores three case studies of programming that took a variety of approaches to representing race relations: from gritty, socially relevant drama in 1963 to light-hearted family comedy in 1968 to more gritty socially relevant comedy in the post–civil rights era in 1974. We begin our exploration, however, by examining entertainment television in the immediate pre–civil rights period, focusing on *The Beulah Show*. This may seem like an odd place to start an examination of television in the civil rights era, but *Beulah* displays television's first attempt to imagine the "black and white together" theme that so animates televisual representations of race relations as we move more firmly into the civil rights years. *Beulah* did not, of course, give viewers a concept of black and white on equal terms. However, the show did not trade in merely the conventional old minstrel-based stereotypes. Network television in its earliest days, particularly before its coaxial cables linked up the Deep South and the other more rural parts of the country into a nationwide web, was seen as a potentially more progressive force among the major media. Responding to the currents gathering force in the post–World War II years pushing for black equal opportunity, television executives circulated rhetoric suggesting that television might be a more welcoming place for a new generation of African Americans. The furor around *Amos 'n' Andy* may have indicated something else, but the huge amount of attention given that show and the controversy surrounding it has diverted attention from explorations of the more "integrated" world of *The Beulah Show* and questions about of how pre–civil rights television attempted to figure the relationship between whites and blacks in domestic space.

Amos 'n' Andy along with *Beulah* (to a lesser extent) did result in high-profile, organized protest by blacks, particularly through the NAACP. In this period the politics of representation garnered significant attention in the political work of black organizations, whether the NAACP or the national black press. This concern with media imagery dissipates as we move into the key years of civil rights activism and campaigning. Clearly, the black press and civil rights groups were less concerned with the politics of media representation when issues of desegregation, voting rights, and equal opportunity assumed center stage.[25] While segregationists deconstructed their televisual representations and railed against network television as a propagandizing medium disseminating false material about the South to a national audience, blacks tended to remain largely silent on how television portrayed the freedom struggle. So long as television imagery was not a "problem" for the movement, the medium *as* a medium tended to become invisible. This changes in the later 1960s when television as a representational technology implicated in the status of African Americans again becomes an animating issue for black commentators, critics, and viewers. It happens as the civil rights movement fragments and loses much of its political and organizational force as attention moves North and as nonviolence as a governing philosophy and strategy withers.

Part 1 opens with an examination of the recurring themes that animate network news documentaries on the civil rights story, most of which aired in prime time, from the late 1950s to 1962. These prestige documentaries, produced to show the networks' commitment to their public service requirements and also to demonstrate that television could be a serious journalistic institution, display a seriousness and soberness in covering the medium's first ongoing domestic story of major importance. Rather than emphasize dramatic confrontation, flamboyant and quotable spokesmen, or extreme polarization of positions, these news programs searched for a moderate middle, even when it was rather hard to find. Over and over again network news elevated Southern white moderates, as reporters and news producers searched for some figures of consensus. Paired with these white moderates, network news programs gave viewers not Southern black civil rights activists working within collective social and political movements to demand their rights, but rather individualized, often mute, worthy black victims of discrimination and brutality. In general, television news was uneasy, if not hostile, to black demonstrators and activists acting as part of social change campaigns, even if nonviolently.

Chapter 3 shifts attention from textual analysis to production and reception as we look at two high profile news programs reported by two of the medium's most respected and acclaimed correspondents: Chet Huntley at NBC and Howard K. Smith at CBS. In both cases, the newsmen attempted to editorialize about race relations and desegregation in the Deep South, and in both cases their resulting news broadcasts generated heated controversy and protest. In the former case, when Huntley editorialized that the NAACP should step out of the school desegregation battle because of its "militancy," we will see how the organization and its supporters geared up to take on the network and its star reporter. Unfortunately, the NAACP attempted to navigate image politics at a moment when it found itself under rather hostile attack in a medium that supposedly was on its side. We will also see how segregationists responded with surprised delight. Paired with this news report is Howard K. Smith's reporting from Birmingham, Alabama, in an attempt by CBS to report in a "fair and balanced" way about the race relations in that most segregated of Southern cities. Smith's attempt to editorialize unstintingly about the evils of segregationist violence and those who tolerate it resulted in far harsher treatment to Smith than resulted from Huntley's castigating of the NAACP. We will also explore the wholly undelighted response from whites in Birmingham about the representation of themselves and their city that Americans around the country (but particularly "Northerners") saw. In particular we will explore the extreme media self-reflexivity among white segregationists grappling with their mass-mediated image.

Chapter 4 explores the way the networks handled the televising of the March on Washington, which all three networks broadcast live during the day on August 28, 1963. Presented to the viewing public as a celebratory and ceremonial "media event" as defined by media studies scholars Elihu Katz and Daniel Dayan, we will explore how the march functioned as a paean of "black and white together," as the networks invited viewers to share in a utopian taste of achieved equality.

Chapter 5 rounds out our examination of news coverage by exploring in depth television's reporting of the most crucial and momentous of the Southern non-

s: the Selma campaign for voting rights that led directly to the
Voting Rights Act. If the presence of television cameras ever
for successful political change, their presence on the Edmund
nday March 7, 1965, did. Those cameras captured the beating,
brutalizing of marchers by Alabama troopers and sheriff's posse men
as the procession of voting rights demonstrators attempted to march to Montgomery. The uproar generated by that footage brought the civil rights movement more
support, volunteers, and moral clout than it could have dreamed of in helping
speed the implementation of rigorous voting rights legislation. But the famous
Pettus Bridge footage needs to be contextualized with the rest of the coverage
that viewers would have seen night after night as the Selma campaign developed
over the span of three months. This chapter examines how the *CBS Evening News
with Walter Cronkite* presented the Selma campaign as an ongoing nightly news
story. We will see the recurrence of familiar themes of mostly mute, worthy black
victims, a celebration of "black and white together," and a frequent unease with
activist, marching, demonstrating black bodies—particularly when those bodies
were young. We will also examine in depth the response of white Selmians in the
"glaring light of television." As with Birmingham's whites in chapter 3, we will see
extreme self-reflexivity about television as a medium, along with anxieties about
how television was challenging a previously naturalized Southern worldview. By
examining the reception practices of ordinary white Selmians and their press
commentators and editors, we get a sense of just how revolutionary, dislocating,
and shattering television imagery of the movement for black empowerment was
for these white Southerners.

Part 2 shifts the focus from news to entertainment, but some of the key themes
we see in news coverage continue. Until the mid-1960s, it was rare for viewers
to see blacks in entertainment programming. This set up a bizarre disjunction
between news programming, which focused increasing attention on the Southern
black struggle, and fictional shows that presented mostly all-white worlds. This
situation began to change slowly, initially with a spate of "socially relevant" programming that television historian Mary Ann Watson has dubbed "New Frontier
character dramas" for their channeling of the Kennedy administration's service-
to-society ideals. Shows like *The Defenders, Mr. Novak, Dr. Kildare,* and *East Side/
West Side,* which we examine in chapter 6, all occasionally explored themes of
race relations and presented viewers with African American characters. But the
networks were not quite ready to break the prime-time color line until 1965, with
the international espionage series, *I Spy,* which co-starred Bill Cosby in a mostly
dramatic role, and then *Julia* in 1968, subject of chapter 7, in which Diahann
Carroll assumed star billing of her gentle, family-oriented comedy. Beginning
in the mid-1960s, ensemble-style programs also began featuring a token black as
part of the team—from Communications Officer Uhura in *Star Trek* to Corporal
Kinchloe in *Hogan's Heroes* to Greg Morris's Barney Collier in *Mission: Impossible.*

All these "integrated" shows had one thing in common: they did not take place in the American South. Visions of "black and white together" could be displaced into the distant future of the twenty-third century or into the immediate past of an alarmingly livable German prisoner-of-war-camp in World War II or, in the case of *I Spy,* into cold war hot spots around the globe.[26] However, prime time's South—Mayberry or Hooterville remained thoroughly segregated. In fact, Jim Crow worked so well for these towns that the bumbling but gentle and good-humored white folks who lived there never seemed to encounter black people at all. It was much the same with TV westerns. As Alan Nadel has shown, viewers engaged with thoroughly whitewashed landscapes. In *Bonanza,* that quintessential western of the era, "the estate that exemplified the American Dream, materially, politically, and theologically, came to be in a territory virtually devoid of blacks that was aligned with neither slavery nor abolition."[27] Network news told viewers that the center of social change and turmoil around race relations resided in the South; entertainment eschewed race entirely in its imagined Southern locales so as not to discomfort white viewers at all. Nadel observes, "The fictional mode of these Westerns allowed far more latitude in representing the South favorably than, for example, news footage of federal marshals escorting children to school amid mobs of angry white protestors. . . . [P]rime-time programming inverted the news/drama relationship so that the news coverage . . . could be seen as the anomaly, no more typifying normal American life than a tornado typified normal American weather."[28]

Since network television wanted to tell a story of moderate racial progress, celebrating the possibility of color blindness and equality based on white norms, situating such narratives in the South could not be particularly convincing. But, as we will see with our three case studies of entertainment programming dealing with race relations in Northern and West Coast urban locales, the production, reception, and representational issues remained explosive.

We start in chapter 6 with *East Side/West Side,* a 1963–64 CBS series about a white social worker attempting to right the urban wrongs of greater New York City. We examine this embattled but acclaimed series' two most famous episodes dealing with race matters in the urban North: one on deplorable ghetto housing conditions and another on suburban racist "blockbusting" tactics. Both episodes were remarkably prescient about issues that would animate racial struggles when the nation's attention turned from the South to the vicissitudes of the Northern inner-city ghetto—and yet, as we will see with reception practices, viewers often framed their meaning making of these episodes as if the narratives were really about the civil rights struggles in the South. We will also examine another recurring theme in "equal time television": the attempt to situate whites and whiteness at the center. *East Side/West Side,* however, has a difficult time navigating the sign of whiteness. Our social worker hero trying to ameliorate racial crises was typically an "impotent hero" unable to solve the social woes he encountered in order to give viewers a narrative closure of achieved equality. As a realist drama of social problems, the series was thus out of step with the story that television really wanted to tell.

With NBC's *Julia,* subject of chapter 7, we will see precisely the story of color-blind equality that the medium preferred to pursue. Along with *I Spy, Julia* is the most significant entertainment show of the civil rights years—the network's showcase for how prime time could fully welcome the Negro into the living rooms of the nation. Unlike the Bill Cosby spy series, *Julia* presented viewers with whites only as supporting characters; widowed nurse Julia and her precocious six-year-old son, Corey, occupied the narrative center. But even as network television finally starred an African American successfully in an ongoing series for the first time since *Beulah* and *Amos 'n' Andy* left the air in 1953, the politics of representation again became problematic. Series creator Hal Kanter attempted to construct a thoroughly innocuous sitcom touching on race and "prejudice" with only the lightest hand. However, in 1968, the year of the series' high-profile premier, the image *Julia* provided viewers with could only clash uncomfortably with dominant news imagery of exploding ghettos, Black Panthers and other non-nonviolent militants, and the generalized chaos and upheaval characterizing that most searing of periods. *Julia* was to be both a self-conscious refutation of *Beulah* and *Amos 'n' Andy* and a fictional vision of the "black and white together" utopia promised in the networks' March on Washington coverage. Many white viewers embraced it as such, celebrating its portrayals of Negroes who were "just like us"—with whiteness as the unexamined norm of definition. But viewers tended to be quite self-conscious about race, both whiteness and blackness, and they used the series to work through what race and race relations meant within the context of both the integrationist civil rights movement and the contemporary turbulence of Black Power and Northern urban uprisings. Black viewers, in particular, struggled with the show and strategies by which they could take ownership of a representation so clearly produced by whites.

Finally, in chapter 8, we turn to an example of the spate of ghetto-situated black sitcoms of the 1970s to explore the legacy of the civil rights movement at a moment when prime time was seemingly awash with highly rated programs starring black performers—from comedies like *Sanford and Son* and *The Jeffersons* to variety shows like *The Flip Wilson Show* to the mini-series phenomenon *Roots.* If *Julia* was to some extent an "answer" to *Beulah* and *Amos 'n' Andy* as an attempt to substitute a "positive image" of black middle-class achievement and successful integration into the white world, *Good Times* "answered" the vehement criticisms about *Julia.* To return to Harper's distinction between "mimetic" and "simulacral" images: *Julia* gave viewers a simulacral "Super Negro" to inspire blacks and comfort whites; the Evans family, living in a graffiti-filled Chicago housing project, presented a more "realistic" image of the challenges, struggles, and poverty that many blacks actually encountered in their daily lives. If black viewers were encouraged to aspire to live like Julia, they could, conversely, iden-tify with and find personally relevant the lives of the Evanses. If *Julia* mostly avoided grappling with social and political issues around race, *Good Times*, a sitcom in Norman Lear's stable of "socially relevant" hits, pointedly addressed hot-button issues like school busing, teen pregnancy, and street gangs. *East Side/ West Side*, a decade earlier, had explored many of the same urban problems but, as Lear, the 1970s television producer-extraordinaire, discovered with hits like *All in the Family*, audiences were much more likely to embrace entertainment programming that dealt with such subject matter within the context of com-edy.[29] *Good Times* is a particularly useful case study to examine as a television legacy of the civil rights movement in part because it was created by two African Americans and in part because it attempted to respond to previous representa-tions. Yet representational politics became particularly heated over this program in ways that echo protests of the *Amos 'n' Andy* days when Jimmie Walker's J.J., the family's elder son, developed into a sensation with audiences at least partly because of his minstrelsy-inspired comic antics.

Black and White Reception

A central concern for this project is how audiences, Northern and Southern, black and white, responded to the representations of race and changing defini-tions of race relations under the impact of the civil rights movement. But when we speak of television audiences, what are we actually talking about? When we speak of audiences in the past responding to an activity as seemingly ephemeral as television viewing, how can we talk about such audiences at all?

Media scholars and researchers have been preoccupied with trying to under-stand the impact of media on audiences since the rise of cinema and radio broad-casting in the 1920s. The advent of television certainly intensified these concerns. Cultural studies approaches that are grounded in the work of the Birmingham School and particularly the scholarship of Stuart Hall and David Morley provided crucial innovations in conceptualizing audiences as meaning makers who nego-tiate locally relevant meanings based on sets of discourses both available to the reader and also available to be activated in the text. As Morley argued, "The mean-ings of the text will be constructed differently according to the discourses (know-legdes, prejudices, resistances, etc.) brought to bear on the text by the reader, and the crucial factor in the encounter of audience/subject and text will be the range of discourses at the disposal of the audience."[30] In Stuart Hall's original formula-tion, audiences could adopt reading strategies either in basic agreement with the meanings, perspective, and ideological positions encoded by the text's producer, in stark opposition and resistance to the encoded meaning, or, as Fiske suggests is the most widespread practice, audiences could adopt negotiated stances, accepting some of the positions offered by the texts while rejecting or ignoring others. This general approach to studying television audiences has served as a foundational logic for the study of media reception practices within the humanistic tradition for close to thirty years. It is assumed that audiences are in fact active makers of meaning rather than passive vehicles to be filled up with meanings imposed on them by media texts and their producers. And, more important, it is assumed that it *matters* what audiences do with media texts, whether it is producing localized pleasures or a sense of community in difference, for instance.[31]

The literature in media and television studies is replete with audience reception analyses in which the audiences studied are contemporary. Media ethnography, unfortunately, is not of much use to the historian. A recent book-length historical survey of media reception studies has nothing to say regarding historical reception studies beyond a discussion about memory.[32] But unlike Steven Classen's book *Watching Jim Crow* on the civil rights movement in Jackson, Mississippi, and WLBT-TV, which relies on participants' memories of television in that period, *Equal Time* does not use oral histories to reconstruct how viewers made sense of what they were watching in the civil rights years. Television historian Lynn Spigel points to the dilemma faced by the researcher who wants to uncover the reception context around television in the past: "Routine events such as television viewing are part of the often invisible history of everyday life, a history that was not recorded by the people who lived it at the time. In order to understand such historical processes, it is necessary to examine unconventional sources, sources that tell us something—however partial—about the ephemeral qualities of daily experiences."[33]

Most television viewers did not record their responses to what they were viewing and thus leave a documentary record for historians. But some did. And some of those responses, typically letters written to program producers or networks, have ended up in the collected papers of those producers. In other instances, letters ended up published in newspapers. *Equal Time* relies heavily on such documents in its attempt to make sense of how variously situated Americans, using their engagement with television, grappled with racial change during a turbulent era.

But what do letters to the producers of *East Side/West Side, Julia*, and *Good Times* or to journalists like Chet Huntley or to newspapers like the Selma *Times-Journal* or the Birmingham *News* ultimately tell us? Letter writers are always a more motivated group of viewers who clearly feel particularly called upon to voice their sentiments than the general public. To quantitatively oriented social scientists, this documentary evidence may lack in statistical certitude. To the historian, however, who always struggles with an incomplete record, a jigsaw puzzle that will surely have many, many missing pieces, an embrace of partiality is inevitable. Audience letters, wherever one finds them, are a form of evidence that allows us to conjecture about the larger whole to which we will never have access.[34]

Another set of jigsaw pieces we can use to fill in the reception terrain is critical commentary in the press, particularly African American newspapers and, in specific instances, white Alabama newspapers—and, more generally, the mainstream popular press. Media coverage and opinion is useful for a variety of reasons. Popular press materials can set up a dialogical relationship with their readers, as Spigel points out, in order to actively engage them in thinking through a period of change.[35] In the case of the black press and the white segregationist press, we can uncover particular dominant, emergent, and residual discourses to help us track a social group's structure of feeling through the recurring debates and perspectives that crop up.[36] Particularly in the case of African American reception strategies, the discourses in the black press are often the only clues we have to help reconstruct how blacks made sense of the televising of their freedom movement. Other documents, such as letters, are few and far between, although we will see some of these materials in the NAACP papers, as supporters responded to TV coverage that specifically concerned that organization. Inevitably, the discourses of educated and middle-class African Americans, a relatively small segment of the black community in this period, will be given more weight. Nevertheless, used together and analyzed symptomatically, letters and press commentary provide us with a rich, complex, and eye-opening view of how ordinary Americans of both races and from various corners of the country grappled with and processed the vast changes that literally transformed their country under their very eyes.

CHAPTER 1

Propaganda Tool for Racial Progress?

In June 1950, *Ebony* magazine had good news for its African American readers about television: the new medium looked to be a strong ally to the black community in its struggle for racial equality and opportunity. Pointing out the popularity and frequency of black performers on television programming, *Ebony* argued this was "a sure sign that television is free of racial barriers. Negro footlight favorites are cast in every conceivable type of TV act—musical, dramatic, comedy. Yet rarely have they had to stoop to the Uncle Tom pattern which is usually the Negro thespian's lot on radio shows and in Hollywood movies."[1] The magazine touted for the coming fall season two new "top rate" shows that would feature black talent: *Amos 'n' Andy* and *Beulah*.

Ed Sullivan, "New York columnist and CBS-TV showman," gave *Ebony* readers his own rosy view of television and racial progress: "Television not only is just what the doctor ordered for Negro performers; television subtly has supplied ten-league boots to the Negro in his fight to win what the Constitution of this country guarantees as his birthright. It has taken his long fight to the living rooms of Americans' homes where public opinion is formed and the Negro is winning! He has become a welcome visitor, not only to the white adult, but to the white children, who finally will lay Jim Crow to rest."[2]

Four years before the Supreme Court's *Brown v. Board of Education* decision outlawing segregated schools, five years before Rosa Parks and the black citizens of Montgomery refused to ride segregated buses, and long before the nonviolent, direct-action campaigns and the leadership of charismatic figures like Martin Luther King and the organizing of young people in group like the Student Nonviolent Coordinating Committee (SNCC) impelled the U.S. government to pass the Civil Rights and Voting Rights Acts in 1964 and 1965, there was television. And in its earliest days it was being touted as a key influence in the movement for black civil rights and desegregation.

Ed Sullivan and *Ebony* magazine were not the only voices proclaiming television's promise to consign Jim Crow to the grave. In 1952, Georgia Governor Herman Talmadge condemned television for promoting the "complete abolition of segregation customs in these shows which are beamed to states of the South."[3] He railed against the "mixing and mingling" of black performers and whites, especially white females, and the more general image of blacks and whites interacting "on a purely equal social status."[4] He even threatened a massive boycott of television advertisers by white viewers if the medium did not respect the sensibilities of Southern white segregationists.

Talmadge's rant led to a gleeful response by a columnist in the *Pittsburgh Courier*, the prominent, nationally distributed, African American weekly newspaper:

> When Talmadge shrieked out that the South's system of segregation would be disturbed by the television portrayal of colored Americans in respectable roles, he inadvertently gave proof to the contention of this commentator that TV will soon become a dynamic instrument in racial progress. . . .
>
> It has been possible to bar moving picture films, showing colored folks as decent, intelligent, upright souls, but the South has run into a snag with television. If they do not like what they see they can turn off their sets, but when pictures are thrown on Southern TV screens from New York, Chicago, Los Angeles and 'Frisco, all the rabid Talmadgites can do is bellow and wail. . . .
>
> TV will prove to be a powerful propaganda medium. Talmadge thinks so, and so do we.[5]

All these commentators assumed that televising images of nonstereotyped Negroes and showing blacks and whites together in integrated situations would have direct pedagogical effects.[6] Broadcasting such representations to the nation, and especially to the South, would compel fundamental change in race relations. Network television as a national medium privileging presumably more progressive, Northern, urban approaches to race relations would foist those images and sensibilities on the backward South, which would inevitably end up absorbing and adopting them.

That television would inspire idealistic hopes about African American advancement and racial justice in this period is not particularly surprising. J. Fred MacDonald, in his history of blacks in television, notes: "The politics of postwar America . . . encouraged many to envision a bright, bias-free future in television."[7] The Truman administration exhibited a certain amount of support for civil rights issues. The president used executive orders to desegregate the armed forces and required fair employment practices in hiring and promotion for government jobs. In the years leading up to the 1954 *Brown* decision, Thurgood Marshall and the NAACP Legal Defense Fund steadily chipped away at the *Plessy v. Ferguson* "separate but equal" doctrine with successful Supreme Court decisions on graduate education. Returning black veterans came home having embraced the "double V for victory," asserting victory against fascism abroad and against Jim Crow and second-class citizenship at home. The postwar period seemed to herald significant advances for African Americans.

As the newest mass medium, it was predictable that those with a stake in racial politics could assume that television might be some kind of player in the unfolding situation. These early discourses on race and television are noteworthy, not so much for their optimism that the medium would avoid disseminating familiar and degrading stereotypes, but rather for their conviction that the medium would do so much more: it would be a mechanism for overturning the racial caste system, dismantling Jim Crow, and enabling blacks to achieve social equality.

Of course, that was asking a lot of a commercial medium built on the model of radio broadcasting and structured in similar ways. And network radio had certainly never been a force for racial amelioration and uplift. Network radio's first phenomenal hit show beginning in the 1920s had been *Amos 'n' Andy,* voiced by two white men engaged in minstrel ventriloquism.[8]

Unlike radio, early network television appeared to take seriously obligations to present African Americans in respectful ways. Bob Pondillo has explored how, in the early 1950s, NBC's politically progressive chief censor worked to eradicate offensive black stereotypes from programming by scrubbing references to "darkies," images of Stepin Fetchit–style characters, and even taking on Eddie Cantor and his blackface routines. According to Pondillo:

> All hackneyed notions that depicted African Americans as tambourine-shaking minstrels, derelict sociopaths wielding concealed weapons, simpleminded loafers, excessive drinkers, drugged-out zombies, addicted gamblers, infrequent bathers, and easily freighted stooges—that is, "Feets don't fails me now!"—were cut. [Chief censor] Helffrich admonished his editors to "anticipate [these] kind[s] of [racial slurs] from writers and agencies, . . ." suggesting that "[such] sloppy and lazy clichés are out of date, are not fair, and are anything but a pretty face of America to the rest of the world." He pointedly wrote, "I can't very well poke my head in the sand to avoid reminding you not only of the century we are living in but of the nature of our audience."[9]

NBC also pursued a policy of "integration without identification" in the early 1950s, whereby African American actors and extras would be cast in roles without drawing attention to their race.[10] The other networks may not have been as proactive as NBC on matters of race representation, but they followed, at least on paper. In 1951, the National Association of Radio and Television Broadcasters put forth its Television Code. Among other areas of programming conduct, the broadcasters pledged: "Racial or nationality types shall not be shown on television in such manner as to ridicule the race or nationality."[11]

If early television encouraged optimistic hopes that it could be a progressive tool for black advancement, the medium could also lead to great disappointment. Much has been written about *Amos 'n' Andy,* which, as a television series, joined the CBS prime-time lineup in June 1951 after a heavily publicized search for an all-black cast. The show's representation of blacks and the NAACP's high-profile boycott are often used to exemplify how television reneged on the promise that it would provide a new deal for blacks. But *Amos 'n' Andy* was not the first nationally broadcast, fully sponsored, prime-time series starring African Americans to hit the TV airways. Joining the ABC lineup almost a year earlier in October 1950 was *The Beulah Show*. Initially starring Ethel Waters, then Hattie McDaniel for a short period, and finally Louise Beavers as Beulah, the show followed the homey adventures and mishaps of a maid, or "kitchen queen," to the white Henderson family with their young son Donnie. Unlike traditional mammy figures, Beulah had a steady boyfriend in Bill Jackson, the owner of a fix-it shop. She also had a best friend, Oriole, a featherbrained fellow maid initially played by the child-voiced Butterfly McQueen, then later by Ruby Dandridge. The show tended to provide more or less equal narrative attention both to the Hendersons and their dilemmas and to Beulah and her friends; however, Beulah and Bill's lives thoroughly revolved around the dilemmas of Beulah's employers.

Beulah has received surprisingly little attention, considering its popularity with viewers and its three-year run. Within the context of postwar race relations and an environment of nascent civil rights concerns, *Beulah* and the varied responses to it, particularly in the black community, merit a closer look. Unlike *Amos 'n' Andy*, *Beulah* provided viewers with an "integrated" environment where blacks and whites interacted and where black characters were privileged. *Beulah* exemplifies early television's initial foray into the arena of race relations and black representation and does so with some degree of awareness that these matters needed more careful treatment. Examining *Beulah* helps us begin a story about the fraught and complicated relationship between television and the developing black freedom movement that would explode onto television screens later in the decade and throughout the 1960s.

Who's Bawlin' for Beulah?

Beulah's beginnings on radio were similar to those of *Amos 'n' Andy* and the minstrel tradition of whites "blacking up" to enact a pleasing and comforting fiction of blackness for white audiences. The creation of white actor Marlin Hurt, Beulah made "her" debut on the *Fibber McGee and Molly* radio show in 1944. The character was so popular that the following year CBS gave Hurt his own radio show built around Beulah.[12] A year later Hurt died, but rather than give the role to another white actor, CBS asked Hattie McDaniel, who had a long and illustrious career playing maids, to take over the part. McDaniel thereby became the first (and only) African American to star in a sponsored network radio series, playing the role until her death in 1953. The movement of black performers into previously blackface roles created by whites became a notable phenomenon in the evolution of the minstrel stage. Robert C. Toll, in his history of American minstrelsy, has argued that black performers working within established minstrel traditions and parameters attempted to modify the stereotypes and bring the influence of their lived culture to bear on the roles. The appearance of black entertainers on the minstrel stage began to bring large numbers of black audiences to the theaters.[13]

McDaniel's *Beulah* achieved the same with radio audiences, and the show was very popular with African American listeners. *Pittsburgh Courier* readers voted it their favorite radio show in 1952 and their fourth most-liked show in 1953.[14] In 1950, *Beulah* had the blessings of the Los Angeles chapters of both the NAACP and the Urban League (the show was produced and aired in the city). However, the heads of both organizations qualified their praise of Proctor and Gamble for sponsoring a show starring an African American by noting that Beulah "could not be accepted as the ultimate in Negro roles."[15] Nevertheless, the Interracial Unity Committee honored the show for its "contribution in the field of race relations."[16]

How could a show about a black domestic to a white family who always puts their needs first garner all these accolades from civil rights groups? The *Courier* article provides some clues, arguing that Beulah was not a stereotype because she "had beaten the Hendersons out on quiz programs, had helped Donnie pass history exams, bested psychiatrists, and helped put over the town's charity carnival."[17] Beulah, therefore, was not "culturally incompetent" like Amos, Andy, and the Kingfish. Michele Hilmes has argued that what separated the ethnic humor of *Amos 'n' Andy* from the plethora of other such programming on network radio is that these black rubes would never be able to assimilate or integrate into white America. Comic Jews, Italians, Irish, or "Dutch" were often performed by entertainers who belonged to the ethnic group being lampooned, and the humor suggested a process of assimilation as the rube learned the ways of white America. The characters of *Amos 'n' Andy*, on the other hand, were "our nation's 'permanent immigrants,' always arriving, never arrived."[18] But if Beulah was seen as smarter than her white employers and white professionals and was organizationally competent enough to intervene in the public sphere of the local town, then perhaps Beulah was ready for political integration and assimilation into white society. The *Courier*'s emphasis on Beulah's skills outside the kitchen suggests that what made *Beulah* pleasurable for blacks was her apparent superiority to the white people who surrounded her. Whites appeared inferior and especially intellectually challenged in contrast to Beulah. More generally, they were helpless without the black woman's active control over situations.

The article continued the integrationist theme by quoting one of the show's cast members: "The Beulah show has done wonders for the cast. We don't think of race, creed or color, we're simply good friends."[19] The *Beulah* set was, therefore, a fully integrated work environment wherein color blindness prevailed. And this encouraged harmoniousness and a congenial workplace: "There is genuine enjoyment at both rehearsals and during the broadcast. It's such a healthy atmosphere to work in."[20]

Black listeners may also have taken pleasure from the fact that the voice they heard belonged to a black performer—and the *Courier* made much of the fact that the show starred a renowned black entertainer and not a white man doing radio minstrel ventriloquism. In another indication of the show's move away from the comedy of cultural incompetence, radio scripts for the show suggest that neither Beulah nor the other black characters were supposed to deliver their lines in "dialect." The scripts contain no "sho-nuffs or "yas 'ums" or much comedy revolving around malapropisms—elements which so defined the aural world of *Amos 'n' Andy*.[21] Thus the markers of ignorance—lack of proper education, acculturation, and thus assimilability—did not characterize the world of *Beulah* on radio.

Beulah did receive vocal and very significant protest from at least one segment of the African American community. In 1951, black troops in Korea objected to the airing of the show on overseas broadcast. According to the *Chicago Defender*—like the *Courier*, a nationally distributed black news weekly—"the protest calls the program extremely offensive to Negro personnel, bad influence on service morale and dangerous to the promotion of interracial goodwill."[22] Black troops may have been particularly sensitive to the show's more traditional and ultimately servile representations of blacks, no matter how smart and accomplished they were, because those troops were serving in the first federally desegregated American institution. The politics of integration and equal opportunity would have been particularly palpable for African American soldiers. Black audiences in all-black communities may have found satisfaction in the ways that Beulah "bested" the white folks. However, black soldiers in an integrated environment sharing images of a black maid whose life seemed to revolve around solving the problems of her white employers while trying to cajole matrimony from her commitment-averse and essentially lazy boyfriend might take on decidedly different meanings.

Onto this somewhat conflicted stage came the television version of *The Beulah Show* in October 1950. While Hattie McDaniel continued the role on radio, another African American luminary took over the part in the new medium. Ethel Waters had achieved an almost-unprecedented level of acclaim and stardom within and outside the black community. One of the great jazz and blues vocalists of the 1920s and 1930s, Waters also conquered the Broadway stage as the first black actress given a starring role in a dramatic production. She went on to triumphs in Hollywood cinema, playing complex characters in films such as *Cabin in the Sky* (1943), *Pinky* (1949), and *The Member of the Wedding* (1952), a film version of her Broadway triumph. Waters received two Academy Award nominations for her cinematic performances. In 1950 she published her autobiography, which quickly became a bestseller. Waters had, thus, achieved stunning successes across a remarkable array of entertainment platforms. With *Beulah*, it looked like she would add television to her list of media successes.[23] In fact, as Waters took on the role of Beulah, not only was her book recounting with brutal honesty her poverty-to-wealth story riding the bestseller lists, but she was also reprising her signature role of Bernice in the Broadway version of *The Member of the Wedding*.

Commentary in the black press tended to emphasize the spectacular nature of her success. The *Baltimore Afro-American* noted her lavish Harlem apartment, her maids, big car, chauffeur, and her ability to command purportedly $76,000 for a role. But the article also noted: "Ethel spends a large part of her income on charity, remembering her own early days."[24] The *Pittsburgh Courier* pointed out that Waters had been named by the Boston Chamber of Commerce as one of their twenty-five most outstanding women in America.[25] The *Chicago Defender* celebrated Waters's ability to juggle the demands of Broadway and television roles simultaneously.[26] Thus, Waters was a shining example of black achievement. Her foray into television augmented her successes, further cementing her status as a role model of racial advancement.

However, opinion in the black press quickly turned against Waters. The *Courier*'s columnist Joseph Bibb voiced the most outspoken concern. Bibb had considered television to be a powerful "propaganda" tool for race relations and he had high hopes for it. But racial propaganda could go either way. He accused Waters and her co-stars of defiling and desecrating black people with buffoonish and slaving stereotypes that were "impressed upon the minds of ever-growing television audiences. Herein is great peril and inherent danger. . . . Through this medium the stereotype can be preserved indefinitely."[27]

The very qualities of television that promised blacks a new deal in representations could also extend the pernicious old ones. Television's visual nature and its mass penetration into all sectors of the population could just as easily entrench destructive images. The medium's potent hypodermic drug of minstrel stereotypes could inject another white generation particularly effectively with racism and another black generation with low expectations and self-hatred. Bibb went on to condemn Waters in particular: "Miss Waters, we regret to note, is establishing a most disgraceful precedent. Her Beulah presentation does nothing to advance the cause of the darker minority. To the contrary, it gives succor and aid to those who advocate second-class citizenship." He went on to compare Waters's choice of roles to that of other notable black women performers: "Ethel Waters and Josephine Baker do not see eye to eye on the types they portray. Lena Horne, likewise, has refused to lend her talents in roles that will reflect upon her people. In the opinion of his reporter, Miss Waters deserves condemnation, while orchids should be bestowed upon La Baker and Miss Horne." For Bibb, the stakes were very high: "Radio had a strong impact upon people, but nothing like TV. That is why colored Americans should unite . . . in a bold and valiant effort to establish a high TV level in presenting a lowly people." Referring to Arthur Godfrey and other television personalities who "present colored people as gifted American citizens," Bibb was not going to give up the struggle to seize television as a political tool for black empowerment, but Ethel Waters, *Beulah,* and the upcoming *Amos 'n' Andy* threatened this entire project.

Despite Bibb's vehement criticism of Waters and a number of other condemnations of her role as Beulah scattered throughout the black press, the bulk of the controversy around *The Beulah Show* found its mark elsewhere. The most significant flashpoint of attention centered not on Waters and her character but rather on her co-star Bud Harris and his character, Bill Jackson. In one episode after another, Bill would shower Beulah with hyperbolic expressions of devotion, but he always found a reason why the two of them could not marry just yet. In the midst of the show's first season, Harris abruptly left the show, refusing to continue to play the character as written. He then took his case against the show to the pages of the black press.

The *Chicago Defender* highlighted the controversy with a banner headline story based on a letter Harris had forwarded to the *Defender* explaining his departure. To black readers, Harris declared:

> The writers for this show are sending scripts that require Bill Jackson, Beulah's boyfriend, to eat chicken, use dialect, fight, and things that are really degrading to my race. This I refused to do. . . . I didn't make my reputation on Uncle Tom roles and I won't do it now.
>
> In every script they had me eating chicken, pork chops or something. Then they had me coming in the kitchen where Beulah worked, going in the refrigerator, and taking food out. You know people just don't do that.[28]

The *Courier's* Joseph Bibb jumped to Harris's side, declaring, "Bud Harris should be awarded a vote of thanks. He has won the accolade. He has taken an heroic role that will pay his people much higher dividends in the long run than playing on the Beulah show." Bibb condemned black performers who continued to play such roles and expressed befuddlement that "the majority of the colored American citizens have not expressed uniform resentment" over the perpetuation of Mammy and Uncle Tom caricatures. He tried to convince his readers about the political stakes of such imagery:

> Down South, where such fawning characters are cherished and adored, the relations between the races are sorely strained. The Southerners would like to perpetuate the bowing, scraping type of colored citizens.
>
> These wily Dixiecrats have no use for red-blooded, upstanding colored citizens. That is why they ban first-rate pictures where colored people are permitted to play respectable roles.[29]

The Bill Jackson character also elicited criticism from another black periodical that appeared to want to shield Waters from condemnation. According to *Our World*, "It is unfortunate that a great actress like Miss Ethel Waters is forced into such a show. Her attempts to dignify a menial role are wasted when Bill appears. He's called a business man. That's just a malicious slander on all Negro businessmen."[30]

A number of themes emerge from these responses: a focus on the representation of a male supporting player rather than the female main protagonist; a concern with the representation of the black professional class; and anger that black audiences were not collectively rising up against these images. Similar concerns circulated when, a year later, *Amos 'n' Andy* joined *Beulah* on television in June 1951. They provide revealing clues about the status of black representational politics, television, and civil rights during this period.

The NAACP, *Amos 'n' Andy* . . . and *Beulah*

Melvin Patrick Ely has argued that the timing of *Amos 'n' Andy*'s TV debut at the very moment that the NAACP was holding its annual meeting in Atlanta may have helped galvanize the organization's move to protest the series, which had been heavily promoted and publicized in the press (including the African American press) in a way that *Beulah* had not. Thus: "The premier broadcast of the show . . . allowed NAACP delegates from all over the United States to watch together, reinforcing each other's negative responses and influencing the views of members who otherwise might not have reacted or even tuned in."[31] Ely suggests that there may have been no coordinated campaign against the show had it not been for that accident of timing. Certainly *Beulah* received no protest or condemnation from the civil rights group when it first came to the television airwaves the previous year. However, when the organization voted unanimously to censure *Amos 'n' Andy* and threaten its sponsor, Blatz Beer, with a consumer boycott, *Beulah* got thrown into the resolution as well. The resolution stated: "WHEREAS, radio and television programs, such as the 'Amos 'n' Andy' and 'Beulah' shows, which depict the Negro and other minority groups in a stereotyped and derogatory manner, definitely tend to strengthen the conclusion among uninformed or prejudiced peoples that Negroes and other minorities are inferior, lazy, dumb and dishonest. . . ."[32]

Beulah, of course, was anything but lazy, dumb, dishonest, or inferior to her white employers. Bill Jackson, on the other hand, could fit some of those characterizations. Certainly, the main characters in *Amos 'n' Andy*, with the exception of Amos who had long since been relegated to a more marginal status even in the radio version, fit the resolution's description. Kingfish, the ever-scheming, shady businessman with no visible source of income; Andy, the forever-bamboozled victim of Kingfish's antics and presumed owner of a taxi company; and especially Calhoun, the shyster lawyer, excited NAACP delegates' ire. In part this was because of a decision CBS had made in its development of the show for television. In an attempt to avoid alienating or angering audiences, CBS elevated the class status of the show's characters. According to Ely, CBS was highly conscious of black racial sensibilities and their increasing demands for change: "CBS therefore made a conscious decision that sets and wardrobe on the new TV series would reflect middle-class tastes as indulged on middle-class budgets."[33] Ironically, the network appeared to be attempting to adhere to the newly passed Television Code and its strictures against ridiculing a racial group.

The problem for the middle-class NAACP members was that these images of buffoonish and incompetent middle-class blackness seemed a direct jab at their own identities and hard-won class status: the so-called "talented tenth," who viewed themselves as the political, social, and economic leaders and role models for their more "lowly" brothers and sisters. *Beulah*'s Bill Jackson, as a business owner, appeared to be in the same category, yet here he was, a businessman who managed to spend most of his time in Beulah's kitchen, raiding her employers' icebox, and, when needed, preoccupying himself with her employers' needs rather than that of his own enterprise.

But what about Beulah? In NAACP protest materials railing against the depictions of black doctors, lawyers, and other professionals, there was no mention of the portrayals of black female domestics. The closest the organization came to protesting the representation of black women was a condemnation of female characters "shown as cackling, screaming shrews, in big-mouth close-ups, using street slang."[34] Most likely this referred to Kingfish's wife, Sapphire, or Sapphire's mother. Beulah did open each episode with a close-up direct address to the camera delivering one-liners like: "If marriages are made in Heaven, my guardian angel has sho' been loafin' on the job!" Beulah would then either smile broadly or engage in a hearty, but not cackling, laugh.[35]

The NAACP's characterization could only with great elasticity presume to refer to Beulah. More generally, criticism of Beulah in the black press tended to be vague on exactly what about the character was objectionable, whereas, as we have seen, the black press and the NAACP tended to be quite specific about what they found objectionable about black male representations. With respect to Beulah,

Beulah's direct address at the beginning of each episode: no "cackling" or "big mouth close-ups."

no specific points were raised about how the character may have insulted African American women and notions of acceptable femininity. Bud Harris and Joseph Bibb made it very clear how Bill Jackson functioned as an "Uncle Tom." Beulah may have been an "Aunt Dinah," but what that was supposed to communicate to black and white audiences about black womanhood was less clear. In the critical discourse, Beulah's "Aunt Dinah" was invariably linked with "Uncle Tom" to signal the kind of stereotype the commentators found objectionable. However, "Uncle Tom" tended often to predominate in the analysis. One could easily forget that Beulah was the star and central character around which the program revolved.

The middle-class male writers and editors of the black press along with the middle-class male NAACP delegates could not get particularly exercised about Beulah because, as black feminist theorist Patricia Hill Collins has observed, "adhering to a male-defined ethos that far too often equates racial progress with the acquisition of an ill-defined manhood has left Black thought with a prominent masculinist bias."[36] Few black women held leadership positions in any of the black organizations of the postwar period.[37] In the early 1950s, the question of black female representation was not a significant arena for struggle in the image politics of black advancement. Outside the select group of black cultural commentators and civil rights officials, it is not clear that representational issues had significant salience for many within the black community.

The NAACP went into high gear promoting its campaign against *Amos 'n' Andy* and Blatz Beer; *Beulah* may have figured in the original resolution but was quickly dropped from further consideration and protest. The black press gave significant attention to the NAACP campaign, but African Americans more generally were not unanimously against *Amos 'n' Andy*. Some middle-class and working-class blacks agreed with the organization, but very many of all social and economic strata vehemently opposed the boycott and voiced no particular concern about the show as a debilitating factor in black advancement.[38] A *Pittsburgh Courier* sampling of local "person in the street" responses suggests the range of perspectives. One woman admitted, "I liked it. Sure it was corny. So is 'Luigi,' but we all know that 'Luigi' isn't typical of all Italians. We should be able to see our funny side, too." A man countered, "I thought it was completely derogatory. I tried to compare it to the 'Goldbergs,' which has never been derogatory of Jewish people. The show last night had too much stereotyping and eye-rolling. I never listen to 'Amos 'n' Andy on the radio." Another woman observed, "It was pretty good . . . Some of the characters put on too much. I didn't like the Kingfish's actions in his office."[39]

These responses suggest a mild degree of unease with the representations, but not the full-throated outrage of the NAACP. Joseph Bibb joined the fray, fulminating at the millions of African Americans who did not see eye to eye with the NAACP:

> Amos and Andy have their supporters among the darker minority—some
> of them folks of status and importance. Others, who are just plain dumb and
> dense, [are] not keen enough to recognize the psychological effects of the Amos
> and Andy drivel. . . .
>
> [I]t is no longer funny nor laugh-provoking to see colored people forever de-
> picted as scapegoats, ghost-fearing, half-baked, chicken-stealing, crap-shooting
> scamps and rascals. Neither the Kingfish, Andy, Calhoun, nor Beulah can pro-
> mote the best interests of the darker minority.
>
> It's puzzling, indeed, that colored people are not united on this point.[40]

The politics of black representation on television in the civil rights era was of
enormous concern to various constituencies, both black and white, particularly
as the civil rights struggle emerged as a grassroots mass movement on the national stage—in large part because of the new medium of television. However,
responses to those representations were never united, singular, or predictable.
African American viewers, to the extent that we can find clues about their decod-
ing strategies, defy predictable reading stances. African American elites such as
the officials of the NAACP and cultural commentators like Joseph Bibb wanted
to launch a mass movement around questions of derogatory television representations in order to hold on to the promise of the medium as a potential tool for
racial advancement. But, as Ely notes in his summary of black response to the
boycott campaign:

> Afro-Americans were still not of one mind on *Amos 'n' Andy* as they were on
> lynching or job discrimination. . . . In the real world of 1951, the NAACP . . .
> could put together neither a true mass protest nor a united front among the
> Talented Tenth. Some, perhaps many, Afro-Americans in every social stratum
> grumbled about *Amos 'n' Andy* or certain aspects of the show, but few protested
> publicly—in part, perhaps, because they knew that many of their peers disagreed
> with them. . . . [T]he Association could not convincingly claim to represent an
> Afro-American consensus, and its threat of a boycott thus rang hollow from
> the first.[41]

As with *Amos 'n' Andy*, black viewers were not of one mind about *The Beulah
Show*. *Beulah* as a text presents us with a somewhat contradictory, ambivalent,
and unstable representation of blackness and race relations. Based on an evalu-
ative judgment of comedic performance, *Beulah* does not match the brilliant,
if ideologically troubling, work of Tim Moore as Kingfish or Spencer Williams
Jr. as Andy. There is a fluidity to the comic timing and sparkle to the writing in
the televised version of *Amos 'n' Andy* lacking in *The Beulah Show*, wherein the
writing is flatter, the repartee among the show's characters is duller, the comedy
is muted. However, *Beulah* did not engage in the kind of broad slapstick that was
Amos 'n' Andy's stock in trade—and also the source of much of its controversy.
What did *The Beulah Show* look like for viewers in the early 1950s?

Three Beulahs and Two Bills Negotiate Blackness

The Beulah Show comprises at least two, if not three, different series. The Beulahs created by Waters, McDaniel, and Beavers are quite distinct personalities. Each engages with the Hendersons differently and each has a distinctive relationship with Bill. Bill also becomes a different character, depending on which of the three actors took on that contentious role. Finally, the series gave viewers two different Alice and Harry Hendersons with distinct images of white, middle-class family and heterosexual relationships.

Of the three Beulahs, Ethel Waters's version is the most dignified, nonservile, and emotionally complex. Donald Bogle, in his analysis of the three Beulahs, suggests that black viewers would have been well aware of the struggles and triumphs Waters had encountered (certainly the black press emphasized her biography) and that this awareness would have informed their reading of Beulah and their satisfaction with the show.[42]

An episode from later in the show's first season, after Bud Harris had left, gives us a glimpse into how Waters attempted to deepen and complicate the character.[43] Alice has given Beulah the night off, assuming that Harry will agree to take her out since Donnie is away at a friend's house. Beulah smiles her gratitude for the time off, but she displays no obsequiousness. When Alice discovers that Harry has made a plan for them to go out with a boorish business associate and his monosyllabic wife, we focus on Alice's very disappointed face. Beulah enters the scene and says to the saddened Alice, "If it's all right with you, I'd like to go to Sadie Harris." Beulah informs Alice that she wants to get some knitting instructions for a sweater she is making for Bill's birthday. Waters delivers the request more as a statement than as a question; there is no hint of deference in her manner or her line reading—she is not asking Alice's permission. Of course, the Hendersons end up complicating Beulah's plan. Harry agrees to take in his business associate's daughter under the assumption that Beulah would be available for babysitting, even though Alice yells out a sharp "No!" Alice tells Harry that Beulah has the night off. The scene provides us with a provisional sort of female solidarity across the race and class divide. If Alice cannot have her night out as planned, then at least Beulah should have hers. However, positioned between her two employers, Beulah acts as the compromiser.

Beulah volunteers Bill's services as a babysitter for the time she will be at Sadie Harris's. While on the one hand, Beulah, as usual, has to come to the rescue of her white employers, turning Bill into an extension of herself, on the other hand, she does not relinquish her desires: a night out to focus on her wants and her goals. In a subsequent scene, we see Beulah lovingly caress a wrapped up bundle containing the material for the sweater she is making. The gesture is suffused with tenderness, desire, and emotional warmth—and has nothing whatsoever to do with the Hendersons.

Beulah mediates between her two employers and finds an acceptable compromise to their dilemma.

Beulah's emotional focus for the entire episode is on Bill and completing the sweater for him as a gesture of her love and devotion. In this way, Waters's Beulah attempts to undercut the otherwise taken-for-granted assumption that Beulah, as a descendant of Aunt Dinah and Mammy, cares first and foremost for the white folks, and lives her life only to serve and please them. This Beulah has her own life separate from the Hendersons, and the dilemmas and problems they encounter end up impinging on that separate life.

The series' other Beulahs display far less independence and desire to protect their own time. In "The Hendersons Go Camping," Louise Beavers's Beulah excitedly tells Bill that she has the next two nights off because the Hendersons are going on a camping trip. Asking if Bill will be off work, she launches into a litany of evening activities for the two of them: a trip to the beach, a matinee, dinner at Tony's Place. Bill quickly informs her of his depleted financial situation, but what really scuttles Beulah's plans is Alice Henderson, who informs Beulah and Bill about her worries that Harry and Donnie have gone off on their wilderness adventure without food and that their tent will not stand up to a coming wind storm. Beulah and Bill immediately offer to bring food and a sturdier tent from Bill's shop out to the two. Suddenly, Beulah's days off disappear, but in this narrative the white folks come first, and Beavers's Beulah never even hints at regret at the loss of her time off.[44]

In an episode with Hattie McDaniel, Harry Henderson decides to economize by firing the gardener under the assumption that he, Alice, and Donnie will do the gardening chores, which he divvies up among the three of them.[45] Of course, all three end up with other things they have to do. McDaniel's Beulah obligingly agrees to do all the gardening chores. After having been told how wonderful she is by each one in turn, Beulah muses to herself, "Everyone keeps telling me I'm wonderful today. I wonder why?" McDaniel delivers the line straight with no indication that she is being thoroughly exploited. Later in the episode, as the demands of the gardening cause her to burn the dinner, we see her slap the ruined roast on the table in front of the Hendersons and grumble that the food "was prepared by a field hand not a cook," and she exits back into the kitchen. The pointed reference to slavery provides a potential moment for viewers to ponder Beulah's labor and the power dynamics between her and her white employers/owners. But that discursive opening needs to be shut down immediately. When Harry comes up with a solution whereby Beulah can serve them cold cuts on the Saturday set aside for gardening, Beulah metamorphoses into McDaniel's traditional Mammy character: "Mister Harry, I'll dig the yard if I have to, I'll lay a brick wall for you, but I'm not going to serve my family no cold cuts for Saturday night," and she harrumphs back into the kitchen. In these scenes there is precious little distance between the professional, salaried housekeeper and cook circa 1952 that Beulah is supposed to be and the antebellum house slave that McDaniel portrayed in *Gone with the Wind.* Her Mammy and her Beulah both engage in a certain amount of talk back and criticism of the white folk, but both also display an unending appetite for work and a perverse sense of ownership of their white taskmasters.

The episode gives us a glimpse into Beulah's own separate world when, in a telephone conversation with Oriole, Beulah laments not going to the dance with Bill, not because he did not invite her, as Oriole assumes, but because "I got a misery" from all the gardening labors. The visual image of Hattie McDaniel makes that line particularly poignant. McDaniel was herself suffering from late stage breast cancer that would kill her the following year. She looks physically exhausted, weakened, and spent. In her dialogue with Oriole, she adopts a long-suffering posture. Rather than refuse to continue doing the exploitative labor, Beulah resignedly tells Oriole that she will take it easy tomorrow (presumably her day off) and rest up during the week.

"I got a misery." Poignant visual representation of McDaniel's Beulah looking exhausted and spent from her added labors for the Hendersons.

Beulah's predicament here would likely resonate strongly with black female audiences who had experience with domestic work. As Jacqueline Jones, a historian of black women workers has noted, "Although mistresses dubbed their employees with the titles of maid, cook, or nurse, they in fact placed little value on labor specialization within their own households. Thus a 'nurse' could find herself 'watering the lawn in front with the garden hose, sweeping the sidewalk, mopping the porch and halls, dusting around the house, helping the cook, or darning stockings.'"[46] Beulah was mostly a cook, but in episode after episode, she is called upon to do many other tasks for her employers, and as was the experience of black domestic workers, the time commitment expected by employers was voluminous. Beulah's availability to the Hendersons seems to know no bounds, and, in general, they exhibit no qualms about expecting her to be at their beck and call. In the traditional Mammy representation, however, the black domestic has no outside life and in the white imagination exists only to serve and nurture her white folks. *Beulah,* in a variety of ways, negotiates that familiar stereotype and insists that the domestic does have a life separate from her employers even if we still have the pleasing fiction that the domestic is more or less content to subordinate that separate life to the white folks, or, as was often the case in *Beulah,* bring that separate life into the service of the white folks.

The most obvious way Beulah brought her own life into that of the Hendersons was through her boyfriend, Bill. As a representation of black masculinity, the character certainly presents difficulties. Although Bill runs his own business, viewers rarely see him in his shop; typically, we see him in Beulah's kitchen. Placed in this "feminine" space where he, like the young Donnie, comes to be fed by Beulah, Bill is inevitably emasculated and infantilized. Everything about Bill undermines traditional notions of appropriate masculinity. Although well into middle age, he refuses to pursue the appropriate role of husband and father, despite constant invitations from Beulah. In one episode in which Beulah mistakenly assumes that Alice is pregnant, Bill builds a wooden cradle for the nonexistent baby. At the end of the episode, Bill and Beulah wistfully look at the cradle as Bill says, "The folks ain't going to have a baby after all. And I was in de mood. Made this crib with my own hands. Wooden pegs, so the little one wouldn't scratch itself." Louise Beavers's Beulah smiles and, putting her hands on her middle-aged hips, informs Bill, "Someday it might come in handy." Bill immediately shuts her down by muttering, "Let's not bump the apple cart befo' the horse is loose." Visually, Bill and Beulah present a ludicrous image of a couple well past prime childbearing years. Within the world of *Beulah* and the minstrel tradition to which it harkens, blacks are there to care for white children such as Donnie and the imagined Henderson baby. By casting older actors to play both roles and by insisting on Bill's marital and paternal recalcitrance, the show participates in the longstanding white image of black men as problematic husbands and fathers.

The show also undercuts and lampoons Bill as a romantic partner for Beulah. In the babysitting episode, when Bill first enters Beulah's kitchen, he greets her with his typically excessive expression of affection. In this instance: "Here's your love apple falling from the tree of romance." The excessiveness and silliness of Bill's lines render parodic any notion of Bill and Beulah as sexual partners. Viewers saw noncomedic expressions of love and desire from Beulah, but not from Bill. Certainly the fear of black male sexuality has been deeply entrenched in the white imagination, and clearly the producers of *Beulah* continued to circulate that fear by presenting viewers with a thoroughly desexualized as well as demasculinized figure.

Dooley Wilson's Bill was also made to look ridiculous and clownish. In the babysitting episode, viewers are treated to numerous scenes of a monstrous little white girl bedeviling Bill. She sticks a lighted match in Bill's shoe as he sleeps in a chair. After she has smashed dishes and pots all over Beulah's kitchen, she causes Bill to take a comic pratfall over all the debris. As he lies unconscious on the floor, she sprays his face with white whipping cream. This action results in a bizarre twist on blackface conventions. The little girl has black chocolate smeared over her face while Bill has been put into whiteface. Later she falls down the coal cellar further "blackening" her.

As the emasculated black man, Bill mostly has to take the abuse from the white child. However, he delivers a number of lines that help to undercut or at least comment upon the traditional power dynamic that places any white—even a child—over any black person. As the girl runs into the kitchen, he mutters to himself, "Maybe she'll electrocute herself on that stove." In the kitchen, he opens the refrigerator and beckons her: "And if you crawl inside, close the door, you'll find out what makes that little light go on." The dynamic between this child and Bill inverts the traditional Uncle Tom/Little Eva relationship. Bill's murderous imaginings, considering the white and feminine object of his homicidal musings, has an almost subversive quality. As Patricia A. Turner has pointed out, historically it was images of black children who were imaginatively imperiled.[47] A veritable pop culture industry developed around images of little black pickaninnies threatened by alligators. In this imagery, it was perfectly reasonable, not to mention humorous, to show black children terrorized, victimized, ill clad, dirty, and parentless. The *Beulah* episode seems to gesture, at least tacitly, toward an inversion of the pickaninny stereotype. But, then again, by "blackening" the white girl, that inversion goes only so far. Nevertheless, by allowing the otherwise buffoonish Bill to voice murderous designs on a white girl, *Beulah* did suggest that at some level it was permissible for blacks to condemn the white people who mistreated them.

If Dooley Wilson's Bill engaged in some physical slapstick and buffoonish antics, Ernest Whitman's Bill developed as a much different character. Bogle has praised Whitman's performance: "Whitman understood how to play with a line, and he was able to suggest a wily intelligence, leading the viewer to believe that Bill knew more than anybody thought."[48] Among existing episodes, none had him engaging in physical comedy; none made him look ridiculous as did the episode with Wilson's Bill. If Whitman's Bill appeared to be lazy and only interested in Beulah's food, those behaviors often functioned as tactical means to evade exploitative work for the white folks. In the gardening episode, Mc-Daniel's Beulah informs Whitman's Bill, as he sits at her kitchen table, about the Hendersons' plan to do their own garden work on Saturdays. Bill casually informs Beulah that he will not be around on Saturday. To Beulah's accusation that he is deserting a sinking ship, Bill wryly informs her that he understands her remark, but that rats only swim when they have to: "And when we do, Olympic team, look out." Unrepentant, he sweeps out of the kitchen, taking a piece of pie with him. Whitman's line reading is defiant, his body language purposeful; the response not of a shiftless good-for-nothing but rather of a wily man who knows that the white folks are about to exploit Beulah and himself, and he is searching for a way out.

Of course, Bill ends up assisting Beulah in her labors, and there is nothing comical in the shots of Bill digging up Harry Henderson's prize rosebush. In fact, whenever we see Whitman's Bill laboring for the Hendersons, Whitman portrays that labor as dignified and requiring skill and knowledge, and Bill often comes across as more physically competent than Harry. Whitman attempted to negotiate a more complicated and nuanced version of the very limited representation of black masculinity allowed him.

Similarly, Ethel Waters brought more depth and nuance to her Beulah than did either Hattie McDaniel or Louise Beavers. McDaniel's personal illness may have made her too weak to struggle with the material given her; Beavers often appears mechanical, as though merely going through the motions. However, Bogle notes that "more than either of the other actresses who played the role, Beavers often made Beulah a proper Black matron. Without a trace of dialect, she was always well groomed, well coifed, and well mannered, looking like a woman ready to go off to church every Sunday. . . . Beulah seemed capable of dealing with an integrated society, even though she could function only as a servant in that world."[49]

Ultimately, the two actors who brought the most dignity, complexity, intelligence, and humanity to their roles—Ethel Waters and Ernest Whitman—never played Beulah and Bill together. Waters was saddled with the clownish Dooley Wilson and Whitman with the weakened McDaniel and lackluster Beavers. Had Waters and Whitman been cast together, *Beulah* may well have offered viewers a quite revolutionary representation of a loving black couple. Unfortunately, network television would have to wait over two decades for a fully realized, committed black couple: Florida and James Evans in *Good Times*.

And what of the Hendersons? *Beulah* differed fundamentally from *Amos 'n' Andy* by portraying direct interaction between black and white worlds and black and white characters. Both sets of Hendersons, the former from the show's first year with Ethel Waters and the second from the series' last two years with McDaniel and Beavers, are upper-middle-class suburbanites who would fit right in with the

Cleavers of *Leave It to Beaver* and the Andersons of *Father Knows Best*. However, the earlier incarnation of the Hendersons did not fit the white sitcom family ideal as well as the later ones. Earlier in the series, the couple is decidedly middle-aged and not physically attractive. In the one extant episode featuring this couple, Alice also does not appear to be a particularly contented wife. Harry sabotages her visions of a romantic night out, and she is quite helpless to do anything about the situation. In her discontent, she tells Harry, "Every time we go out, it's for business." We have already noted the instance of female solidarity between the white female employer and her black housekeeper in this episode. That image of solidarity was mostly a pleasing white fiction of domestic labor. Jacqueline Jones has shown how white women employers "[c]aught up in a patriarchal world of their own, deprived of formal economic or political power, and convinced of their own racial superiority" often managed their black female servants with a heavy, and at times violent, hand.[50] This particular episode gestures toward Alice's powerlessness within a patriarchal structure, but her response to Beulah is not quite what might typically transpire when a housekeeper assumed she had the night off.

The second Alice Henderson more closely fit the picture of the perfect sitcom wife and mother. This Alice represents the promise of the postwar suburban ideal for women. She can display herself as a sexual being in her domestic space because like June Cleaver and Margaret Anderson, the modern housewife is no longer a household drudge. Of course, Alice has not only the labor saving devices and good design features that assist these TV housewives; unlike them, she also has a more old-fashioned labor-saving device in her black maid.[51] Like June Cleaver, Alice Henderson wears ubiquitous pearls, perfectly coifed hair, and elegant dresses with high heels. Unlike June Cleaver or the other 1950s sitcom moms, Alice Henderson is far more overtly glamorous.

Family sitcoms of the period, along with the marketing industry, may have promised white women leisure, domesticated sexuality, and consumer pleasures, but even if new appliances could cut the drudgery out of housework, it was assumed that suburban white women did their own housework. Alice Henderson's glamour was made possible by the domestic labor of another woman. In the political economy of postwar America, this setup would become increasingly residual. In fact, a Proctor and Gamble ad that appeared in the show's first year suggests the emergent postwar ideal.[52] A beautiful, white, aproned model extols the benefits of Dreft self-cleaning dishwashing suds. As we see an animation of hard working little bubbles sucking up grease and grim off of dishes, the model proclaims, "I don't do any work." The product does it for her. In the old order that *Beulah* harkens back to, the black servant supplied the labor; in the new postwar consumers' paradise, a commodity does the work. Alice's over-glamorization might serve as a marker that her particular domestic ideal was headed for extinction, hurried into the dustbin of history by the gathering strength of a black freedom movement that first burst into public consciousness in 1955, when scores

Alice Henderson displays the glamour and leisure available to the white housewife with a black maid. Neither June Cleaver nor Margaret Anderson could match this level of haute couture.

of black maids and domestics like Beulah refused for an entire year to board buses that consigned them to the back.

Conclusion

When both *Beulah* and *Amos 'n' Andy* went off the air in 1953, neither did so because of protest and boycott threat. They left the air because the networks were moving toward a new vision of programming exemplified by new family situation comedies focused on blandly white, suburban, and consumerist families like *The Adventures of Ozzie and Harriet,* which debuted on ABC in 1952, and *Father Knows Best,* which joined the CBS lineup in 1954. By the late 1950s, the networks' "ethnic" and working-class comedies such as *Life with Luigi, The Goldbergs, The Honeymooners,* and *Life of Riley* had largely disappeared, no longer ideologically useful for providing a sense of memory and connection to the past in order to legitimate the new medium and its celebration of a new phenomenon of postwar consumer capitalism.[53] Black performers largely disappeared from prime time. NBC displayed the last gasps of its early 1950s attempt to integrate its programming with nonstereotyped black performers when it presented the urbane and sophisticated Nat "King" Cole in his own variety show in 1956 and ended up sustaining it for a year when no national sponsor elected to pay for the show.

By the mid-1950s, the networks had established their nationwide reach, linking up affiliated stations in all segments of the country by coaxial cable. Before 1953, an FCC freeze on new television licenses issued in 1948 (so that the broadcast regulator could figure out a set of technical matters) meant that many markets in the Deep South and in rural areas had no television service whatsoever. The states of Mississippi, Arkansas, and South Carolina were entirely outside television reception.[54] But with television's ability to reach almost all Americans by mid-decade, the medium assumed a more central role in the national imagination.

Alan Nadel has argued that network television served as a key Cold War medium that helped to solidify shared images and narratives of what it meant, within the Cold War context, to be American. Diversity, heterogeneity, and difference had no place in the new sensibility, and neither did controversy. Television and its advertisers increasingly gave viewers a vision of America as a homogenous and neutral *white* nation:

> They were promoting the notion of a stable, transparently normal nation, unambiguous and without controversy or dissent. Lacking partisan emotions, political positions, or minority opinions, much less minority complexions, the Americans featured by television mirrored the products they were supposed to consume: white bread, vanilla. In this sense, whiteness means the absence of emotional, political, or philosophical pigmentation. Cold War television—in regard to anything but communism—was white in the sense that white is the most neutral of colors, deployed by a medium that had honed the craft of equating neutrality with normality.[55]

The quintessential genre of 1950s programming, the western, imagined an American West depopulated of people of color and celebrated the triumph of white men, especially Southern white men, in conquering this new frontier for white normality.[56] Suburban family sitcoms celebrated the relatively new phenomenon of the insulated nuclear family, and by normalizing this vision of suburban whiteness, they implicitly supported real estate and banking tactics of redlining and neighborhood covenants that kept nonwhite families out.

But suddenly, in September 1957, nine African American students attempted to integrate Central High School in Little Rock, Arkansas. Television news, still in its infancy as a journalistic medium, found itself with its first major story, providing the national television audience with saturation coverage. Blacks and the questions surrounding race relations may have been whitewashed out of prime-time entertainment, yet, in a bizarre case of the return of the repressed, they reappeared with spectacular drama and poignancy in the developing genre of television news. News coverage of the burgeoning civil rights movement, to which we turn in the next section, may have heartened those champions of the medium who earlier in the decade had touted television for its unique ability to function as a propaganda tool for racial equality and who by the mid-1950s could only despair about their earlier utopian hopes. If the entertainment side of the medium had crushed those hopes, could the news side redeem them?

PART 1

Network News
in the Civil Rights Era

CHAPTER 2

The Chosen Instrument of the Revolution?

Seventy-five newsmen convened at the University of Missouri's School of Journalism in 1965 to grapple with ethical dilemmas arising from television news and its coverage of the civil rights movement. To what extent was broadcast journalism actively participating in events it was supposed to be observing? One CBS reporter affirmed: "The Negro revolution of the 1960s could not have occurred without the television coverage that brought it to almost every home in the land."[1] NBC Washington Bureau Chief William B. Monroe went even further: "Negroes are the architects, bricklayers, carpenters, and welders of this revolution. Television is their chosen instrument." And even as he initially qualified this statement by noting that television did not "set out to integrate the nation or even to improve the South," he acknowledged that "network television newscasts brought in the message day after day that integration was overtaking other Southern cities and that it could not be prevented."[2]

Implicitly and explicitly, these TV newsmen suggested that their medium made the civil rights movement possible and, despite obligatory nods to disinterestedness, television news was an agent of change in the struggle for integration and racial justice. Decades later, a number of television journalists advanced these same assertions in their memoirs. Howard K. Smith, whose coverage of the beating of freedom riders in Birmingham resulted in his firing after a long and illustrious career at CBS, declared: "Television pictures of recurring horrors such as the attacks that bloodied Freedom Riders—and incidentally unhorsed me—had become nightly fare. Even indifferent citizens were beginning to feel and to say, 'Something must be done.'"[3]

Was television news "the instrument of the revolution" during the civil rights era? Did this new medium amplify and publicize the goals, politics, and agendas of the movement, its activists, demonstrators, and spokespeople for the cause of voting rights, desegregation, and black empowerment? Was TV news a sympathetic cheerleader for the movement's direct action and nonviolent civil disobedience philosophies and strategies during its ten-year heyday from the 1955 Montgomery bus boycott to the 1965 Selma campaign?

Evidence from a variety of prime-time documentaries and news reports that aired between 1957 and 1962 provides a more complex picture than what is suggested by the assertions and reflections of these journalists. While news coverage took a generally sympathetic stance toward the idea of desegregation, especially with regard to the Supreme Court's *Brown vs. Board of Education* ruling and to voting rights, television news during this period generally did not constitute a cheering section for the civil rights movement. Close textual and thematic analysis reveals that, in general, network television news at the time told a story of sectional reconciliation around a constructed figure of the Southern white moderate. Southern blacks typically appeared as sympathetic but objectified figures rather than subjects in their own empowerment struggle.

News reporting, whether print or television, is obviously not a neutral mirror reflecting reality. Reporters have to select, categorize, and package events and details in some sort of patterned manner. But as Gaye Tuchman noted in *Making News: A Study in the Construction of Reality*, television newsfilm presents a "web of facticity" that tends to militate against seeing newsfilm as a representational system with its own imposed rules and penchant for defining and redefining social reality.[4] Journalists rely on media frames—sometimes acknowledged, often not— to organize the segments of reality they package as stories for their audiences. Todd Gitlin has cogently defined media frames as "persistent patterns of cognition, interpretation, and presentation of selection, emphasis, and exclusion, by which symbol-handlers routinely organize discourse, whether verbal or visual."[5] During the civil rights years, TV news personnel employed a fairly stable and persistent set of media frames to make sense of events in the South. And while they often, but not always, benefited the movement, those frames certainly had ideological implications.

The Dawning of Television News and the Civil Rights Story

Middle-class Americans began buying television sets in huge numbers during the 1950s, but the three major networks waited until late in the decade before investing much financial and human capital in their news divisions. Establishing the entertainment infrastructure and its programming came first. Early television reporters, schooled either in print or radio, had to come to terms with their new visual medium. Former print reporter Robert Schakne, for instance, covered the 1957 Little Rock school desegregation crisis for CBS as if he were still a newspaperman.[6] Attempting to interview one of the black students wanting to integrate Central High School, Schakne seemed oblivious to the effect of the broadcast journalism paraphernalia surrounding him: a large microphone, a cameraman with a cumbersome camera hoisted on his shoulder and battery belt around his middle, a soundman with a recording deck connected via heavy cord to the cameraman. A print reporter with discreet notepad and pen would not attract the attention—in this case from a mob of angry white segregationists—that focused on the highly visible broadcast crew. Schakne noted, "The whole process of changing television into a serious news medium happened to coincide with the civil rights movement."[7]

Schakne's reporting from Little Rock also highlights some of the ethical dilemmas in using this unwieldy visual medium for journalism. The CBS cameraman had gotten his camera set up too late to record a white mob yelling racist invectives at Elizabeth Eckford, a frightened but stoic fifteen-year-old African American girl who had been separated from the rest of the group attempting to integrate the high school. According to Gene Roberts and Hank Klibanoff in their history of the press during the civil rights years, "When Schakne realized he didn't have the footage, he did something that revealed the raw immaturity of this relatively new medium of newsgathering: he ordered up an artificial retake. He urged the

CBS reporter
Schakne attempts
to interview a
frightened Eckford.

crowd, which had fallen quieter, to demonstrate its anger again, this time for the cameras. 'Yell again!' Schakne implored as his cameraman started filming."[8]

Before the late 1950s, television news shows like NBC's *Camel News Caravan* or CBS's evening news with Douglas Edwards were little more than fifteen-minute bulletin services backed up with visuals typically from newsreel companies. Only Edward R. Murrow's prestigious prime-time news documentary series *See It Now* and Sunday afternoon "cultural ghetto" programs provided much serious, in-depth network news and public affairs programming.

Things began to change significantly in the 1959–63 period. The networks feared political backlash and potential FCC interference when critics, such as CBS's own journalistic luminary Murrow, castigated the networks for putting profit over public service, contributing to a poorly informed American public unable to deal properly with Cold War challenges.[9] In 1960, a new, activist FCC head, Newton Minow, appeared ready to take action against the networks for perpetrating a "vast wasteland" on the American public. In response to this criticism, as well as crises such as the quiz show scandals, the networks began to fund the infrastructure costs of their television news operations, inaugurating high-profile, prime-time documentary series such as *CBS Reports* (1959–71), *Eyewitness* (CBS, 1959–63), *Bell and Howell Close Up!* (ABC, 1961–63), and *NBC White Paper* (1960–80). These documentaries were to be a "key genre for transcending the superficial and commercial aspects of the medium" and served to signal the networks' abiding commitment to their public service responsibilities.[10] Then, in the fall of 1963, NBC and CBS inaugurated half-hour nightly news programs.

Television historian Michael Curtin points out that during the early 1960s, the networks produced and aired more documentaries in prime time than they ever would again. In *Redeeming the Wasteland,* he focuses primarily on how this plethora of documentary programming engaged with the Cold War and American foreign policy. However, this zenith for network documentaries falls within the key years of the civil rights movement. The sit-ins, the freedom rides, James Meredith's integration of the University of Mississippi, the Birmingham campaign, the March on Washington, and Freedom Summer all happened between 1960 and 1964. Sasha Torres points out the "historical coincidence" of the rise of the movement and of the medium as an "authoritative force in American public life."[11] Reporting about the Cold War may have been an organizing principle of much news and documentary programming (and numerous news stories brought the Cold War ideological frame to the civil rights story); nevertheless, the civil rights movement was the networks' first major, ongoing domestic news story, and as such, network news organizations had to come up with a narrative frame, recurring themes, familiar characters, as well as picture-friendly visuals as the novice journalistic institution learned to tell an unprecedented story with novel news tools. Torres points out, "Telejournalism, obviously, needed vivid pictures and clear-cut stories; less obviously, it also sought political and cultural *gravitas.*"[12]

Establishing the Civil Rights Story:
See It Now (1957)

No news broadcaster exuded gravitas like Edward R. Murrow, even as his seminal news documentary series, *See It Now,* faced cancellation by 1957. Murrow's team had not explored the civil rights situation much beyond a 1954 examination of segregation in two Southern towns.[13] However, a broadcast from January 1957 provides and early model for how network news and documentary programs would treat the Southern desegregation story.

In an episode titled "Clinton and the Law," Murrow explored a school desegregation crisis in Clinton, Tennessee.[14] In August 1956, in the wake of the Supreme Court *Brown v. Board of Education* ruling, twelve black students registered to attend the previously all-white Clinton High School. According to the report, while local whites were not necessarily happy about the situation, but most respected the new law and would obey it. Enter John Kasper, an "outsider" from Washington, D.C., and a white supremacist, who declared that the townspeople of Clinton did not have to obey the law.[15] The previously unharassed black students began to suffer intimidation. Eventually, the town descended into chaos with an attack on a minister who accompanied the black students to school, and with riots, mob actions, and National Guardsmen called in to restore order.

How did *See It Now* represent the conflict? Over and over again, the report emphasizes that the townspeople of Clinton wanted to obey the law. From the town's newspaper editor, who originally opposed integration, to a judge who, before *Brown,* ruled against integration, to the high school principal who originally fought against desegregation, to the high school football team captain who admitted his lack of enthusiasm for integration—all these representations of the white Clinton establishment spoke the discourse of law and order. If *Brown* was now the law, they not only planned to obey it, they would fight to obey it. John Kasper embodied segregationist intransigence—but he was not of the community. He was the low Other, the lawbreaker, the alien presence in this otherwise peaceful and tolerant white community. *See It Now* marginalized white supremacist politics by suggesting it was a foreign manifestation, infecting the community from outside. The spokespersons representing Clinton were all white moderates, struggling to come to terms with the new racial landscape.

Against this abundance of white moderate voices, the report then gave viewers almost seven full minutes of Kasper delivering an incendiary speech in Kentucky. Television audiences heard him rage against the threat that civilization would be turned over to a group only eighty years from slavery and a few hundred years from "savagery." He referred to President Eisenhower as a "hollow pumpkin" and suggested that impeachment efforts were useless, but that assassinating Supreme Court justices who had life terms on the bench might be more productive. He went on to describe his approach as "metaphorically" throwing a lit stick of dynamite at local judges, school principals, and newspaper editors and then letting them decide what to do with it. The sheer length of time that Murrow turned over to Kasper might suggest a problem for broadcasters giving demagogues and terrorists a video platform for their incitements to violence.

However, immediately after this sequence, the report shifts to Murrow as he describes Clinton's "worst day"—the beating of the Baptist minister who had been escorting the black students. The minister spoke the law-and-order discourse again: since the law allowed the students to attend Clinton High School, they should be able to attend unharassed. Clearly, Murrow wanted to draw a direct connection between Kasper's hate-mongering speech and the violence and turmoil that followed in Clinton. So, while on the one hand *See It Now* provided Kasper with a platform to speak, his words are contextualized to the most reprehensible of violent acts: an assault on a heroic clergyman who happens to be white and happens to be protecting worthy, innocent black children.

At the end of the report, Murrow returned to the newspaper editor who had opened the broadcast with his remarks about not supporting desegregation. Now, after the beating of the minister, the editor affirms the need to stand up for law and order. Within the context of the report, this seemed a roundabout way to indicate the editor's newfound support for integration.

Moderates, Worthy Victims, and Deviants

See It Now created a strategy to privilege the white moderate, and it serves as a template for most future reporting on the civil rights story. These Southern white moderates were thoughtful, law-abiding, and earnestly trying to come to terms with challenges to their previously naturalized segregationist common sense. Dyed-in-the-wool segregationists and white supremacists, when presented, were typically shown as deviant.

Along with the white moderates and deviant segregationists, there was a third figure completing a tripartite structure that recurs in TV news coverage of the civil rights movement: the "worthy," black victims not affiliated with the movement. Like the white moderates, worthy black victims were thoughtful and articulate; their representations carried signifiers of middle-classness, from the suits and ties and modest skirts they wore to the educated speech patterns they employed and the recognizable aspirations for the American Dream they espoused.

The *CBS Reports* September 26, 1962, episode, "Mississippi and the 15th Amendment," displays this tripartite structure in its examination of the denial of black voting rights in the Magnolia State framed within the context of the James Meredith crisis.[16] Viewers were introduced to a number of worthy black victims—all sincere, well-spoken African Americans who merely wished to exercise their Constitutional rights to the franchise. Cast in the role of exemplary Negro was David Robertson.[17] Shown at the head of a classroom diagramming a chromosome on a blackboard, Robertson, as reporter David Schoenbrun described him, was a "math teacher, college graduate, Master's student at Cornell University, member of the National Science Foundation," and technically illiterate, at least according to Mississippi voter registration tests. Robertson stood in for all disenfranchised Mississippi blacks, although most would not share Robertson's prestigious academic accomplishments. Rhetorically, it made sense for *CBS Reports* to feature this exemplary figure in order to highlight the injustices of the Mississippi system and to ensure viewer sympathy. Robertson was middle class, educated, and, within the context of the documentary report, not affiliated with any civil rights organization. He was thus not too different from the program's presumed audience.

Juxtaposed to images of Robertson was Theron Lynd, registrar for Forrest County and the official responsible for denying Robertson and most other blacks in that part of Mississippi the right to vote. Lynd appeared standing atop the steps to the county courthouse in an extreme low angle shot. The framing is significant because Lynd was grotesquely fat; the low angle accentuated his morbid obesity. Over a cut-to-close-up of his doughy face, reporter Schoenbrun observed that Lynd was one of the most powerful men in the country because he had the authority to decide who could and could not vote. Lynd, who never spoke, is presented as the "low Other," his visual excessiveness offered as a marker of the deviance of Jim Crow, the strangeness and inscrutableness of the Deep South, and the corrupt nature of Southern law. Theron Lynd could have easily come from central casting so effortlessly did his visual image suggest the stereotype of the bloated, corrupt Southern sheriff of popular culture.[18]

Much of the report focused on a number of individual black Mississippians and their hardships in attempting to register. One section of the report followed Hattiesburg resident Mattie Bivens. Using cinema verité techniques, the *CBS Reports*

"Worthy black victim": David Robertson, the science teacher and Cornell University graduate student, deemed by Forrest County registrar as illiterate and thus not qualified to vote.

The grotesqueness of Jim Crow: Theron Lynd framed to emphasize both his morbid obesity and the deviance of Deep South laws and customs.

crew trailed her with a hidden camera to the Forrest County courthouse. Bivens was well dressed in a white frock and purse and provided articulate voice-over commentary about her quest for the franchise. She noted the dust that accumulated on her otherwise neat shoes as she walked down a dirt road, pointing out that if Negroes had the vote they would not have unpaved streets. The hidden camera showed her at the courthouse taking a registration test in which she has to interpret a section of the legalistically complicated Mississippi state constitution. In an interview afterward, Bivens recounted her answer to the reporter. Schoenbrun then informed viewers that after consulting expert legal advice, he could assert that Bivens interpreted the statute well. Like Robertson, Mattie Bivens was an ideal representation of engaged citizenry: knowledgeable, educated, aware of the power of political engagement for societal improvement.

Both Robertson and Bivens are quintessential examples of Herman Gray's concept of "the civil rights subject." Although Gray examines the circulation of this cultural trope in televisual texts that nostalgically remember the civil rights era from the vantage point of the 1980s and 1990s, this figure is not merely a representation of a past remembered in a particular way to comfort contemporary viewers. The civil rights subject was already present in network television's representational strategies as a means to soothe and reassure the medium's white audiences about the worthiness of Southern blacks in their quest for equality and political rights. For Gray, the civil rights subject encompassed "largely middle-class benefactors who gained the most visibility as well as material and status rewards from the struggles and opportunities generated by the civil rights movement." The civil rights subject was "an exemplar of citizenship and responsibility—success, mobility, hard work, sacrifice, individualism."[19] It is this image of the worthy Negro, one that middle-class whites could feel comfortable welcoming into their living

Mattie Bivens: another "worthy black victim." In neat white dress and high heels, she notes the dust accumulating on her shoes from the unpaved streets.

rooms, either in news coverage or, as we will see when we turn to entertainment programming, in fictional material, that network television privileged over and over again in the civil rights years.

Balancing its "worthy" Negroes, the report featured a few segregationists talking about the question of who could vote. Schoenbrun got one Mississippi lawyer tied up in knots trying to explain how someone like David Robertson, working toward his Masters degree and licensed to teach in Mississippi, could be deemed illiterate. The lawyer, scratching uncomfortably, hemmed and hawed about facts and assumptions in the case and whether the individual was of good moral character, before finally getting honest and stating that the country would be better off if there were legal means to keep all Negroes off voting rolls. Schoenbrun's camera comes in for an disconcertingly tight closeup, one that violates traditional norms of interpersonal distance. As John Fiske has noted, this extreme closeup has been conventionalized to represent villainy.[20] We are encouraged to interrogate the motives of the speaker in this framing.

More significant, however, was the report's attempt to find white moderates to speak. Considering the political situation in the state during the civil rights era—Mississippi was generally considered the most closed of the Jim Crow states and the most violent—*CBS Reports* producers managed to find a number of white moderates to speak on camera. While the report privileged the worthy black victims over the white moderates in screen time and narrative emphasis (whereas "Clinton and the Law" did the opposite), *CBS Reports* clearly felt the need to give viewers some indication that white moderates did, in fact, exist in the Magnolia State. Schoenbrun interviewed a former head of the White Citizens' Council who indicated his pride in the accomplishments of some Negroes in the area and affirmed that they should be permitted to vote. Highlighted was

Choker close-up: segregationist lawyer interrogated in uncomfort- able close-range, encouraging viewers to question his motives.

a white attorney, who functioned similarly to the Baptist minister in "Clinton and the Law." Introduced toward the end of the report as a graduate of Ole Miss and Harvard (thus bridging the Mason-Dixon divide), he was shown leaving his modest bungalow.

This framing humanized and individualized him; like the worthy black vic- tims, he was a person, not merely a representative of a political position. In his interview, he provided a class analysis of the Jim Crow system that suggested he might actually be a political radical, not a moderate. However, given the struc- ture of civil rights reporting and the desire to show Southern white moderates working with blacks to ensure their rights, this possibly Marxist lawyer was cast

White Southern moderate: this lawyer who takes voting rights cases is presented as a human being (we see his house), not just a political position.

as the exemplary white moderate to counterbalance the deviant and benighted Southern racist and segregationist.

Televising the Crisis at Ole Miss

"Clinton and the Law" and "Mississippi and the 15th Amendment" went out of their way to provide representations of Southerners who could be brought into the frame of moderation. Indeed, this search for moderation extended to coverage of the crisis at the University of Mississippi even as Oxford, in the fall of 1962, was an inauspicious venue for moderation in any form.

The James Meredith crisis at "Ole Miss" was a significant moment for the maturing medium of television news. The turmoil in Oxford received an unprecedented amount of television coverage during September and October 1962. *Broadcasting*, the industry trade journal, noted that the networks forfeited $400,000 in ad revenue with their many broadcast hours given over to Oxford coverage and the resulting preemption of regular programming.[21] *Variety* ballyhooed the networks' massive news juggling act with not only the ongoing crisis at Ole Miss, but also a highly dramatic baseball World Series matchup and a heavily anticipated manned space shot from Cape Canaveral. The trade paper reported on the "costly" decision NBC made to present a one-hour special report from Oxford in prime time, thus preempting the premier of a new drama series. This caused concern at NBC because of "the danger involved for a commercial hour called 'It's a Man's World,' which, being so new, is subject to all the vagaries of the sensitive viewership barometer, one of which is early preemption for something else."[22] NBC took out a two-page ad in the trade journal to trumpet its public-mindedness to other industry insiders. The ad tellingly displays how the network and its developing news division wished to be seen, particularly in the wake of condemnations from FCC commissioner Newton Minow.[23] Under images of two TV screens, one showing an image of James Meredith being escorted by officials and the other showing an image of the jubilant New York Giants, NBC exulted:

> We expected Monday, October 1 to be a big day for NBC Television. It *had* to be. "David Brinkley's Journal" was starting its new season with a full-hour chronicling of corruption in highway building. Johnny Carson was making his debut as the star of "Tonight!" And our afternoon schedule was opening its doors to the nighttime goings-on of "The Merv Griffin Show."
>
> So we *expected* it to be quite a day. But two unexpected news happenings the day before—one grimly serious and the other a sports story—made our Monday's television programming even more unusual.
>
> The violence at the University of Mississippi (and its aftermath) could not have been covered properly without our cutting into and changing our prepared schedule. This was done. Reports on the Southern crisis reached NBC viewers throughout the day and evening. On the "Today" show alone, there were five

up-to-the-minute newscasts on the situation. And in the evening, "It's a Man's World" was preempted for a special, full hour program highlighted by exclusive interviews with key figures in the controversy. First things first.[24]

Pointing out the preemption of five hours of regularly scheduled programming on this unusual day, the network then crowed, "It's comforting to know that when such days come, NBC's resources are *ready.*" The network then hyped itself as "*the largest single source of news, entertainment and information in the free world.*"

The network proclaimed that in the contest between commercial programming and public service news reporting, the latter would win out every time. It was also signaling a degree of maturity to its newsgathering institution and an obvious self-satisfaction with its approach to handling news. That all three cases of breaking news upending the entertainment schedule just happened to be highly dramatic, suspenseful, and visually exciting certainly did not hurt. In fact, this moment in the evolution of network news may merely have helped solidify conventions of television news that would always privilege these characteristics.

In this flurry of television attention, what did the coverage from Oxford look like? An examination of a number of television reports about the crisis suggest that, even in this highly polarized situation, television news still went out of its way to find white Southern voices of moderation. On September 28, CBS's Friday night documentary news series, *Eyewitness,* sent senior reporter Charles Collingwood to Oxford to report on Gov. Ross Barnett's refusal to allow Meredith to register at the University.[25] Much of the report focused on dramatic filmed sequences of the confrontation between Meredith and Barnett on the grounds of Ole Miss as Barnett refused Meredith's admission, along with footage of students cheering Barnett as he urged the students to remain "dignified" as the eyes of the world were upon them and would judge their conduct. Viewers also saw a tense confrontation as federal official John Doar, with Meredith, attempted to enjoin the Governor to obey federal law. And, most disturbing, viewers witnessed footage of crowds yelling at Meredith as he was forced to retreat. Collingwood, in voice-over, emphasized that these were not college students but older townspeople and high schoolers from Jackson. By emphasizing that this mob was not made up of Ole Miss students but rather of "outsiders" to the campus, Collingwood performed a maneuver similar to one used by Murrow in the Clinton story: the extremists and rabble-rousers were not of the community. The Ole Miss community may have been staunchly segregationist, but Collingwood attempted to negotiate the incendiary quality of the crisis by suggesting that the bad guys came from elsewhere.

Collingwood then extended this search for moderation by telling viewers: "But on the campus the rebel yell is not the only voice to be heard. There is a much more subdued voice that reflects the views of [inaudible words] and perhaps some students." Collingwood then interviewed a campus Episcopal minister and a colleague who both affirmed that they wanted Meredith admitted because otherwise the university would be shut down. Like the moderate townspeople highlighted in the Murrow report, these moderates emphasized that the courts have ruled; therefore, Meredith must be allowed to attend. In a standup after the interview, Collingwood admitted to his viewers: "What you've just heard is obviously a minority view in Mississippi." Collingwood did not interview any Mississippi whites who spoke the majority discourse of resistance to federal law. The only other players interviewed were Meredith, explaining why he wanted to go to Ole Miss, and his cotton farmer father, who was clearly uncomfortable confronting Dan Rather in a cotton field. Barnett spoke only in the documentary footage, not in the more privileged space of the formal interview.

Why the emphasis on the Episcopal minister? Within the ideological frame Collingwood brought to the story—a consensual value that the rule of federal law and the courts must be obeyed—Barnett's refusal to recognize that law was too disruptive. In constructing the parameters of legitimate debate, it made more sense for Collingwood to search for the moderate voices that, on the one hand, would make sense to the correspondent's own sense of the allowable political positions, but also, on the other hand, allowed Collingwood to portray a rational, thoughtful, accommodating South—a "new" Southerner who could be knitted into a new shared common sense about race and national values.

Barnett, on the other hand, was the deviant Other—the law breaker who "symbolizes the old and deeply held convictions in the South about the proper place of the Negro," according to Collingwood's tailpiece. Counterpoised to Barnett was Meredith who "symbolize[s] the new thrust of the American Negro for equal opportunity." Collingwood, however, did not give viewers a polarization of equally legitimated forces. The struggle may appear to be between Barnett and Meredith, but Collingwood needed to give viewers a moderate alternative that we see over and over again: a white Southerner who accepted that the ideology of equal opportunity provided the ultimate solution.

A few days later on NBC, *Chet Huntley Reporting* provided a similar frame to its story about the continuing crisis in Oxford—even using the same Episcopal minister. Between the CBS report and Huntley's October 2 program, Oxford had descended into chaotic violence as mobs rampaged through the campus, overwhelming the few hundred federal marshals sent by the Kennedy administration to protect the newly registered Meredith. Barnett inflamed the mob further with a fiery radio address, and their number grew as the evening progressed. Before the arrival of thousands of army troops to reinstate calm, scores had been wounded, and two lay dead, including a French news reporter.

Huntley's prime-time report began with correspondents Bill Ryan and Richard Valeriani reporting from the Ole Miss campus.[26] Ryan briefly questioned Meredith, described as traveling everywhere with federal marshals and troops, about his resolve to "stick it out." Valeriani then interviewed the Episcopal minister "who tried to prevent campus violence." The minister again spoke the discourse of law and order, but also the discourse of "outside agitators." He argued that students who did participate in the violence were incited by outsiders to the university and would never have done so on their own. Correspondent Ryan interviewed a total of two students: one who discussed the feeling of tension on the campus and, with the prodding of Ryan and echoing the minister, suggested that any further violence would be coming from outsiders. Ryan described the other student as "critical of school officials and grateful for the Federal presence." The student admitted that most students did not share his view. "I feel most of them feel as if, just as Barnett said, they said, well, we were invaded, which is ridiculous. We would have been destroyed without them [the federal troops]."

So, although the majority of students on the Ole Miss campus were surely opposed to Meredith's admission, and although sizable numbers may have participated in the September 30 rioting and would be deeply hostile to the presence of federal force, Ryan and Valeriani did not highlight—or even present—these perspectives, except filtered through the eyes of more moderate subjects.

The report did not entirely silence the voices of those opposed to the federal government. Viewers heard from Ross Barnett's second-in-command, Lieutenant Governor Paul Johnson, who, like Barnett, faced federal contempt-of-court citations. However Johnson's interview was narrowly focused mostly on the issue of why Mississippi patrolmen left the scene of the violence rather than help quell the mob. In a rather surprising maneuver, the report then turned to Arthur Krock, the *New York Times*' Washington correspondent and columnist to speak for the Mississippi position. Filtered through the legitimated institution of the Northeast newspaper of record, Krock's discourse was, like Johnson's, narrowly drawn. In heavily legalistic terminology, Krock questioned whether the state of Mississippi had received due process of law in the Meredith case. By focusing debate on whether the federal government and the Supreme Court acted appropriately and correctly, the broadcast managed to nudge an aspect of the conflict (state's rights vs. federal power) into the sphere of legitimate controversy. It helped that this discourse was spoken by someone not of the South but who was instead affiliated with an institution typically associated with the liberal, urban North.

Outside of the crisis at Oxford, the broadcast networks hunted for Southern white moderates to champion. In August 1962 Chet Huntley found some in Farmville, Virginia. The report dealt with the aftermath of Virginia's "Massive Resistance" to school integration of 1959. Although the resistance evaporated after less than a year in other parts of the Commonwealth, in Prince Edward County, students were into their third year of closed public schools. Huntley described the plight of Farmville's black children who had received no formal, professional instruction for more than two years, compared to white children, who had had a special private school built.[27] Huntley identified the leader of Farmville's segregationists—the publisher of the local paper. But, not surprisingly, Huntley's attention went elsewhere. Over film footage of the local teachers college, he stated, "Here at Longwood State

Teachers College was the only white citizen we could find in Farmville willing to oppose publicly the segregationist leadership. Others, and there are others who disagree, are inhibited by business and family considerations." Huntley introduced the dean of the college, Dr. Charles Moss who, in turn, introduced three Northern student volunteers—one from Harvard Law, one from Yale Divinity School, and a New Haven music teacher—all of whom had come to provide education to the town's black children. In this narrative, Huntley offered viewers Northern volunteers coming together to make common cause with a Southern white moderate in service to worthy black victims of segregation.

Another news report put together during the Meredith crisis could serve as network television's major celebration of the Southern white moderate. "The Other Face of Dixie," produced by *CBS Reports,* returned to the sites of four major televised school integration battlefields: Clinton, Tennessee; Little Rock, Arkansas; Atlanta, Georgia; and Norfolk, Virginia.[28] All had been subjects of CBS news coverage. The point of the broadcast was to demonstrate the success of integration and, just as important, to portray the ascendance of a Southern white integrationist common sense. In interview after interview, viewers encountered Southern whites speaking the discourses of color blindness, progress, success, and optimism. Over and over again, white moderates from these battlegrounds noted in upbeat tones that the South was in a period of transition and that the changes were positive and necessary. The color-blind theme was particularly emphasized. The Clinton High School principal (who had already been cast as an exemplary white moderate in the *See It Now* piece five years earlier) responded to a reporter's question about the number of blacks in his school by saying he was embarrassed to say he did not know: "We register them only as students." A teacher from a high school in Norfolk, Virginia, which had been shut down for half the school year during the "Massive Resistance" campaign of 1959, noted that one of the best football players at the school was black. When students cheered him, they were not cheering a race, but rather the best player and the best team. The postintegration South earnestly celebrated here eschewed difference, ignored diversity, emphasized commonality. The best way to integrate blacks into white institutions was to ignore their blackness.

Blacks, when represented at all, appeared only as silenced schoolchildren, singly or in small groups, surrounded by larger numbers of white peers. As objects in the struggle to bring white Southerners into an integrationist consensus, these blacks were not active agents in the narrative. The struggle was between and among whites. In this report, the narrative trajectory led viewers from the deviant and backward recesses of Arkansas' Orville Faubus, who was briefly interviewed as a still-unreconstructed segregationist, to Georgia Governor Ernest Vandiver, the reluctant but pragmatic recruit to white moderation. In an interview with Harry Reasoner, the reporter almost cheered the Governor's enlightenment. Vandiver grudgingly appropriated the law-and-order discourse by admitting that in Georgia, "our problems have been solved" by complying with the courts and adhering to law and order. He even pointed out that in an upcoming election there were some "Nigra" candidates and that the State Legislature might soon have some "Nigra" legislators. A smiling Reasoner replied, "You may have a desegregated legislature then." With a tight smile, Vandiver conceded, "That's correct. If the people vote that way."

"The Other Face of Dixie" presented a new South that conformed to postwar liberalism and was comprehensible to Northeastern-based network reporters, producers, and executives. It could be melded easily into the new mass audience so necessary to the postwar media and consumer industries. The documentary report also represented race relations in this new South (and presumably already the status quo in the already "enlightened" North) in easily comprehensible ways. Just as white Southerners could change quickly to join consensus politics around race and social progress, so too could Southern blacks. Integration was easy, once rational leadership held sway, because ultimately there were no significant economic, cultural, historical, or class differences among Southern blacks and whites that could not be erased through progressive mass institutions—whether public schooling or broadcast media and the consumer culture. "The Other Face of Dixie" was the story the networks wanted to tell because it was a story of inevitable progress toward the homogenous mass culture, untroubled by regional sectarianism or racial identity politics or caste systems that would challenge this undifferentiated new monoculture of TV viewers and consumers.

Covering the Movement: Network News Ambivalence with Black Activism

As we have seen in our exploration of TV news coverage of civil rights and desegregation activities, Southern white moderates were frequently paired with noble, suffering, well-spoken, middle-class-seeming black victims of segregation. From the earnest and well-educated franchise-seekers in "Mississippi and the 15th Amendment" to the beleaguered school children of Clinton and Farmville wanting only an education as good as their white peers, network news tended to prefer representations of Southern blacks as either paragons of respectability and potential and of demonstrable achievement or as silenced objects of mistreatment whose cause needed to be championed by enlightened whites.

Network news programs seemed particularly comfortable with black seekers of desegregation if they did not appear closely aligned or affiliated with a black civil rights organization or activist group. Herbert J. Gans, in his study of news values, has pointed out that journalists tend to emphasize individuals and individualism over groups. According to Gans, "The ideal individual struggles successfully against adversity and overcomes more powerful forces."[29] TV news producers may have been particularly drawn to James Meredith because he was so demonstrably on his own. In CBS's *Eyewitness* report of January 1963, titled "Color Line on Campus," Dan Rather pointedly asked Meredith (who was reconsidering whether he would continue at Ole Miss after a semester of isolation and harassment) if he had been paid by the NAACP or if he was their "tool."[30] Meredith denied he was in the employ of the organization but admitted to accepting its legal help. Later in the broadcast, viewers were introduced to another black student attempting to integrate a Southern college. The broadcast used the case of Harvey Gantt and his experience at South Carolina's Clemson University to contrast the deviant and violent extremism of Mississippi with the peaceful moderation of this other Deep South state. A reporter asked Gantt whether he was "led into" his actions by the NAACP.[31] "This was entirely my brainchild," Gantt replied emphatically. "No one has influenced me." He admitted, like Meredith, to using the organization's legal assistance. The thrust of the questions to Meredith and Gantt suggests that there would be something dubious or suspicious had these men been movement-affiliated activists—had they been anything but lone individuals wanting to exercise their individual rights to nondiscriminatory educational opportunities.

Network news reports and documentaries often appeared quite uncomfortable with representations of activist mass movements of blacks advocating and protesting for civil rights and desegregation. Organizationally affiliated blacks were less easy to cast in the role of individualized worthy victim. However, when covering mass-movement activism, TV news was most comfortable with material that they could celebrate as scrupulously peaceful and nonconfrontational. Unfortunately, the medium's ideological stake in peaceful, moderate moves toward accommodation around desegregation at times blinded reporters to the real story. In coverage of the Albany campaign, this ideological positioning caused CBS to thoroughly misread one of the SCLC's biggest failures.

Getting the Albany Campaign Wrong

By the time CBS *Eyewitness* cameras came to Albany, Georgia, in August 1962, blacks in this small, rural city had been organizing around desegregation of the town's institutions and the integration of its bus terminal since the previous fall. Initially, SNCC and the NAACP had aligned with other local black organizations to form the Albany Movement. However, after an energizing visit by Martin Luther King who led a mass march to city hall, the SCLC decided to use its resources and the organizing power of Dr. King to, in effect, take over the campaign in Albany. The SCLC anticipated that its tactics of passive resistance, mass arrests, and appeal for federal intervention would force Albany's white power structure to relent and integrate its public institutions. Unfortunately, the movement did not factor in the town's police chief, Laurie Pritchett. He refused to play the role of brutal, openly racist, Southern lawman. Despite months of protests, civil disobedience, jailings, and mass marches, the SCLC and the Albany movement never cracked the white segregationist wall they faced. And because there was no chaos, as there was in Oxford, Mississippi, the Kennedy administration never felt compelled to intervene. By the end of the summer, King and the SCLC left Albany in defeat.

Eyewitness's "The Albany Movement" did not appear to appreciate the defeat the activists were facing.[32] The report featured a number of worthy black victims used to encourage maximum sympathy from viewers: black protesters kneeling in prayer in front of city hall, with the focus on one kneeling woman weeping; teenage protesters kneeling and praying in front of a library whose front doors and stacks were barred to them; young girls in church singing and clapping to "This Little Light of Mine"; jailed activists crowded into cells; a protest leader instructing protesters not to speak harshly or chew gum but to emphasize dignity.

Over footage at city hall of the weeping and praying woman being arrested and placed on a stretcher, correspondent Charles Collingwood noted that prayer was a special tactic employed by the Albany movement. He pointed out that this demanded "great discipline" by the Negroes and "great restraint" from the white population. So far, both sides had shown discipline and restraint, which had made Albany different. The city had not negotiated with black protesters, he admitted, but it had not allowed violent retaliation. For Collingwood, the lack of white violence was good news. It suggested a successful and admirable model for future confrontations in the civil rights struggle. Within an ideological frame that celebrated moderation, Collingwood could not see that the SCLC and the Albany movement required extremism and brutality on the part of Albany whites and especially its police force for its campaign to hope for success. Pritchett was inconveniently cast by CBS as a white moderate and shown being restrained in confrontation with King. In an interview immediately after this footage, Pritchett was asked what instructions he gave his men in handling demonstrators. Pritchett replied, "We knew their theory was nonviolence, so we base our theory on nonviolence also. This has stunned them. They were expecting police brutality. They were expecting the police to come in on them."

Pritchett was, of course, not a moderate. A staunch segregationist, he realized that the best way to ensure no federal intervention, national condemnation, and negative national media attention was to maintain law and order. So, like the white moderates we have seen in other news reports, Pritchett seemed to speak the consensus discourse. Collingwood did not appear to recognize that Pritchett was messing up two scripts: one used by the SCLC and the other used by the TV networks. Pritchett refused to play the brutal Southern sheriff of King's script or either of the recognizable roles constructed by the networks: deviant white Other or embraceable white moderate.

"The Albany Movement" differed from numerous other TV documentary reports in that it focused sympathetic attention on civil rights activists as participants in a movement rather than as worthy, aggrieved individuals. The documentary uses some strategies similar to the *NBC White Paper* report "Sit-In" examined by Sasha Torres. Both present orderly, nonviolent protest as "forms of African American activism most palatable to powerful northern whites." Therefore, "Sit-In" (and "The Albany Movement") are both documentary reports "able quietly to lend [their] support to the integration of public accommodations through nonviolent means."[33] Both reports also allow a significant amount of agency to the blacks they present to viewers. Torres notes how some sequences of "Sit-In" seem to allow activists, using a black idiom, to speak directly to black audiences and to do so in ways that might be unintelligible to whites. Torres points to one sequence in the report in which we hear a nondiegetic voice-over of an unidentified black male speaking in revival-meeting cadences about the need to wake up and rise up as we see a montage of images of black protest, arrest, picketing, and white onlookers. Torres argues that sequences like this are not addressed to NBC's imagined audience of white opinion leaders but rather to "potentially insurgent black subjects."[34]

"The Albany Movement" is notable for a very unusual moment in which an unidentified demonstrator narrated and explained footage of a public library demonstration. Standard news procedure would be for Collingwood or another presumably objective reporter to narrate the footage. Instead, we see film of teenagers kneeling and praying in front of the library; then footage of Chief Pritchett; then of his police carrying the teens to the paddy wagon. As this dramatic material unfolded, a leader of the action explained how the doors were barred and how the students kneeled and prayed and that they all did this (including being arrested) of their own free will. There was no omniscient anchor or correspondent shaping the sequence or eliciting comments from the demonstration leader. The activist spoke directly to audiences without any standard journalistic filters to signal that viewers were hearing a specific, interested point of view.

Televised news reports and documentaries that allowed African Americans to speak in their own voices and to assume active subject positions were, however, rare in TV reporting. There are a number of other notable cases featuring more active black subjects. The Robert Drew/Richard Leacock films for ABC's *Bell and Howell Close Up!*—"The Children Were Watching" and "Walk in My Shoes"—both used verité approaches to give audiences black protagonists who speak from their own social positioning about the discrimination and oppression they suffer.[35] However, as Michael R. Winston has noted, "Television had more to say *about* blacks in American society [in the 1960s], but very seldom was any of this said *by* blacks. Even when the messenger was black, in fact, the message was usually from a white point of view."[36] Winston's argument is a bit sweeping, but it is fair to say that, usually, but not always, black civil rights proponents needed to be structured within dominant white, liberal, Northeast consensus notions of racial progress and deference to the law. As we will see with CBS's coverage of the 1965 Selma campaign, black voting rights activists, marchers, and demonstrators rarely spoke for themselves. Quintessential worthy victims, they served as objects of concern whose plight was spoken for either by legitimated spokesman and leader, Dr. King, or by a white TV reporter.

Conclusion

By 1963, network news seemed to have solidified a general script for its civil rights coverage: search for worthy black victims of racial discrimination who could be individualized or, if in groups, kept largely silent, and have either Martin Luther King or a white reporter speak for them. Search also for representations of white Southern moderation and signs of progress and privilege that discourse. Remain suspicious and uncomfortable with instances of black people in mass movement and, when interviewing, ask demonstrators if there is any suggestion that the situation could become violent. Accept that the following issues are fully within consensus politics and thus not subject to journalistic balancing: school desegregation, integration in public places, voting rights for Southern blacks. As the network news divisions continued to mature and to accumulate more resources and time on air, and as the civil rights movement—particularly the King-led Southern nonviolent campaign—intensified in the next few years, this news script remained mostly in place. When we turn our attention to television news coverage of two of the movement's peak moments—the March on Washington, which helped ensure passage of the 1964 Civil Rights Act, and the Selma campaign, which led directly to the swift passage of the 1965 Voting Rights Act—we will see how this script, in sometimes complicated ways, worked to the benefit of the Southern black freedom movement.

CHAPTER 3

Fighting for Equal Time

Segregationists vs. Integrationists

Mississippi Congressman John Bell Williams was deeply troubled by the state of network television and its regulatory body in 1963. To him, most of the FCC's commissioners were supporters of "race mixing," a matter he wanted investigated by the Communications Committee chairman. He was also alarmed at the way those clearly biased commissioners were wielding the power of the Fairness Doctrine against local Mississippi broadcasters, demanding that they physically go out into their communities to find representatives with views opposed to segregation. Congressman Williams said, "We know of no responsible person in Mississippi who would go on the air and speak for integration." And any Mississippian who did hold such views and agreed to voice them on local television could be nothing but an "agitator."[1] Along with such unwarranted and unjust demands on local Mississippi broadcasters, Congressman Williams was particularly upset with network programming:

> [I have] yet to see a network documentary designed, planned and programed for the purpose of giving the prosegregation side of the race problem, yet we are continuously bombarded with the other.
>
> I consider this an act of intimidation on the part of the FCC against a selected group of broadcasters and an attempt to use radio and TV as a propaganda vehicle for socialism, the New Frontier and forced race mixing. It is an attempt to brainwash the American people into conforming to a preconceived idea of a majority of the commissioners."[2]

The Congressman's particular perspective about television was widely shared among Southern white segregationists. Yet he refused to resign himself to the situation and accept that network programming would be less than sympathetic to the Jim Crow cause. The call for "equal time," for "balance," and for the presentation of "our side" was an ongoing battle throughout the civil rights years.[3] But while white segregationists most frequently positioned themselves as the aggrieved party suffering from "biased" coverage, this was not always the case.

Civil rights activists and supporters of integration could also find themselves protesting network coverage as unfair and as "propaganda" for the other side. From the earliest days of network news coverage of what was happening in the South, constituents from both sides of the black empowerment movement, as well as television viewers from all parts of the country, struggled over and debated to what extent television was giving their side "equal time." Along with the political players and ordinary viewers, network news personnel—journalists, producers, and executives—also struggled and battled with each other over what constituted balanced coverage that gave various voices equal access to the national airways. They also grappled with the ethical conundrum of what reporters could say about the situation and the extent to which network news journalists could or should present on-air opinions and analysis.

Chapter 2 focused largely on textual analysis to uncover how television attempted to negotiate the civil rights story to heal sectional rifts by elevating the white Southern moderate; here we shift our attention to audience reception and production practice. The evidence of audience response suggests that the sectional and political rifts around race were not being assuaged by television coverage—in fact, television coverage served as another battlefield where the politics of race, region, and integration played out. The following case studies of audience reaction to controversial news programs show that what it meant to be "Southern" and "Northern" became particularly fraught questions. Network television's defining quality as a national medium may have made these issues of regional identity particularly salient. But also television's status as a regulated medium required by federal law to broadcast controversial issues according to a doctrine of "fairness" may have further engaged partisans and activated viewers in a struggle over how the new medium ought to be representing the Southern racial situation to the nation. Network executives, news producers, and on-air reporters were also highly sensitized to the fact that regulatory pressures were on them, particularly once the new Kennedy administration took over and its FCC head, Newton Minow, proclaimed a new era of active oversight. More generally, TV news personnel found themselves having to figure out how journalism would work in this new medium even as they covered the most significant domestic story of their generation under the eyes of Washington officials and partisans on either side of the Jim Crow line, as well as a vast national audience.

Fair and Balanced: Using the Fairness Doctrine

How could the networks provide balanced coverage of the deeply polarizing situation in the South? What strategies would be acceptable to the network bosses, to the audience commodity the networks were attempting to construct, to FCC regulators, and to the reporters and news producers trying to use television as a new journalistic medium? The Fairness Doctrine would appear to provide some guidance to networks in their approach, but instead, the regulation incited mostly discord and controversy. Promulgated by the FCC in 1949, the Fairness Doctrine required broadcasters, as "public trustees," when covering controversial matters of public concern to present contrasting positions and to be fair, balanced, and equitable in their journalistic treatment. Although the Fairness Doctrine appeared to mandate standard, professional, journalistic protocol, TV journalists found the regulation to be frustrating and limiting to their news judgments. One journalist at the 1965 symposium (discussed at the beginning of chapter 2) addressed the issue of balance and who the reporter put on air representing Southern whites. Should it be the head of the White Citizens' Council? Should it be the mayor? "Frequently, you wind up with the most belligerent white leader around; the others refuse to comment."[4] Another speaker at the symposium, the president of a local Florida TV station, echoed the argument that the Fairness Doctrine allowed racist views to command more air time than would be warranted by the number of whites in the population who shared those extreme views: "It has . . . allowed minority racist factions to obtain air time on stations that are trying to combat bigotry and extremism."[5] We have already seen that network news journalists maneuvered around this dilemma by overemphasizing the voices of white Southern moderates while using a developing arsenal of narrative and visual tropes to marginalize and vilify hard segregationists.

But even as television news personnel agonized about providing airtime to racists because of Fairness Doctrine requirements, segregationists did not see the Fairness Doctrine as a means for white supremacists to command the airways and disseminate their arguments to local and national audiences. Congressman Williams of Mississippi saw national television as integrationist propaganda abetted by biased FCC commissioners. Williams's colleague in the Senate, South Carolina's Strom Thurmond, also launched a campaign against the Fairness Doctrine. In response to the FCC's recent notice to Southern stations directing them to present the views of black representatives when covering stories about desegregation, Thurman declared on the floor of the U.S. Senate that the Fairness Doctrine was "a most dangerous threat to freedom of thought and the right of the public to have more than just the left point of view presented over the nation's airwaves."[6]

The wariness with which Southern segregationists regarded network television is well illustrated by the NBC public affairs program *The Nation's Future,* which ran in the 1960–61 season on Saturday night during prime time.[7] The series clearly (and perhaps mechanistically) displayed the Fairness Doctrine in action by presented each week a formal debate between speakers taking opposite positions on a contemporary issue of the day. Inspired by the explosion of lunch counter sit-ins sparked by the actions of four African American students in Greensboro, North Carolina, who spontaneously decided to try to integrate the local Woolworth lunch counter in February, the debate question for the November 26, 1960 show was "Are sit-in strikes justifiable?"

Martin Luther King quickly accepted the show's invitation to speak for the proposition. The show's producers encountered much more difficulty finding a debater to take on Dr. King and argue against sit-in demonstrations. Program staffers compiled an extensive list of prominent Southern segregationists, all of whom either outright refused to participate or excused themselves as "out of the country." The list of public figures the show attempted to lure included Strom Thurmond, Mississippi Senators John Stennis and James Eastland, Alabama Governor John Patterson, *Montgomery Advertiser* editor Grover Cleveland Hall (characterized by a show staffer as a "rabid segregationist" but "excellent speaker"), all of whom found reasons to not appear.[8] With only a few weeks remaining before airdate, the show finally garnered prominent newspaper editor James J. Kilpatrick of the *Richmond News Leader*. Kilpatrick expressed ambivalence about his appearance, however, and in a letter to the show's producer, he asked to clarify the debate topic and the ground rules for the program. "Forgive me if I ask for an understanding on these things in advance. The last time I appeared on television with Martin Luther King, I got boobytrapped by David Susskind into the short end of 5–1 odds. I don't propose to walk into a rigged situation again if I can avoid it."[9] Like Strom Thurmond and John Bell Williams responding to the Fairness Doctrine, Kilpatrick considered network television to be a generally inhospitable terrain for segregationists. He worried that the debate would center on the issue of the "morality" of sit-ins and felt that such a framing would stack the deck in King's favor.

Whether or not the debate ended up favoring King, numerous TV stations in Alabama, Louisiana, and Mississippi did not bother to find out. They blacked out the broadcast—the presence of an articulate and highly educated segregationist not being enough to counter the hated image and words of Dr. King. Interestingly, both Kilpatrick and Wyatt Tee Walker, King's right hand man at the SCLC, wrote to show producer Robert Allison about the censorship of the show. Kilpatrick described a friend of his from Camden, South Carolina, who complained that South Carolina stations were "too yellow to carry the debate."[10] Walker noted, "I was in Montgomery and your outlet there blacked [the show] out. I called my wife and listened via long distance telephone. Expensive, but well worth it."[11] For segregationist broadcasters, even an exercise of "equal time" debate such as this could not be trusted. The show came from the network and thus carried signifiers of "the North" and "outsiders." Also, if it was settled opinion in places like Mississippi that only "agitators" spoke in favor of integration, then any program that professed to debate the issue could only be irresponsible propaganda even if a well-spoken, respected, and admired representative for segregation appeared prominently. Even with that appearance, there could be only suspicion over the televisual tactics the network would employ to "booby trap" and undermine the position.

The Southern stations should, perhaps, not have been so quick to censor the program, as it appears that Kilpatrick more than held his own against King.[12] One participant from the broadcast (presumably a member of the studio audience) described comments he received about the show and in particular the statements of Kilpatrick. According to this Manhattan-based writer, "Northerners have too little opportunity to see and hear well-informed and sincere segregationists defend their positions and express their convictions. It was therefore a reality shock for many of the viewers to discover that 'bigots' look, and talk like 'civilized' people."[13] In a letter to Kilpatrick, producer Allison discussed the heavy volume of mail the show generated and noted that "even in the con letters, there was a grudging admiration reflected over the skill with which you defended your position."[14] In a similar letter to King, Allison noted, "[B]oth the program and your contribution to it was overwhelmingly favorable. . . . [I]t is very clear that the public was immensely gratified with the high level contributions that you made and that outside the deep South, you have overwhelming support."[15]

Some young activists within the movement might have disagreed with this assessment of King's performance. During an executive meeting of SNCC members in Atlanta, the group took a break from their organizing work to watch the program. Ella Baker, the SCLC's executive director, who made no secret of her dissatisfaction with King's leadership style and who was instrumental in helping to give birth to SNCC seven months earlier, watched the program with the young activists. All were disappointed with King's performance, according to King biographer David J. Garrow. In their estimation, King was "no match" for Kilpatrick. Ella Baker remembered: "The students were sitting there in front of the TV, waiting for him to 'take care' of Kilpatrick. Finally, some got up and walked away." According to Garrow, King's televised performance provided "the first occasion where the students' unhappiness with King 'finally broke open to the surface.'"[16]

The response of the SNCC activists, along with that of other viewers, suggests that network television may not have fully deserved the suspicion and hostility Southern white segregationists heaped on it—at least not all the time. Nor should we assume that a movement figure like Dr. King always commanded the medium and bent it to his will.

Professionalizing TV News:
Objectivity and Commentary

If the civil rights movement became television journalism's first major story during its formative years, then how would the new medium conduct itself as a journalistic institution? How would viewers respond to network television's unique characteristics as a journalistic enterprise with national reach? Television news historian Michael Curtin suggests that one of the reasons the networks turned to documentary and news genres as their means of asserting public service accomplishments was because news required "professional expertise" that could be supplied by the network's in-house journalists whose grounding in the profession's codes of objectivity would garner trust from television viewers, both in the journalists and, by extension, in the network.[17] Curtin points out that the ideology of objectivity was fraught with contradictions, however. "Documentarists relied on facts, and yet they manipulated the facts in order to draw conclusions. They were unbiased, and yet they promoted a broadly defined political agenda. They were disinterested, and yet they sought to educate, convert, and reform public sentiment. And in the end, the contradiction that would prove the most troublesome was that documentarists were professionals, and yet they were not autonomous."[18]

These sets of contradictions can be seen in stark relief in the production and reception of two controversial news documentaries about civil rights that aired in 1959 and 1961; one reported on "massive resistance" to school desegregation and the other on violence against Freedom Riders, the integrated groups of activists who rode into the Deep South on interstate buses to test compliance with federal law requiring desegregated facilities at bus terminals. Both documentary reports starred two of early TV journalism's most popular and highly regarded reporter/celebrities: Chet Huntley and Howard K. Smith. Both Huntley and Smith engaged in editorializing about desegregation and Southern race relations in their programs. Both shows elicited large volumes of viewer mail reflecting outrage at the "biased" and "unfair" way in which the viewers felt "their" side had been represented. In both cases, network executives intervened in the news division and dictated to the news staff how it would present its coverage. The controversies that swirled around these broadcasts reveal the difficulties reporters, anchors, and broadcast networks faced in covering Southern race relations in the civil rights era.

"The Second Agony of Atlanta"

On February 1, 1959, NBC's popular Sunday evening news program with Chet Huntley explored the threatened "massive resistance" against school integration in Georgia. Newly elected governor Ernest Vandiver, a staunch segregationist, planned to follow the lead of the Commonwealth of Virginia and close any school or district that agreed to admit African American pupils. At the time of reporting, no schools had actually been closed because federal court cases were pending, but the situation looked to repeat what happened in Norfolk and other places in Virginia where public schools had been forced to close, leaving students, black and white, without any form of organized, publicly funded instruction. According to the *New York Times'* television critic Jack Gould, the first part of the broadcast "offered a generally well-rounded summary of opinion among white people in Georgia on the school controversy" and was presented "with commendable calmness."[19]

Some African American viewers disagreed. An NAACP field secretary noted an imbalance of Negro and white opinion in the show with an overemphasis of white opinion supporting continued segregation over white opinion favoring open schools.[20] An African American clergyman from Atlanta was incensed enough to provide a detailed textual analysis of the documentary's lack of balance and damaging representation of young black schoolchildren. He noted that only "one Negro adult was given the privilege to express his views over against many white adults who came from various walks of life" and included the governor. Gould noted the fact that only one adult Negro appeared but did not express the same degree of outrage at the lack of balance this implied. Demonstrating an exquisite sense of the politics of racial imagery, the clergyman pointed out the contrasting ways a group of white and black high school students were presented to NBC's audience: "The white high school students introduced were seated at a table and were evidently prepared formally for the interviewer." The black students, however, appeared "casually as they stood at a soda fountain at a drug store. . . . Their minds were not at all on the question, because as young people they were gathered at a drug store to buy drinks." Exacerbating this negative image of black youth was an interview with a black twelve-year-old who, in the clergyman's reading, was quizzed and grilled with "difficult questions" no child of that age could possibly answer. The interview "could not help but create in the minds of the Negroes who observed, the impression that there could possibly have been a trap set before the kid to make him say something that could be offensive to the white viewers and listeners."[21]

Because images of black people were rare on nationwide television in 1959, any appearances were likely to receive intense scrutiny within black viewing communities. Among those in the civil rights and black leadership class (such as this Atlanta minister), black televisual representations, whether they were entertainment images such as *Beulah* or *Amos 'n' Andy* or news footage, could have profound implications for black advancement—or its opposite. The minister saw NBC deliberately constructing images of black school children as either uninterested in desegregation or not worthy of being integrated with white kids. Hanging out at soda joints rather than at school like their white counterparts, the black students were represented as not serious, not studious, and not well versed in the politics of the integration battle, unlike the white students.

The documentary report itself, however, received only a small amount of commentary. A veritable explosion of protest—and some praise—greeted what followed it. Chet Huntley, who had introduced the report, returned with a provocative tailpiece in which he told his viewers that the movement toward school integration had ground to a halt because the debate was being conducted "in an atmosphere of increasing tension and conflict, dominated more and more by extreme groups and irresponsible spokesmen." The integration issue, he suggested, needed to be taken away from "the unyielding elements which have taken control on both sides" in order to allow moderates to "do the decent thing." Huntley then suggested that precisely because Negroes were the deprived group and as "the price of its own success," present Negro leadership needed to withdraw. He then zeroed in on the NAACP. This was a surprising editorial move, considering that the previous news report contained no reporting about the organization's activity in the Atlanta desegregation issue. Huntley observed, "The NAACP may have outlived itself, because the white Southerner who must prevail, if anyone will, consider it an unacceptable symbol. Nor is it fair that militant Negro leadership must be abandoned while militant white leadership can continue. But just as the Negroes have the most to gain, it is they who must make the unfairest sacrifice to achieve it. I also suggest that if militant Negro leadership is removed, militant white leadership will in time atrophy and disappear."[22]

A number of the recurring themes we have already seen in television coverage of civil rights are on display in Huntley's tailpiece. Most obvious is the discomfort with organized "extremists" and "intransigents" and the elevation of the "moderate" not connected to organized, activist groups. Huntley's describing the NAACP as "militant Negro leadership" is a startling characterization. During the civil rights era, activists frequently criticized the NAACP for its caution, its discomfort with mass protest, and its focus on using the courts as the primary venue for addressing black citizens' oppressed status. Huntley comes uncomfortably close to constructing a moral equivalence between the NAACP on one side and the Ku Klux Klan, the White Citizens' Councils, and other white supremacist groups on the other. Both sides are organized and vocal and impassioned. Thus both sides are dangerous. But the NAACP is even more dangerous because the white Southerner refuses to engage with the group. Although it is clear that Huntley supports desegregation in principle, his commentary aligns the reporter rather closely to Southern segregationists' views of the NAACP. If Southern whites consider the group to be militant, then the NAACP must be militant. If white Southerners want the group to disappear, then the NAACP must disappear.

Having constructed a story of opposing forces, Huntley's solution is a vague, unorganized, silenced, moderate middle. He alludes to Americans, Negro and white, who have talked to him and other reporters "in hotel lobbies and railway stations, in formal meetings and on the street" about wanting to do the right thing, but not in the present climate. It is these moderate individuals, not spouting a party line, not getting their marching orders from an agitating collective, who will solve the problem, ensuring that children get educated and that the law is upheld.

Viewers Respond

Huntley's report was not unusual in the general themes it advanced, but it was atypical in its overt criticism of a black civil rights organization. Immediately following the Sunday night broadcast, NBC received a deluge of letters, telegrams, and phone calls both praising and damning the broadcast. Newspapers around the country carried reports about Huntley's opinion, including Southern outlets like the *Birmingham News,* which reported the controversy on its front page. White Southerners in particular flooded the network with letters, many expressing surprise and gratitude that for once the national broadcast networks were siding with segregationists.

One viewer from Fort Worth wrote: "This is to express my admiration and astonishment that a northern newspaperman, commentator or *whatever* could give as cogent and understanding a review of the south's position in the racial issue as you did in your recent broadcast."[23] A viewer from Albany, Georgia, noted: "Your Sunday program . . . was as nearly unbiased as any program that I have seen on the usually biased networks."[24] In a clear case of negotiated meaning making, large numbers of white Southern letter writers neglected to hear Huntley's approval of school integration and interpreted his criticism of the NAACP as supportive of continued segregation. Repeatedly they used the term "unbiased" to characterize Huntley's commentary. For many of these writers, Huntley was not expressing an editorial position but rather reporting in a fair, balanced, and objective manner about the facts of the situation in the South. They viewed this "unbiased" reporting as a departure from the slanted, hostile coverage Southern white segregationists were used to getting. Gratified letter writers discursively then embraced Huntley as one of their own. Wrote another Georgian on the broadcast's controversy: "Perhaps you can better realize now the reaction we Southerners get to our ideas or opinions. You see, [three-quarters of] the country considers us terribly uninformed and biased. Welcome to the fold!"[25]

If segregationists embraced Huntley as one of their own, letter writers supporting integration (mostly from Northern, urban areas) expressed outrage that this highly respected reporter could be "brainwashed." A Brooklyn viewer wrote: "Tonight, you showed yourself as no longer an impartial reporter—you have now become a victim of the group which feels that, left alone, the 'southerners' can work it out; that 'time' will solve all."[26] A Jamaica, New York, letter writer observed: "I have heard many stupid things on TV but yours was the most asinine and illogical suggestion yet to emanate from a single network. . . . It is evident that you have been wined and dined and brainwashed in the homes and country clubs of the white Southerner until you have become a better advocate for them than they could be themselves." Yet another New Yorker fumed, "If the states of the South which are spending money to educate the North on the virtues of segregation wanted a nationwide network show to present their case, they could have done no better than to have bought the hour you devoted last night to the Atlanta story."[27]

A number of civil rights and social justice activists, in particular, emphasized the charge that Huntley was furthering the public relations work of the White Citizens' Councils and other segregationist groups. The Fellowship of Reconciliation's field secretary, in a letter to the NAACP, noted that it was not so much Southern white extremists who posed a danger to desegregation, but rather "the selling job that white 'moderates' are doing in the north, and I think Chet's comments were a partial reflection of how frightfully successful some of their efforts have been in this direction."[28] The NAACP regional secretary quoted above also worried about the "anti-NAACP and anti-Negro propaganda that has been flooding the country under the aegis of the White Citizens Councils and the States' Rights Committees of the South."[29]

For these activists, the mass media was a crucial terrain of struggle, and they feared the prospects of outlets like national television being captured by segregationist forces. In fact, segregationists did pursue strategies to make the South's race policies appear "respectable" for national audiences. According to television historian Steven Classen, the White Citizens' Councils, using Mississippi taxpayer money, began in 1955 to produce a TV talk show titled *Citizens' Council Forum* that was syndicated across the United States to apparently three hundred stations in forty-one states.[30] According to Classen, the program appropriated the conventions of the networks' sober public affairs shows in order to appear credible and evenhanded, but the only guests who appeared were white supremacists who couched their arguments in the language of "states rights."[31]

Neither the NAACP nor any other civil rights organization had this kind of direct access to the nation's airwaves. They had to rely on the justice of their cause in persuading broadcast journalists, commentators, and producers to report sympathetically on issues such as school desegregation. The Huntley controversy suggested that civil rights activists could not assume that network television necessarily would serve as their ally and advocate.

For viewers—Northern and Southern, segregationist and integrationist—the stakes were high in television coverage. Television viewers, critics, and activists saw the young medium as a significant player in the unfolding political struggle over desegregation. White Southern segregationists assumed the networks and their reporters (coming from outside the South) to be both uninformed and hostile toward the Southern way of life. Northern supporters of integration (typically from middle-class, urban areas) assumed the networks and reporters shared an anti–Jim Crow common sense. Civil rights activists worried that the news media could be captured by savvy segregationist propagandists. The controversy around Huntley's broadcast highlights the uncertainty about the role that national network television would play in the unfolding struggle over civil rights in the South. It suggests that we need to question the conventional wisdom that network television served unproblematically as the "instrument of the revolution" wielded by the civil rights movement.

As the broadcast networks completed their push to achieve nationwide reach through the mid to late 1950s, the networks needed to rethink how they addressed their diversifying audiences. In the earliest days of television broadcast, stations were limited to major urban areas in the Northeast, Midwest, and California coast. Programming during this period tended to assume a more culturally sophisticated, ethnically diverse audience.[32] However, as Southern and rural areas joined the network web, especially after the FCC lifted its licensing freeze in 1953, the networks had to take into account the sensibilities of audiences and affiliated stations in those areas. The networks used their new policy of "least objectionable programming" as a way to deal with a diverse, regionally identified, heterogeneous audience by addressing it as an undifferentiated, nonregional, nonclassed (or naturalized middle-class) mass. Regionally distinct understandings about race relations could be taken care of by ignoring blacks in prime-time programming: removing shows like *Amos 'n' Andy* and *Beulah* from the airwaves was one response.

News and documentary programming presented a more complicated situation. Sasha Torres argues that the networks needed a national audience who shared core values and assumptions about citizenship and the rule of law. This conception of audiences was necessary for the networks if they were to sell their audience commodity to advertisers efficiently and successfully. "In this regard," Torres argues, "the networks shared common cause with the movement, which sought to produce precisely such a national consensus."[33]

But, of course, the networks did not necessarily embrace the activist, marching-in-the-streets movement. In fact, the networks were not really committed to making common cause with the civil rights struggle from the standpoint of the movement and of African Americans at all. In general, the networks, when engaging with civil rights and the black empowerment movement, searched for ways to make the process of change in race relations less uncomfortable to whites. The networks (in this case, NBC) were less than fully committed to ameliorating the outrage of a civil rights organization such as the NAACP. Huntley may have intended to make his white audience feel more comfortable about school desegregation by appealing to Atlanta moderates who would somehow appear out of the woodwork if the NAACP and other "militants" fell away to ensure that the rule of law stood and that desegregation ultimately succeeded; however, his botched editorial merely heartened segregationists and outraged the civil rights community. Rather than construct a consensus position, Huntley's editorializing heightened polarization.

Responding to the Controversy: Equal Time

The intense reaction to Huntley's editorial forced NBC to act. It also spurred the NAACP: Henry Lee Moon, the organization's publicity director, jumped into action as soon as the broadcast ended. Unable to reach Roy Wilkins, executive secretary and public face of the NAACP, Moon managed to confer with Thurgood Marshall, the organization's chief counsel. Marshall advised Moon to get in touch with all field staff, state presidents, and heads of large local branches, urging them to wire their protests to NBC and demand that the NAACP be granted time to reply to Huntley's comments. In making his calls, Moon discovered that most everyone had seen the broadcast.[34]

Over at Rockefeller Center, network president Robert Kintner ordered into his office the news program's producers, including Reuven Frank and news head William McAndrew. Kintner demanded they turn over next Sunday's broadcast to a debate between Roy Wilkins and a noteworthy Southern segregationist.[35] While the original broadcast had been one hour, the follow-up would be half an hour. The network offered Wilkins ten minutes of time for a statement; the other ten minutes would go to Thomas R. Waring, the staunchly segregationist editor of the *Charleston News and Courier*.

Outraged, the NAACP initially balked at NBC's offer. Under this scenario, not only would Wilkins have to rebut Huntley's arguments, but he would have to counter whatever Waring happened to lob at him. The NAACP argued that Wilkins would need a full hour to properly repair the damage done by the previous week's hour-long broadcast. NBC's McAndrew argued that the network was being generous in giving Wilkins ten minutes of rebuttal time, since Huntley's original editorial was a mere four minutes long.[36] Realizing they were not going to prevail over the network, the NAACP grudgingly acquiesced to NBC's terms. Wilkins did so under protest, though. To McAndrew, he wrote: "We do not believe that NBC is really convinced that a half hour divided between a re-cap of his position by Mr. Huntley, a statement by an avowed segregationist, and a statement by a representative of the NAACP provides this organization with a genuine opportunity to deal with the points raised by Mr. Huntley on February 1."[37] This was not "equal time" for the desegregation position. Rather, along with rebutting Huntley, Wilkins would have to "take care of a fresh segregationist onslaught."[38] For members and supporters of the organization, the entire episode seemed weighted in favor of the segregation position and against the NAACP.

During the week before Wilkins's appearance, the NAACP worked hard to make the most of its ten minutes of TV time, knowing that with all the press attention heaped on the original broadcast, the follow-up show would likely draw large audiences. Wilkins and his team worked over his statement line by line, even word by word, focusing in particular on matters of image—both of blacks in general and the NAACP in particular.[39] The organization understood the politics of representation, and Wilkins and Moon were both media savvy. They had only a short moment to visually and verbally recast the image of the NAACP from "militant" and thus frightening to white audiences, to "righteous" and thus acceptable to whites. Wilkins and his team were also very aware that they would be speaking to two different audiences: blacks, who were expected to watch in large numbers due to the organization's vigorous publicizing within black communities, and whites. According to Wilkins, the task before him was "soft selling the white audience" and "hard selling the Negro audience."[40] Unlike the broadcast networks, which had no particular economic rationale for concerning themselves with black audiences, the NAACP saw Wilkins's appearance as an important opportunity to do some television organizing around civil rights issues directed at black audiences: "hard selling." But how to do that without missing the opportunity to appeal to the vast white audience? This was a quandary that civil rights organizers would encounter again and again as they found themselves playing on the national stage. Only Martin Luther King seemed, at least for a time, to have perfected the balance.[41]

Wilkins and Moon's quandary in attempting to speak to two audiences and provide a representation of blackness that articulated African American strivings in distinct ways suggests W. E. B Dubois's influential concept of "double consciousness." Television would increasingly function as yet another terrain upon which "two-ness" would be enacted: "this sense of always looking at one's self through the eyes of others," as Dubois described the phenomenon. "One ever feels his twoness—an American, a Negro: two souls, two thoughts, two unreconciled strivings; two warring ideals in one dark body. . . ."[42] In this case, Wilkins would provide the dark body that would have to encompass the warring ideals, presenting himself for white inspection and scrutiny while also reaching out and mobilizing his other constituency.

On February 8, Huntley opened the broadcast by recapping the most controversial of his comments from the previous week. He then emphasized, seemingly in direct answer to his Southern letter writers, that his suggestions were not intended to espouse preventing desegregation of Southern schools, but rather work toward making desegregation easier. "My interest was and is to get all children to school." Huntley then introduced Waring, who argued that forced integration led to lowered standards and created "blackboard jungles," all for the sake of "a sociological experiment." He lambasted the NAACP for creating and exploiting division and animosity, insinuated that it was riddled with communists, and accused it of mandating racial censorship so that magazines, books, and newspapers could no longer use Negro dialect. Huntley then turned things over to Wilkins, who quickly dispatched Waring's red baiting by noting that the FBI's J. Edgar Hoover had affirmed that the NAACP was not communist. He then focused most of his attention on Huntley's comments about the organization's "extremism." He pointed out examples of the organization's call for moderation after the *Brown* victory and the extremism of segregationists who used a variety of tactics, from revocation of mortgages and jobs to dynamiting in order to punish Negroes attempting to petition for access to public schools. He emphasized the NAACP's goal of "orderly legal procedure" and its belief in law and the court: "If that be extremist, then we are extremist." He also pointed out that there were no "moderate groups" to enter the school desegregation situation were the NAACP to bow out.

Wilkins and the NAACP were showered with congratulatory messages in the aftermath of the broadcast. Numerous branch reps, members, and church pastors wrote in about the successful group viewings they had set up or publicized. A Detroit member informed Wilkins that she told everyone she knew that he was going to be on the program: "[I]n this way quite a few people stayed home from Church so they could be able to see the program, [and] after the program there were many good comments stated about you."[43] In Atlanta, the pastor of the Zion Hill Baptist Church polled his congregants on how many of them had watched the broadcast: "Nearly every hand in the auditorium went up, so you see: 'We were listening.'" A reception at Atlanta's Clark College scheduled for Sunday evening fizzled as "nearly everyone made a 'beeline' for television sets as soon as they could get out of there."[44] Many of the letters attesting to these group viewings came from more urban and educated supporters, but not all did. In tiny, rural LaGrange, North Carolina, a pastor who either could not navigate a typewriter keyboard well or was only moderately literate informed Wilkins, "I maid A announcement at my Church that Sunday and all that I talk with was very glade to see and here you."[45] The congregation of the Gillfield Baptist Church in Petersburg, Virginia, thought the broadcast so important that they shifted the schedule for Holy Communion, brought a TV set into the church annex, and arranged for everyone to watch or listen together.

Wyatt Tee Walker was pastor of that significant congregation. He was also a cofounder of the Congress for Racial Equality and a key member of the Southern Christian Leadership Conference. A year later he would become its executive secretary and an architect of that organization's phenomenally successful media strategy. But even in early 1959, Walker was already showing off his media savvy in a letter to Wilkins. He noted that with the continuing controversy about the desegregation issue, "[T]his medium of a national forum, nation-wide affords us the best public relations possible."[46] In the years to come, the SCLC perfected strategies that appealed to network television news, particularly with the 1963 Birmingham campaign that Walker helped coordinate against segregated public services, and then finally with the 1965 Selma voting rights campaign. Network coverage proved key to those successes, and years earlier Walker already understood, as Wilkins and Henry Lee Moon appeared to grasp as well, that their organizations had to think carefully about how to cultivate this new medium for their own "public relations."

Walker also sent a telegram to Huntley that demonstrated Walker's canny cultivation and strategic appeal to the embattled NBC commentator. While Huntley received nothing but rebuke and condemnation from black viewers and white civil rights supporters, Walker adopted a more conciliatory approach. He praised Huntley and NBC for providing rebuttal time and the "fair presentation with equal time for both sides of the coin."[47] Why did Walker feel the need to reach a hand out to Huntley and to the network when no one else in the civil rights community was doing so? Walker appeared to want to establish an amicable relationship with a very powerful broadcaster who commanded a national forum, which Walker knew the movement needed now and in the future. By appealing not once but twice to "fairness," Walker must have been hoping to bank enough good will so that when the need arose, NBC and Huntley would indeed provide not just fair but ample national coverage to the civil rights struggle. It was all about establishing good relationships, and Walker, in these very early days, understood that he and other civil rights organizers would need to cultivate respectful and mutually beneficial bonds with network television.

While Chet Huntley dealt with concerted outrage and protest from the NAACP and from supporters of racial integration, two years later his counterpart at CBS would suffer similar charges of unfairness from supporters of "segregation forever." Smith would suffer far more than Huntley though. Huntley's high profile jibe at the foremost civil rights organization of the time caused him nothing but momentary professional discomfort. Smith's attempt to castigate Southern segregationists led directly to his firing from the Tiffany Network after an illustrious twenty-year career there as one of "Murrow's boys." The difference in these two cases tells us something about the limits of television's embrace of the black struggle.

"Who Speaks for Birmingham"

In April 1960, *New York Times'* star reporter Harrison Salisbury penned a hard-hitting, front-page exposé about Birmingham's racial situation. He described a city gripped by "fear and hatred." *CBS Reports,* the network's flagship prime-time documentary series, decided to report on race relations in "the Magic City" after Birmingham city officials, including Bull Connor, the public safety director, slapped a libel suit against the *Times* and Salisbury. CBS News wanted to know if Salisbury's characterization of virulent racism in the South's industrial stronghold "reinforced by the whip, the razor, the gun, the bomb, the torch, the club, the knife, the mob, the police and many branches of the state's apparatus" might not be somewhat exaggerated.[48] Edward R. Murrow and producer David Lowe had just begun their investigations in Birmingham when Murrow abruptly resigned from CBS to head the Kennedy administration's U.S. Information Agency. Lowe, who had recently completed acclaimed work with Murrow on the documentary *Harvest of Shame,* about the deplorable conditions faced by migrant workers, provided most of the journalistic legwork for the new documentary. Spending nine months going back and forth to Birmingham, he tried to encourage white and black Birminghamians to agree to on-camera interviews. Eventually, Howard K. Smith replaced Murrow as the report's narrator and correspondent.

The documentary's original motivation abruptly ran up against the nonviolent, direct action movement as a busload of Freedom Riders organized by the Congress of Racial Equality (CORE) happened to roll into town just as Lowe and Smith were finishing up their work. Lowe and Smith received a phone tip encouraging them to go to the Greyhound bus station.[49] Arriving at the station without their equipment in order to avoid calling attention to themselves, they witnessed the brutal beating of the black and white civil rights activists by Ku Klux Klansmen. For fifteen minutes with no police in sight, the Klansmen pummeled and brutalized the nonviolent activists until, by prearranged signal, the Klansmen fled just before police arrived at the scene.

Just as the NAACP had hoped to bring their perspective to national television audiences in the aftermath of the "Second Agony of Atlanta" controversy, Birmingham segregationists had hoped to use "Who Speaks for Birmingham" to redress the damage done to their city by Salisbury's *New York Times* series. Vincent Townsend, city power broker and media mogul, controlled the *Birmingham News,* the city's most widely read newspaper, along with its most listened-to radio station and a television station duopoly affiliated with both CBS and NBC. He launched a campaign to strong-arm CBS and manage whom Lowe would interview. Townsend wanted to ensure that only a favorable image of Birmingham resulted. He sent a delegation of the city's white power structure to intervene with CBS president Frank Stanton, reminding him that Townsend might not continue his local station's affiliation with Stanton's network in the future. Stanton hoped the removal of Murrow from the assignment and his replacement with Smith, a Southerner from Louisiana, might assuage Townsend's group.[50]

Birmingham's segregationist champions were not fully convinced. John Temple Graves, nationally noted journalist and commentator who wrote for the city's other major daily paper, the *Post-Herald,* noted Smith's Southern pedigree, two degrees from Tulane (as well as his status as a Rhodes scholar), but pointed out "his Southern birth and upbringing are not reflected in his views on the race question." Graves went on in hopeful tones: "That he has a will to be fair, however, and to be an objective reporter when that is his task, I am able to believe."[51] Graves expressed a greater confidence in Lowe and submitted himself for an interview. Lowe had managed to cultivate some trust in others at the *Post-Herald* as well. The paper informed readers that Lowe, "who has become almost a permanent 'fixture' in our town, has promised the program won't be distorted in its viewpoint."[52]

The first three-quarters of the resulting news program seemed to be a primer on the Fairness Doctrine in action.[53] The first part of the show focused on white opinion about Birmingham race relations, from hard to soft segregationist positions; the second half presented the perspectives of black Birminghamians, all affirming Salisbury's description of the city and calling for change. Smith's reporting on the beating of the Freedom Riders formed an addendum to the report. The section focusing on black Birmingham perspectives followed the "worthy black victims" approach we saw in chapter 2. Lowe and Smith highlighted accounts of violence against blacks seeking equal rights, such as a World War II and Korean War veteran who testified about being "beaten with chains till the blood run down" for joining the Alabama Christian Movement for Human Rights.[54] A minister described being sentenced to hard labor and given a $500 fine for "preaching the truth—all men created equal." A highly poised and articulate teenage girl described her arrest at Kress's department store, being dragged to jail, having her dress torn, and being handled "roughly" by the police. All three of these testimonials occurred in an auditorium filled with black citizens who provided verbal affirmations and vigorous head nods as these individuals recounted their stories.

Reverend Fred Shuttlesworth, the city's most high-profile civil rights leader, provided the most drama. In a sit-down interview with Lowe, he described at length the bombing of his home and his miraculous survival. He also discussed being beaten at the hands of a white mob. In both cases, we see footage of the wreckage of his home and film of his beating. This file footage serves both to verify what Shuttlesworth describes and to further dramatize and intensify the narrative of racist violence.

In another sit-down interview, local civil rights leader and clergyman Rev. C. Herbert Oliver described the threatening phone calls he received after a letter he wrote in support of Negro voting rights appeared in the *Birmingham News*. Callers made thinly veiled bomb threats and talked of turning Rev. Oliver's children into "fertilizer." In another interview, Dr. Lucius Pitts, the president of Birmingham's black college, poignantly discussed the inadequacy of the facilities for black education. "It is painful to be a 'reading Negro,' an educable Negro, in the South—with a family. How do you interpret the situation so that [your child] doesn't develop the kind of hatred, fear, and conditioning that I've had to strive to try to get rid of." He pointed to the "brainwashing" of the media, such as newspapers that report on Negroes only as robbers and rapists.

White Birmingham Responds to Black "Worthy Victims"

How did whites in Birmingham respond to the voices, stories, and perspectives of their black fellow citizens?[55] Whites were not used to hearing them. In fact, as Steven Classen points out in his history of local television in Jackson, Mississippi, during the civil rights years, "[T]he rarity of televised black personalities discussing [their] oppression made their appearance an incredibly, almost shockingly, powerful new experience for television viewers, particularly in some Deep South states."[56] Documentary reports such as the ones we examined in chapter 2 were often not shown in Deep South markets, especially when they handled topics

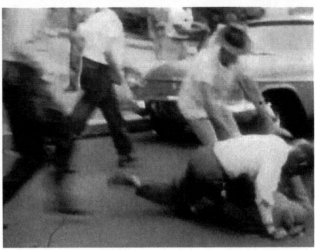

Black voices: Rev. Fred Shuttlesworth describing the violence directed at him by Birmingham racists. CBS validates his words and intensifies the narrative of racist violence by showing footage of Shuttlesworth being beaten by a white mob.

on Southern race issues. In fact, *CBS Reports* was carried by neither Townsend's WAPI-TV nor WBRC-TV, Birmingham's other commercial broadcaster that had recently dropped its CBS affiliation to join ABC. However, the station decided it was worth rearranging the broadcast schedule and dealing with the awkwardness of carrying its spurned network's offering in this instance.[57]

White viewers struggled to make sense of the Negro representations that confronted them on the evening of May 18, 1961. One viewer admitted he did not enjoy watching the program, that it was "not very pleasant." He went on to state, "I was pleased, however, to hear some intelligent Negroes talk, such as the president of Miles College. We do not often get the chance to hear them. Perhaps if we could meet with some of them once in a while to discuss our problems and their problems, and both give in a little, we could find an honest solution. There must be one."[58]

Unfortunately, this conciliatory and open-minded response proved unusual. White Birminghamians (at least those who wrote letters to the newspaper, were interviewed by its reporters, or wrote columns for it) were not ready for dialogue. One woman interviewed by the *Post-Herald* wanted to know why the program could not have shown "one Negro who does not think Birmingham is all bad." Another woman affirmed that they "could have used a plain old Negro off the street and got a better viewpoint." A male interviewee declared the show "real good" but went on say, "The colored people were part of the extremists."[59] Over and over again, with various tactics, whites found ways to avoid grappling or engaging with the black voices they had heard. The perspectives offered could not be representative of "our colored folk" because, as John Temple Graves noted in his final column (he died of a heart attack mere hours after having penned the piece), the program "didn't represent the huge number of responsible colored people who know the South was advancing tremendously in race relations under its own steam before the Supreme Court decision."[60] If the Negroes interviewed in the program were not "responsible" or "plain" folks from the street, and if they could be dismissed as "extremists," then they could easily be ignored as voices not worthy of being heard.

Graves' comment also implied that black voices could be ignored if they did not include the kinds of perspectives white segregationists wanted to hear. Segregationists wanted to hear that "our colored folk" had faith in the South's abilities to manage its own racial issues without federal intervention. Mayoral candidate Art Hanes fulminated about what he did not hear from the program's black voices: "Nowhere in this program was any mention made of the fact that the income of Negroes in Birmingham is the highest in the Southeast, that Negro schools in our city are among the best and that there are many Negro citizens in Birmingham who also believe that segregation is the best pattern of life for both races."[61] Hanes and Graves appeared perfectly comfortable asserting that they knew the thinking of Birmingham's many Negro residents not interviewed by Lowe and Smith, and that those Negroes shared the same worldview as supporters of Jim Crow. Objections came only from outsiders: Graves, for instance, zeroed in on the teenage girl who had discussed her brutal arrest at Kress's. In the opening of the broadcast, she plaintively warned anyone living in Birmingham—"white, black, red, yellow, green—don't live here. Under this, life isn't worth living." Graves insisted that there was no "climate of fear" despite what "the Negro girl from parts unknown" had uttered with "such sinister implications the one sentence 'Don't live here.'" The girl was obviously from Birmingham, as Lowe only interviewed residents, but doubt had to be cast upon her: she had to be an outside agitator, like the Freedom Riders and others who merely riled up "our colored folk" and tried to instill alien, Northern attitudes.

Outsiders (even outsiders from Birmingham) did not have to be listened to because they expressed attitudes that fundamentally challenged white structures of power and taken-for-granted common sense about the Southern way of life. A letter written by a woman responding to the program neatly sums up this attitude. Affirming that watching the report only made her love her city and Alabama more, she declared: "We are a happy people here and want to remain that way, but we cannot if outsiders continue to upset our peace-loving people."[62]

Representing Segregation to the Nation

White viewers were far less vehement in their response to the program's first half with its sampling of white voices. However, Lowe interviewed a number of white students from Birmingham-Southern College and Howard College, and a number of them suggested integration was necessary. One female student, revealing her own evolving political position, declared she was principally against integration but knew that she was responsible for the low economic and educational status of Negroes. Law was needed "to make me do what I ought to do, but don't want to do." Another female student argued that Negro college students could not be equal to whites because they did not have colleges like hers. If Negroes went to her college, "we'd get to know their problems, know them as people." That smart, articulate "coeds" could espouse quasi-integrationist views rattled some viewers. One nineteen-year-old declared himself "shocked" at the appearance of these students. "I was amazed to say the least at their babblings. They willfully stood up before coast-to-coast cameras and condemned and insulted our city, our state, and our sacred way of life."[63] This young man appeared concerned not only that young white Southern women could harbor integrationist leanings but that they would display those views on network television. Not withstanding the unseemly nature of such revelations, it was traitorous to the "Cause" of segregation. Northerners would be watching; the South needed to present a united front in its television spotlight. That, at least, was what Vincent Townsend had tried to mastermind in his attempt to use the CBS program to redeem the tarnished image of his city. Unfortunately, these female students had not quite gone with the plan.

The Birmingham whites who appeared (whether hand picked by Townsend or not) realized the significance of network television as a soapbox. Many of the interviewees used the venue to try and speak directly to "the North." Network television was, for many Southerners, a Northern institution, another form of "outsider" that did not understand or appreciate the unique (and, to many, "sacred") way of life grounded on racial separation. The broadcast served as an ambivalent attempt to use the other side's instrument of national communication to build sympathy and understanding for a besieged position.

John Temple Graves, in his appearance in the program, was the most self-reflexive about the role television could play in the controversy. Complaining about Birmingham's image as the worst city in the South, Graves noted that this assessment could not be disproved through one newspaper, but he said, "[W]e can have it denied if a vast thing like television undertakes to be fair, if, as I think, you mean to be fair to us." Graves recognized the unique power of network television to reach a massive and presumably persuadable audience; he understood this as surely as did the leaders and organizers of the civil rights movement. The question was whether Graves and his ilk could construct for the (always assumed white) television audience a pleasing and captivating representation of the white Southerner.

This had been achieved in the past. Historian Grace Hale notes that in the aftermath of the Civil War, appeals to a "common whiteness" helped recast the war as a "civilized" conflict fought between "our friends the enemy." Activism around women's suffrage and labor issues in the late-nineteenth century helped reunite Northerners and Southerners within shared ideas of whiteness, masculinity, and American imperialism. The national popularity of the "plantation pastorale" in narrative, imagery, and song, along with narratives about the "hell of Reconstruction" best exemplified in D. W. Griffith's *The Birth of a Nation* (1915), helped solidify a general acceptance of the evolving "culture of segregation."[64]

The civil rights movement had undermined the reconciliation around this notion of whiteness and opened up sectional rifts. In the late nineteenth and early twentieth centuries, media such as novels, theater (particularly the minstrel show), popular song, and cinema had helped create a positive, if nostalgic, vision of the South and its peculiar institutions. The question for the latter part of the twentieth century was whether network television would inevitably work to subvert the sectional reunion. Graves, Townsend, and their compatriots were not entirely ready to concede the medium to their foes.

Unfortunately, segregationists had a difficult time representing themselves in a way likely to garner sympathy among those imagined "Northerners." Hugh A. Locke, an elderly attorney, attempted to make Northerners understand the way of life in the South.[65] He reminisced about living down the street from a "nigger" who was born on the very same day as he was and lived on his aunt's farm. As Locke mentioned the boy's name, Jack Finney, we see a close up of Locke's aged face lighting up into a quite genuine, wistful, warm smile as he appeared momentarily lost in memory. "That nigger would do anything for me. And I'd do anything for him," Locke insisted. "And that's just the way we feel about it." The evocation of familial cross-racial closeness, so comparatively absent in the North, might have had some persuasive power had Locke been savvy enough not to use a despised racial epithet. As it was, by calling him a "nigger," many viewers might question whether Locke would do anything for Finney if Finney did not stay in his place.

The segregation cause was not much helped by another interviewee hand picked by Townsend: Mrs. Georges Bridges. Interviewed at The Club, the social center for Birmingham's white elite, Bridges happened to have positioned herself in front of a white cage in which flapped one or more white birds. On her head, Mrs. Bridges wore an elaborate hat fringed with white material similar to the caged birds' feathers. Without saying a word, the mise-en-scène of Mrs. Bridges' interview suggested whites imprisoned by their own system of racial separatism. The framing was probably entirely accidental; *CBS Reports* was not noted for visual creativity and Lowe really did appear to want to be fair with his subjects, most of whom were shot in very neutral set-ups.

As the white feathers flapped behind her, Mrs. Bridges, a local art and culture supporter and Alabama head of UNICEF, insisted there was very little prejudice, "nothing like the people of the North seem to think." She then narrated a story of an art contest for local schoolchildren that she helped organize. The winning artwork was displayed in the city's public library. As it happened, the schoolboy whose work won was a Negro. When he and his family came to the library to see his entry, they were barred from admittance. Mrs. Bridges blithely explained, "It's against city ordinance for the Negro people to come into the white library." But she was able to make a phone call to get "special permission" for the boy and his family to enter in order to see the exhibit. The lesson Mrs. Bridges drew from this episode was that art and culture belong to everyone and that on that level, there was very little prejudice.

Townsend may have been satisfied with this defense of the racial status quo, but Mrs. Bridges then, perhaps not entirely consciously, undercut herself by noting that the Negro used to sing all the time. "He was happy and contented." But she had not heard Negroes spontaneously breaking into song in four or five years. "We're not happy. They're not happy." Mrs. Bridges did not explore why that might be—or Lowe and Smith did not allow her to; her interview ended on those final words.

While the only vehement response to the program's white voices came in reaction to the white coeds, some whites noted that the segregation cause was not much assisted by this presentation. One letter writer to the *Birmingham News*

White voices: Mrs. Georges Bridges in front of a white cage. The symbolism speaks volumes.

protested the "sorely biased" presentation of people representing the segregation side. "Older people, while surely wise, simply are not able to keep abreast of the times and are therefore out of touch. As for the college students—well, they are there to learn." Calling for equal time and "more qualified" speakers, the writer insisted, "We are not ashamed to be ardent segregationists and our only desire is to be able to present a true picture of our area as it is and not as Mr. Howard K. Smith of CBS and Mr. Harrison Salisbury of the *New York Times* would have the world believe."[66]

John Temple Graves sadly agreed in his final column for the *Post-Herald*. He criticized the cross-section of whites as "a lot of nice people making random observations, some of them the sentimental, paternalistic, outworn or purely incidental kind the country laughs at in this modern day."[67] Rather than a platform for the vigorous defense of segregation, network television gave Northerners yet another set of Southern caricatures. Even when segregationists got ample airtime, they did not appear to be able to command the medium in order to curry favor for their positions. The "truth" of the segregationist position just was not being captured by television.

The *Birmingham News*, in a special editorial report on "Who Speaks for Birmingham," zeroed in on a key attribute of the evolving television news format and realized that there was no way for "their side" to prevail: "Inherently it was like a horse opera in its components—the integrationists were the good guys and early had that assigned role. There was nothing left for Birmingham whites to be but the bad guys."[68] The editorialist recognized that television news, far more than any other form of journalism, relied on traditional narrative structure and easily legible binaries of good and evil. This recognition suggests segregationists shared a media savvy with their Southern black antagonists. Being in the television spotlight in these early days of TV news may have helped school its subjects in the medium's conventions more quickly than the general viewing public. Alas for these segregationists, understanding how television news worked to make meaning did not help them bend the medium to their will. As the *Post-Herald* groused in its editorial on the program, "The NAACP itself could not have produced as effective a propaganda piece as did David Lowe and Howard K. Smith."[69] Whereas in 1959, the NAACP and its supporters feared television news could become a propaganda venue for segregationists if they managed to capture a trusted newsman like Chet Huntley; in 1961, segregationists knew that the NAACP had been the victor.

The coincidence of the Freedom Riders' beating while Lowe and Smith were still in town only made the segregationists' position that much more difficult. For many Birmingham whites, it was no coincidence at all. Their distrust of network television boiled over, and collusion between the CBS newsmen and the Freedom Rider agitators could be the only explanation. One letter writer to the *Post-Herald* noted that there were only two sides to be on in the Freedom Rider incident. The media had chosen "to take the side of the renegades sent down here to purposely create a disturbance." He noted that everything had to be carefully planned out in advance with notice given to the media, including Lowe and Smith. "It appears that everyone who could and would give it publicity was notified in advance, but not the police."[70] Another letter writer accused the Freedom Riders of being demagogues and rabble-rousers who required free publicity for their cause. The result of media attention and "free publicity over the nation through television" was "more people are behind the cause of the Freedom Riders. Thus, our position against integration in the South has been weakened."[71] The implication was that the Freedom Riders engineered their own beating and ensured that the cameras would be there to capture the violence.

The beating was, in fact, a set-up for Smith and Lowe, and other newsmen, but the tip-off did not come from the Freedom Riders or CORE. It came from Eugene Fields, the head of a neo-Nazi state's rights fringe organization that had recently moved into Birmingham. Fields, according to Diane McWhorter, "had come to see CBS as a potential collaborator, a vehicle for publicizing the [National State's Rights Party's] first big splash in Birmingham."[72] This story, however, did not fit the script that most segregationists had developed to explain the relationship among network television, the civil rights movement, and Southern defenders of Jim Crow. Increasingly, segregationists insisted that they were the victims of both the black movement and of the national media.

The *Birmingham News* was the first to insinuate collusion between the Freedom Riders and CBS. In a banner page-one editorial the day after the violence, the paper condemned the lack of police presence and proclaimed:

> The business was a 'set up' in a variety of ways.
> The CBS people had their camera ready, aimed at the heart of the Greyhound terminal. The camera, with a constantly attending operator, was in a brilliant red convertible. It stuck out.[73]
> Thus Birmingham yesterday was a drugged turkey—a city ready to be plugged, to be made to seem a city of terror—just as Harrison Salisbury said it was.
> We fell, this city of Birmingham, into the trap like a stupid beast falls into a pit in the jungle.[74]

The victim was the Magic City. CBS somehow conspired with civil rights agitators to make Birmingham look as if it really was the city of fear and violence Salisbury had described for that other Northern media organ. White Birminghamians despaired at their television image and their apparent inability to influence how Northern media portrayed them. One man wrote, "I am a white person. Living in the present day South I am thought of by my fellow Americans as a lead-pipe swinger. At least that's the abstraction made by such media as national radio and television as well as the national press." Arguing that pipe swingers were as much a minority among Birmingham whites as NAACP and CORE supporters were among the Negro population, the man continued, "It hurts me deeply to see the

Northern section of the United States continually 'spit' upon the city I love, my hometown, for being what we are not."[75] Another letter writer fumed that the news media would have a "field day" with the story of the beating. "CBS can go back and select all the worst parts of the film and the country will be only too glad to believe the worst of us."[76]

Within the politics of media representation, white Birmingham segregationists found themselves in a galling position, one that student demonstrators and Black Power activists would face in a few years when the TV news spotlight hit them.[77] Framed with signifiers of violence, brutality, and hatred, segregationists found their positions marginalized in television news. African Americans were (for a few crucial years) framed with signifiers of suffering, dignity, and middle-class respectability. Segregationists, try as they might in the Birmingham example, had no compensating representation to offer—or at least none that network television wanted. White Birminghamians identified as "Northerners" the hegemonic power structure that framed them in deviance. This labeling fit within traditional ways of imagining Southern community and identity as opposition to ideas of "northernization."[78] Because the news media were "Northern" entities and the North did not understand the mind of the South, network news could not possibly represent white Southerners (who were always presumed to be segregationist: representations of local white integrationists could only be scandals). For white Birminghamians, the attempt to use network television to construct a pleasing and persuasive media representation of segregation for the national audience had been a failure. But like political actors who would come after them, they had no choice but to engage the system and attempt to reframe the story that the new media wanted to tell about race and rights. Only after the spring of 1965, when the story moved west to Watts and then north to Detroit and the urban ghettos, would segregationists begin to feel some political and media relief.

The Freedom Riders' Beating and the Censoring of Howard K. Smith

"Who Speaks for Birmingham" entered the annals of broadcast journalism history not so much because of its portrayal of the black and white voices of Birmingham responding to Salisbury's indictment but rather because of what happened to Howard K. Smith when he tried to editorialize about what he had witnessed in the wake of the beatings at the Trailways bus terminal.

The program's addendum about the violence played mostly as a straight news story. Smith interviewed a soft-spoken, business-suited, black Freedom Rider who quietly asserted, "If you want your freedom, you have to fight for it. . . . Some will have to die for it. I am now prepared." This portrait of dignity was juxtaposed to a still photo of Bull Connor (who had refused to participate in the documentary) as Smith quoted Connor explaining that his men were on leave for Mother's Day and thus late in arriving at the bus terminal. Smith also quoted Governor Patterson arguing he could not protect those whose purpose was stirring up trouble. Then Smith, over footage of James Peck, a white leader of the Freedom Ride in a close-up portrait with a bruised and heavily bandaged face looking down in thought, provided the comments of an Alabama Congressional representative: "They got what they deserved."

The report ended with Smith's showing the front page of the *Birmingham News* with its editorial condemning the assault. Rather than conclude in his own voice that Salisbury's characterization of the city was vindicated, he quoted from the editorial and let Vincent Townsend's organ of Birmingham white segregation do that for him. Reading selectively from the editorial, Smith closed out the broadcast by affirming, in the words of the *News,* that fear and hatred stalked the sidewalks of Birmingham.[79] It was a canny move.

While certainly hard-hitting and deeply critical of Birmingham's racism, this addendum was not what Smith had intended. He had wanted to do an editorial tailpiece. In his proposed commentary, Smith observed that in history's great turning points, the victor was usually the one who deserved to win. He then quoted a friend "of proven patriotism": "'When I see events like those going on in Alabama, I begin to wonder, in spite of myself, whether *we* really deserve to win the Cold War.' The answer to my friend is—we *do* deserve to win the Cold War. The Attorney General, Mr. Robert Kennedy, seems about to provide evidence that the rule of barbarism in Alabama is going to be made a temporary exception to the general rule of law and order—and Justice—in America. However, it is no wonder that sensible people can have doubts."[80] His proposed tailpiece also included a famous quote from philosopher Edmund Burke about how evil triumphs when good men do nothing.

The proposed commentary circulates common themes we have already seen in civil rights coverage: the Cold War frame, the emphasis on political officials rather than movement activists as agents of change, the appeal to law and order over disruption in the streets. However, Smith's characterization of white, segregationist Alabama as barbarous and a potential triumph of evil certainly diverged from the norms of coverage. Within the polarization of forces, victims versus villains, the righteous versus the sinful, news coverage typically emphasized the forces in the middle trying to figure out how to navigate the impasse. Huntley's tailpiece attempted to find that center, but stumbled in characterizing a moderate organization as extremist. Smith seemed to suggest that in this Manichean situation, everyone needed to choose sides, and most white Alabamians were on the side of the devil.

CBS quickly intervened before Smith's commentary could reach the air. Concerned about affiliate response in the Deep South, the network demanded Smith cut the Burke quote.[81] More cuts followed as CBS lawyers and VPs argued with

Lowe, Smith, and executive producer Fred Friendly. Smith was then suspended from the network for not being objective, fair, and balanced in his reporting. Smith argued that "giving equal time to Bull Connor and to Earl Warren and leaving it at that was equivalent to saying that truth is to be found somewhere between right and wrong, equidistant between good and evil. . . . [T]he Civil Rights issue was not one over which reasonable minds might differ."[82] CBS executives were unmoved. They forced Smith to resign from the network; he moved over to the less prestigious ABC and spent the rest of his journalistic career there.

The networks found themselves in a contradictory situation. On the one hand, they wanted respected and highly regarded journalists like Huntley and Smith to provide context, understanding, and interpretation about the events of the day. This journalistic work provided the esteem and respectability the networks so desperately needed, considering the criticisms they faced about their entertainment programming and oligopolistic business practices. However, by seeming to take sides in a battle quickly shaping up to be the most divisive and turbulent domestic crisis since the Civil War, TV journalists, as the key figures communicating to the nation about this phenomenon, threatened their network employers: while making an editorial comment, they appeared to be speaking for the network. According to a CBS producer, "It is not appropriate for a television network to take a partisan position and to be seen to be trying to force on an audience a predetermined editorial point of view."[83]

Conclusion

The controversies over Huntley's and Smith's editorializing about civil rights issues reveals important lessons about the limitations television news faced in the coverage of its first major ongoing story. Despite the fact that the networks needed to construct an undifferentiated national audience sharing common norms and values, the networks could not ignore the racial sensibilities of specific regions and groups. The networks' most elite reporters, such as Edward R. Murrow, Chet Huntley, and Howard K. Smith, would inevitably want to provide interpretation and analysis of the stories they covered; however, commentary on matters of race relations within the turbulent atmosphere of America during the civil rights movement could not help but be ideologically dangerous for broadcasters attempting to offend as few viewers as possible in order to maximize audience share.

These two high-profile broadcasts did offend viewers, particularly ones who represented opposing positions in the struggle for civil rights, integration, and black empowerment in the Deep South during its key years. Both civil rights activists and segregationist activists tried to use television as a platform for their sides, realizing the medium's enormous persuasive potential. Both saw the propaganda value that television served for their opponents. Both appeared to assume audiences could be swayed easily by whichever side got the most airtime and the most sympathetic response from well-known news commentators. Network news in the civil rights years would never be a particularly sympathetic instrument for the segregation position, but these case studies should also temper the conventional wisdom that civil rights forces bent television news fully to their cause. Although the news medium was generally sympathetic to the black cause when it was grounded in law and the political agendas legitimated by the White House, that sympathy had limits. The censoring and firing of Howard K. Smith revealed some of those limits. Chet Huntley could get away with calling for the death of the civil rights movement's most significant lobbying organization; Smith could not get away with calling segregationists evil for not opposing violence done in their cause.

CHAPTER 4

The March on Washington and a Peek into Racial Utopia

On a sunny, humid day in late August 1963, a quarter of a million civil rights marchers converged on the nation's capital to press for "jobs and freedom." Television cameras and reporters focused on the demonstrators' placards and signs. One in particular caught the attention of the TV cameras. It read: "Look Mom! Dogs have TV shows. Negroes don't!!"[1]

On that day Negroes did, in fact, have their own TV show. All three networks gave over large chunks of the broadcast day and, in the case of CBS, a significant portion of prime time to the March on Washington. With the exception of presidential inaugurations and nominating conventions, no single event had ever received such saturation coverage on television. Even the NASA space shots, which garnered lots of attention from the networks for their inherent drama, did not compare. The sheer amount of on-air reporting, technical resources, personnel, and forfeited advertising revenue were almost unprecedented. All this for a demonstration, hastily planned in the aftermath of the successful Birmingham campaign, and with no assurance that the anticipated one hundred thousand or so marchers would even turn up. All this for a politically oppositional activity organized by groups representing one of the nation's most politically and socially disempowered constituencies. All this for a march initially disapproved of by 63 percent of the polled U.S. public.[2]

The impact of the March on Washington ultimately was the very fact of its televising to a national audience of millions. Ostensibly, the quarter of a million marchers were in the nation's capital to petition Congress for civil rights legislation and jobs training, but the actual audience for the demonstration was not undecided congressmen considering the Kennedy administration's civil rights bill but a vast media audience that only network television could bring together. How did the networks cover the march both as a live phenomenon and as a prime-time special? If the television coverage of the March on Washington had an overarching theme, it was "black and white together." More surprising perhaps is the coverage's de-emphasis on leaders such as Martin Luther King and an exuberant celebration of the marchers both as a body and as a set of individualized portraits in dignity and racial solidarity.

Why March on Washington?

The idea for a march on Washington did not originate with Martin Luther King or the SCLC but rather with seventy-four-year-old A. Philip Randolph, head of the influential Brotherhood of Sleeping Car Porters, and Bayard Rustin, organizer extraordinaire.[3] With the surge in demonstrations and activism around black civil rights and empowerment sweeping the South in 1962 and 1963, Randolph and Rustin felt the time was ripe for focused activism in the nation's capital. In the wake of the Birmingham campaign and Alabama Governor George Wallace's attempt to "stand in the schoolhouse door" to prevent the integration of the University of Alabama, President Kennedy had been goaded into sending Congress a significant civil rights bill on June 19. With the apparent success of Birmingham behind him, King, along with the SCLC, joined up, and Randolph and Rustin also elicited the support and organizing energies of other key black empowerment organizations such as SNCC and CORE. After some hesitation, the NAACP joined in the effort as well. Eventually, the United Auto Workers and various religious organizations representing Catholic, Jewish, and Protestant denominations also decided to participate.

President Kennedy initially expressed dismay at the prospect of demonstrations in Washington, fearing it would make the already precarious chances of passage for the civil rights bill even more difficult. In a meeting with civil rights leaders, he attempted to persuade them to call off the march, arguing that swing votes could be lost if congressmen felt intimidated. Concerns about intimidation came, in part, from early talk about staging sit-ins at the Capitol and engaging in other nonviolent direct action tactics. Even Roy Wilkins, head of the NAACP, refused to go along with such an approach. The organizers quickly agreed on a simple march from the Washington Monument to the Lincoln Memorial, which would keep demonstrators a comfortable two miles from the Capitol. The Kennedy administration reluctantly and not without ambivalence ceased its opposition, and the president—in public at least—expressed a measure of support. By the end of June, with two months lead time, Rustin began overseeing the task of bringing hundreds of thousands of people to Washington in trains, buses, cars, and planes before 11:00 AM on march day and then promptly getting them out of the city before nightfall.

"Demonstrating and Rioting": TV News Responds

While television news coverage tended to be sympathetic to civil rights activism when news reporters could focus on individualized worthy black victims and white moderates, and when the focus was on obeying desegregation statutes, the news media were less comfortable with coordinated, organized mass activism and demonstrations, even though they produced dramatic and exciting pictures. This discomfort continued in the run up to the march. Early summer happened to be a time of significant racial confrontations, demonstrations, violent clashes, and disorder. The *Huntley-Brinkley Report,* NBC's very popular fifteen-minute news program broadcast nightly at 6:45, tended to collapse the signifiers "demonstrating" and "rioting" together to signify the same chaotic, troublesome mess. Co-anchor David Brinkley, while not unsympathetic to the goals of civil rights politics, over and over again allied his commentary with that of the White House.[4] He quoted President Kennedy and Attorney General Robert Kennedy, rendered silent any spokespersons representing the movement, and appeared to place total faith in the ameliorative effects of legislation.[5]

Brinkley's great faith in the White House and his discomfort with black demonstrators was clear in a May 29 broadcast, wherein he observed, "The President and many of his advisors are now occupied with trying to keep the Negro's increasing demand for equality from turning into generalized riots and violence." Kennedy was constructed as a benevolent father trying to placate an unpredictable, irrational, demanding force that could not seem to control itself. "Negro" was unproblematically equated with "violence." The Negroes' "demand for equality" also connoted violence. Brinkley went on to describe President Kennedy and Robert Kennedy as attempting to "relieve the Negro's distress wherever it exists . . . which is almost everywhere, north and south." Brinkley did acknowledge that Negroes had legitimate grievances; however, the agent of change, the figure to mitigate this distress, was the president and his legislative agenda, not Negro protest and mass movement. Brinkley noted that the Kennedy administration was considering expanding its proposed civil rights bill to include all commercial places involved in interstate commerce and ended by observing, "If Congress passes it, and it may refuse . . . and if it is enforced . . . there would hardly be so much as a segregated hot dog stand left in the United States."[6] Brinkley's enormous faith in the legislative process to solve all the Negroes' civil rights problems was a recurring theme in his newscasts in the summer of 1963. On June 19, reporting on Kennedy's submission of his civil rights bill to Congress, Brinkley asserted that the bill's provisions "are so broad . . . covering so much . . . that if they are passed Congress may never see a major civil rights bill again . . . because there will not be much left to pass laws about."[7] In historical hindsight, the gaffe here is enormous. Neither Kennedy's bill nor the Civil Rights Act that passed in 1964 under President Johnson addressed Negro disenfranchisement and voting rights. Of course, Congress would see another civil rights bill, a bill that became the Voting Rights Act of 1965.[8]

Brinkley showed his faith in legislation and his dislike of protest action again in a piece he narrated on May 30 about the NAACP's campaign against segregated unions in Washington, D.C. Brinkley confidently reported that there was, in fact, little overt segregation at all in the city.[9] Everything that the law could do had been done, and most of the battles had been won. With the exception of the construction unions, according to Brinkley, "what segregation remains here is largely private . . . and largely social . . . an area where neither the law . . . nor street demonstrations . . . can help much, if at all."[10] So the NAACP's campaign appeared irrational and pointless. "Street demonstrations" (with which Wilkins's organization rarely associated itself) were also irrational. Brinkley did not quote any NAACP spokesperson or give any suggestion about why the organization might be engaging in this activity. On the other hand, in the same newscast, Brinkley reported sympathetically on President Kennedy's advocating for his civil rights bill. The message was clear: Americans, both black and white, could and should trust in the office of the presidency to wipe away the last vestiges of segregation and discrimination suffered by African Americans. Blacks themselves, and especially demonstrating and activist ones, merely got in the way at best, and hurt the cause at worst.

Part of the context for framing the March on Washington thus involved this emphasis and privileging of presidential and legislative power. The other part of the frame was a preoccupation with Negro demonstrations. SNCC historian Clayborne Carson has noted, "The protests of the spring and summer of 1963 exceeded in intensity and size anything that had preceded them. . . . [During this period] 930 public protest demonstrations took place in at least 115 cities in 11 southern states. Over 20,000 persons were arrested during these protests, compared to about 3,600 arrests in the period of nonviolent protests prior to the fall of 1961. In 1963, ten persons died in circumstances directly related to racial protests, and at least 35 bombings occurred."[11]

On the *Huntley-Brinkley Report* during June and July, one particular ongoing protest captured the attention of the newscast: Cambridge, Maryland. Seldom discussed in the civil rights literature as a major site of activism, this racially divided city received, in the summer of 1963, heavy and ongoing coverage from the *Huntley-Brinkley Report*.[12] The ugly confrontations and violence that occurred there seemed, for Brinkley at least, to signify the inevitable outcome of civil rights demonstrations. In a June 18 piece, Brinkley again suggested the irrationality of black protest, its inevitable connection to violence, and its negative effect on the legislative process:

> In Cambridge, Md . . . still under something close to martial law . . . there was no settlement yet and none in sight. A good deal of the town is already integrated, but the Negroes have been rioting and demanding more [here was inserted thirty-three seconds of silent film footage, presumably of demonstrating or "rioting" Negroes] and they threatened still another mass march tonight. On hearing that, the state ordered 400 more National Guardsmen into Cambridge . . . and they arrived today, by truck, saying no more mass marches would be permitted. Those already held have produced arson, explosions, and fights in the streets.[13]

Within this analytical frame of Negro "rioting and demanding more," two days later Brinkley announced the proposed March on Washington. Not surprisingly, the frame used to construct the Cambridge story served similar duty in constructing the march story. "Today," Brinkley announced on June 21, "there were several predictions that if there is a civil rights filibuster in the Senate this summer . . . as there almost certainly will be . . . there will be an organized March on Washington by about 100 thousand Negroes. The local police are concerned about it . . . and are doubtful that any march that size would remain peaceful."[14] Brinkley included no comment from march organizers responding to such fears.

Reporting about the Cambridge situation, as well as on other stories involving black demonstrators and racial themes, typically assumed violence and aggression, whether the demonstrators were instigators or victims. Herb Kaplow, NBC's chief correspondent on the Cambridge story found an interesting way to narrate a story that involved nonviolent sit-in protesters entering a restaurant owned by a staunch segregationist. Describing Cambridge as "festering under racial tensions for several weeks," Kaplow pointed out that the National Guard had left the city, even though no agreement had been reached between demonstrators and city leaders over desegregation plans. Kaplow went on: "Shortly after the guardsmen moved out the attack on segregation resumed." His choice of words seems a bit odd. Over silent film footage, Kaplow narrated an attack perpetrated by the restaurant owner against a group of demonstrators trying to sit in at the lunch counter. Kaplow described (and presumably the footage showed) the owner pushing and shoving the demonstrators out the door. As they sat on the sidewalk singing, the owner returned with raw eggs, which he proceeded to break over the head of a white protester. So, what Kaplow actually described and showed was an attack on anti-segregation protesters by a violent white segregationist not an "attack on segregation." Yet somehow, the demonstrators initially were portrayed as the attackers.[15]

Three days later, the confrontation at the restaurant continued and the National Guard had been called back in. This time Kaplow used the passive voice to make it unclear who exactly was perpetrating the violence. Over silent film, he described six sit-in demonstrators, blacks and whites, entering the restaurant. The owner locked the door. "A group of white youths already inside attacked the demonstrators. There was pushing and shoving, hitting." Kaplow began by indicating that the attack started with the white youths, but in the next sentence, it was less clear, as he neglected to identify who was pushing, shoving, and hitting whom. He then noted that some of the demonstrators were bodily ejected from the restaurant and that one was knocked unconscious. He then reported that a group of Negroes gathered across the street had "dared the white to come out."[16] Thus, the Negroes were, of course, fully engaged in the aggression.

This use of the passive voice to frame Negro protesters as perpetrators of violence recurred in other stories about racial matters in the weeks leading up to the march. On August 15, Brinkley read a series of short items on race relations themes. He opened the segment with, "Racial tensions led to violence in several places in the United States today. . . . In Birmingham, Alabama, progress toward biracial accommodation was disrupted when gas was let loose in a department store." After a filmed report from the scene (which perhaps indicated the perpetrator of the intentional gas leak), Brinkley read an item from Chicago where "someone set fire to one of the city's mobile classrooms. Integrationists object to them, claiming they perpetrate segregation in schools." And then, "A racial demonstration approached a riot last night in Goldsboro, North Carolina. It started with a group of [N]egroes marching and a group of whites watching. It ended with rocks and bottles thrown back and forth, and police moving in to break it up."[17]

So in the summer of 1963 on network television news, at least at NBC, black protesters of racial segregation found themselves repeatedly juxtaposed to violence, disorder, turmoil, and the need for law enforcement. Coverage of the proposed March on Washington continued this framing.[18] NBC's *Meet the Press* on the Sunday before the march featured both Martin Luther King and Roy Wilkins receiving a rather hostile grilling by journalists. One newsman noted the belief of "a great many people" that it would be "impossible to bring more than 100,000 militant Negroes into Washington without incidents and possible rioting."[19]

Ensuring a calm, orderly, and peaceful demonstration on the Mall thoroughly preoccupied march organizers who were keenly aware that the eyes of the nation would be on them. Along with working closely with city police, Bayard Rustin organized a massive army of volunteer marshals carefully trained to manage the crowd.[20] He ensured that large numbers of port-a-potties, drinking fountains, and free sandwiches were made available "to feed growling stomachs, and thereby prevent growling people."[21] March organizers understood that they needed to undercut the dominant white image of blackness that yoked active, demonstrating, massed black bodies with violence and disorder. In stage-managing this biggest and most extravagant media event ever in American race relations, the civil rights groups realized that civil disobedience could play no part. As we have seen, network news reporters appeared less than sympathetic to such examples of black activism and tended to implicate nonviolent protesters in the aggression of white perpetrators. With news cameras trained on one hundred thousand demonstrators, the unpredictability of direct-action protests could be disastrous to the movement's goals.

Those goals were set out quite clearly in a statement released by the leaders of the march in the aftermath of a July 2, 1963, meeting, where they formally agreed on their united action. Emphasizing their unanimous agreement to eschew civil disobedience and call on all participants to comply, the leaders affirmed: "We are convinced that tens of thousands of people demonstrating with discipline and dignity by their very presence will create great sympathy with our objectives. We are equally convinced that any disorder, any disruption, will be tragic precisely because at this moment it may well turn public opinion against all we stand for."[22]

The march had to be a visual spectacle of disciplined and dignified black bodies to be viewed by media audiences (assumed to be white) whose sympathy could be garnered at least in part because such an image of rectitude would help wipe away older, more demeaning and damaging images. In sending off final versions of march organizing manuals to field staff around the country, NAACP officials noted in cover letters, "The press and TV coverage of the March is reportedly the greatest ever to take place, exceeding even Presidential inaugurals."[23] Organizers needed to ensure that their marchers were camera-ready.

They were.

Covering the March: The Aesthetics of Liveness

The television networks had been covering live events since the 1948 presidential nominating conventions and had more recently become increasingly adept at handling other unfolding live spectacles, yet in 1963 the medium displayed an uneven grasp of visual aesthetics and the rhetoric of image composition. The civil rights movement had a somewhat more sophisticated understanding of visual semiotics largely because African Americans had cultivated almost a century of sensitivity to how popular media represented black bodies. Yet the movement's media savvy on display this day also included some surprising lacunae.

The grassroots organizing to ensure not merely a large but also a disciplined, orderly, and well-dressed assemblage of marchers paid off handsomely as network cameras over and over again trained their lenses on individual male marchers in suits and ties (despite the increasingly humid conditions) and women in their Sunday-best dresses. On the one hand, network coverage emphasized the sheer spectacle of the huge crowds sweeping past cameras and marching down Constitution Avenue to the Lincoln Memorial or via dramatic crane shots of marchers massed on the grounds around the Reflecting Pool. On the other hand, cameras insistently cut in to frame individualized "portraits of dignity."[24] These portraits were always nicely composed, obviously carefully chosen by the news director calling the shots, and they invariably presented individual marchers in a flattering light. For instance, during a speech by CORE's Floyd McKissick, CBS cut to an elderly black woman at a fence. Behind her we see a large black man's arm gently and protectively cradling her. As Mahalia Jackson sings "I Been 'Buked," we see a black man holding up his young daughter. The girl turns in the general direction of the camera and gives a tiny smile. We cut to a young black woman in a neat black dress and white collar listening intently and motionless to Jackson's singing. As the spiritual comes to an end, we cut to a middle-aged black woman also listening intently. The woman grins and nods approvingly as Jackson concludes. As Jackson moves to an unscheduled encore, we see an older black couple, he in a shirt and tie, she in a formal dress and pearls, both, like so many marchers, sporting sunglasses and standing motionless.

⸱ All these portraits presented attractive images of black people, smiling or emotionally moved. They are all quintessential "civil rights subjects," as Herman Gray
uses the term: eminently worthy beneficiaries of the rights and equality they
demand.[25] These are representations of blackness like David Robertson and Mattie Bivens in "Mississippi and the 15th Amendment" that CBS's white audience
could and should be comfortable with.

However, as network cameras searched the crowds, they were not primarily
seeking black marchers. Three-quarters of the participants assembled on the
Mall were African American, but viewers of network coverage could easily come
away thinking that almost half were white, considering the networks' penchant
for framing shots to include white marchers.[26] Over and over again the coverage would cut into a grouped shot featuring one or more whites, center framed.
Like the black participants, the white marchers typically were formally attired
and presented in dignified stances. Unlike the portraits of dignity we have just
discussed, however, the whites were less likely to be framed individually. Typically, the coverage insisted on locating whites in and among blacks where the
whites were seen mingling comfortably and happily with their black comrades.
The message was clear: blacks and whites could come together in joyful equality and, while the goal of the march was equality rights for blacks, whites were
crucial to the process. The coverage's overrepresentation of the white presence
had clear ideological purposes in line with what we have seen in the network
documentaries and news reports. The March on Washington may have been the
Negroes' TV show on August 28, but the networks insisted on white co-stars.

The marchers, black and white, presented aesthetically attractive and compelling visual images, but the speakers on the podium at the Lincoln Memorial
did not. Network coverage mostly comprised shots of massed, small-group, and
individualized images of the marchers juxtaposed with long-duration shots of
the succession of speakers and occasional entertainers at the podium.[27] Viewers
of the live coverage would have spent a great deal of time looking at the speaker's
podium and whomever happened to be commanding that space for his allot-
ted seven minutes.[28] Considering the length of time the cameras were trained
on that podium, it is surprising (at least retrospectively from a contemporary
vantage point of "photo ops" and carefully orchestrated televisual events) that
the march organizers did not think about what the speaker's podium would
look like on television.

The marchers proved themselves camera-ready, encouraging the networks
to provide beautifully composed shots of them; the speakers' podium, however,
presented a distracting, visually chaotic image. Speakers were hemmed in by a
veritable clutch of personnel—marshals, guests, people coming and going, and
a harried, shirt-sleeved Bayard Rustin fidgeting with the microphone, muttering instructions, and pacing around the stage smoking and perspiring. Marshals
sporting paper hats stood behind speakers sweating, occasionally looking bored,

sometimes chatting or gesturing, apparently completely unaware that they were on camera. In contrast to the crowd shots, the podium has an unstaged quality that certainly heightened the sense of authenticity and immediacy but tended to create visual distraction from the speakers' words—especially from those who were less than riveting in their performance.

Movement organizers were not the only ones with gaps in their full command of televisual semiotics, however. CBS, which was positioning its news division as the preeminent institution for television journalism against its rival NBC, provided march coverage that, at least visually, left much to be desired compared with the less-well-developed ABC. Roger Mudd anchored CBS's coverage, but neither he nor his news producers seemed to give much thought to his on-camera appearance. Mudd stood in the glaring sun in an unidentifiable spot around the Mall sporting a very large, cumbersome headset. Over the hours of coverage, the headset must have generated even more heat than the humid weather because Mudd's hair became increasingly sweaty and plastered to his head. No makeup person seemed to be on hand to freshen up the anchor before he went on camera. Mudd also fidgeted with an array of notes and papers. As the long day wore on, Mudd began to look ever more rumpled, wet with perspiration, and physically uncomfortable.

ABC's anchor Richard Bate and his crew of correspondents, including Howard K. Smith, by comparison, situated themselves in the shade inside the Lincoln Memorial with the grand sweep of the Reflecting Pool and the massed marchers behind them. They remained fresh, cool, and sweat-free. ABC equipped the team with discrete and barely discernable earpieces in contrast to CBS's bulky gear. ABC may have been the less competitive of the three network news divisions, but in the battle over televisuality, ABC's news personnel appeared to understand this central component better than their more prestigious rival.

CBS's and ABC's coverage also differed in their reporting of the event. Mudd, while often focused on trying to get accurate crowd numbers and reporting the lack of violence or disturbance, occasionally attempted to assert his role as a skeptical and disinterested journalist covering a story rather than a moderator celebrating an unprecedented event. As the march got underway, he noted that with the offices of all Southern congressmen closed, CBS News had trouble finding voices opposed to the march: "Obviously, this is not strictly bipartisan; there is a side for this march and a side against it." He noted the controversy surrounding SNCC leader John Lewis's speech. At the end of the proceedings, he itemized the march's list of political goals, noting again and again, "This will be hard to fulfill in this session of Congress." These occasional gestures toward balanced reporting were mostly offset by the sweep of the event pictured.

ABC's team more fully embraced a discourse of celebration. As the marchers, getting ahead of their leaders, began the trek down Constitution Avenue, ABC's audibly awestruck reporter describes the sea of marchers going past network cameras: "Their faces are lit up; they are a happy group, a jubilant group." "All factions, all parts of the country singing spirituals—an inspiring sight." Over a long-duration, high-angle shot of marchers flowing down the street: "A panorama of freedom." Anchor Richard Bate observes that the procession "can't really be called a march; it's a stroll." He encourages viewers to listen to the sound of the marchers singing. After a pause to let viewers do so, he returns to comment: "Wonderful sounds." At the end of the march, correspondent Edward P. Morgan, commenting on the unprecedented, worldwide saturation coverage the event has received, comes to more optimistic conclusions than did Roger Mudd. "The question is whether the news travels two-and-a-half miles from where I sit," he ponders, to the halls of Congress where the civil rights bill was still under consideration. Morgan answers his rhetorical question by asserting that it did. "No crowd could be so disciplined, so dedicated, so single-voiced in what it wanted, that it couldn't be heard that far away and, indeed, around the world."

ABC's coverage provides one of the few instances in network news reporting of the civil rights movement where reporters overtly positioned themselves as cheerleaders and proponents of the black empowerment movement. In fact, two days after the march, Morgan sent Roy Wilkins a handwritten note appended to transcripts of his ABC reporting and an August 29 editorial extolling the march: "Rarely if ever have I been more proud of our American heritage than I was on Wednesday. The demonstration was magnificent—as I tried inadequately to report in the enclosed pieces—and now the problem is to keep the momentum going."[29]

The March on Washington as a Consensus Media Event

One of the most significant issues around television coverage of the march is how, prior to August 28, reporting largely revolved around questions of violence and political effectiveness. The coverage remained firmly rooted in what broadcast scholar Daniel Hallin has termed the "sphere of legitimate controversy."[30] Hallin's mapping of how television news bounds and limits the reaches of "objectivity" is particularly salient for making sense of how network news shifted dramatically before and on march day. Hallin's schema involves three concentric circles: at the center a "sphere of consensus" including "mom and apple pie" issues not regarded as controversial but rather matters to be celebrated; an outside circle, the "sphere of deviance," involving political actors and positions like Communists and Communism, not deemed worthy of being heard; in between, we find the "sphere of legitimate controversy," typically bounded by the discourses and debates encompassed by the two political parties and the established players within the American political process. This is the limited arena where "objectivity" and "fair and balanced" ideals of reporting are manifest.

Throughout the summer, the march was obviously a matter of debate within the Democrat-controlled Congress. This issue did not entirely disappear on march day—both ABC and CBS presented interviews with congressmen responding to the march (discussed further below). The violence frame, on the other hand, which had so animated coverage and which had so defined the legitimate controversy around the march, suddenly lost all its oxygen on August 28. As the March got started and it became blindingly obvious that there would be no disorder from this gigantic and telegenic assemblage, neither CBS nor ABC could use "violence" as a peg on which to hang any subsequent reporting—except to note its absence. Because the marchers presented themselves as disciplined and unthreatening "civil rights subjects," figures that network news programs had already featured as acceptable and worthy, coverage on march day quickly drifted out of the sphere of legitimate controversy—because there was now nothing controversial about which to report. The coverage slid toward the sphere of consensus. Hallin has noted that when operating within this region, "journalists do not feel compelled either to present opposing views or to remain disinterested observers. On the contrary, the journalist's role is to serve as an advocate or celebrant of consensus values."[31] ABC's live coverage provides a quintessential example of this form of consensus reporting and, as we will see particularly when we turn to CBS's prime-time coverage, Walter Cronkite and commentator Eric Sevareid did much the same for its large evening audience.

The march and its political goals continued to be controversial in many parts of the country—the South in particular and among significant numbers of legislators. However, on August 28, it was not covered as a news story within the realm of controversy. Hallin's work provides one means to understand the ideological decision making underpinning network news coverage in its celebration of consensus values of achieved and achievable racial equality. Daniel Dayan and Elihu Katz's influential work on "media events" and the "live broadcasting of history" provides an even more powerful model to help us make sense of what happened on American television screens that day and what the medium told its audiences about race relations, the civil rights struggle, and the purpose of demonstrations at that moment.

Dayan and Katz describe media events as ceremonial television, a break from regular viewing patterns wherein viewers are encouraged to watch reverently and in unison with the entire nation. The media event spotlights television's unique ability to "command attention universally and simultaneously in order to tell a primordial story about current events."[32] Media events tell a story of consensus values. In the case of events like the March on Washington, which culminated a spring of remarkable conflict and strife, "they celebrate reconciliation. Often they are ceremonial efforts to redress conflict or to restore order, or more rarely to institute change. . . . They celebrate what, on the whole, are establishment initiatives that are therefore unquestionably hegemonic."[33]

March organizers may not have seen their mass gathering as hegemonic, but the networks certainly endeavored to present the march that way. The public blessing of the Kennedy administration and the fact of the civil rights bill assisted in that process. The coverage celebrating "black and white together" in peace and harmony pointed to the solution to all the news about racial strife in Birmingham, in Cambridge, and elsewhere that preceded the march; the solution did indeed require the institution of change, but the insistent focus on black "civil rights subjects" and their respectable-looking white allies made change look not only unthreatening but positively desirable.

Dayan and Katz itemize an array of attributes a televised event must include in order for it to pass muster as a media event. First and foremost, it must be broadcast live with most regularly scheduled programming preempted to make way for the event. In signaling its importance, most broadcasting channels participate. This, of course, was a more straightforward feat in the 1960s pre-cable, pre–100-channel universe. As Dayan and Katz note, "Broadcasting can hardly make a more dramatic announcement of the importance of what is about to happen."[34] Broadcasters tend to publicize the complexity of mounting such broadcasts and note that these events are often "hailed as 'miracles' by the broadcasters, as much for their technological as for their ceremonial triumphs."[35]

The media industry trade press crowed about the unprecedented and massive manpower and technical power maneuvered into place to cover the march. *Broadcasting*, the mouthpiece for the National Association of Broadcasters, gushed, "Whatever had been superlative in the past became comparative last week as radio and TV converged on Washington to describe the civil rights march."[36] *Variety* praised, "Logistically it's a Cape Canaveral moon shot, an Inauguration Day and an election night bundled into one and topped off by a total measure of unpredictability."[37] The crowing was not without reason. Nothing like march coverage had ever occurred on American commercial television. And while nobody in August 1963 could know it, the organizing and execution of television coverage of the march ended up serving as a successful dry run for television's next major media event which came, tragically, a mere three months later: the televised funeral of John F. Kennedy following his assassination in Dallas on November 22.

The three networks met on August 14 and agreed to pool their radio and television coverage of the march, with CBS taking charge of the pool arrangements. The plan was to have twenty-two cameras providing shared footage from the Washington Monument, where marchers would congregate; from the parade route; and from the Lincoln Memorial, where speeches and music were scheduled.[38] The networks employed more than four hundred of their Washington-based personnel and hundreds more New York-based employees. District police were inundated with requests for press passes: beyond the twelve hundred passes already accredited for the year, nineteen hundred extra ones were issued—more requests than the D.C. police had ever received for one event.[39] Along with the pooled camera positions, each of the networks had its own exclusive cameras, approximately forty-nine in all for the three networks. International broadcasters from Canada, the U.K., Japan, France, and West Germany were also on hand to cover the march; the new Telstar communication satellite beamed live coverage to Europe. Most Communist countries in Europe and the Soviet Union taped the program. Much was made of the fact that Russia decided not to broadcast the event live.

Liveness is also a crucial element of the media event. Events are perceived to unfold outside the media, which serves merely to record and transmit the usually unpredictable activities. There is also the assumption of a large audience that watches "ceremonially," breaking away from daily routines, just as the networks themselves break from program scheduling routines and flow in providing their live coverage. "Like the holidays that halt everyday routines, television events propose exceptional things to think about, to witness, and to do."[40]

The march was carried live by all three networks during the day on Wednesday. ABC and NBC ran special half-hour reports throughout the day and late night news wrap-ups at 11:15. CBS provided the most extensive coverage, beginning from 10:00 to 10:30 in the morning with pre-march coverage and extensive, uninterrupted live coverage from 1:30 to 4:30, with a prime-time hour-long news special at 7:30.

Ratings for the coverage were high—in fact, significantly more viewers watched coverage of the march than typically viewed weekday television.[41] During some of that time the other two networks went back to regular broadcasting. ABC, for instance, ran *American Bandstand* with one Negro integrating the show's dance floor.[42] *Variety* noted, "If NBC and ABC entertained the notion that fun and games might grab off some ratings points while afternoon numbers leader CBS was tending its public affairs, they were sadly amiss."[43]

What makes a media event significant, ultimately, is the ideological role it plays within the social and political order. Dayan and Katz emphasize its hegemonic function, its celebration of consensual values. They argue that media events typically are organized by entities "well within the establishment" with which the media already cooperates.[44] This often means governmental bodies, national political parties, or international organizations like the Olympic committee. This was certainly not the case with the March on Washington organizers, although they did have the public blessing of the White House. However, Dayan and Katz also point to certain media events that respond to social crises and perform a transformative function providing possible solutions to social problems. These kinds of events function as "previews, foretastes of the perhaps possible, fragments of a future in which the members of society are invited to spend a few hours or a few days. Activating latent aspirations, they offer a peek into utopia."[45]

The march provided a vision of racial utopia. And much to the outrage of Southern segregationists, this vision of a color-blind, desegregated America, already backed up by Supreme Court and other enacted and pending legislative decisions, was largely supported by network news reporters and executives. A national consensus on racial equality was, in fact, good for the networks as they expanded their programming and advertising reach to all regions of the country. A national audience, undifferentiated by significant regional sensibilities, was a necessity for the networks in their attempt to construct one-size-fits-all programming for that audience. March on Washington coverage provided viewers with a vision of what a color-blind America might look like. Yet this vision was organized not by "establishment" players but by activist, social change groups outside the dominant social and political order with the news media, in this instance, sanctioning and amplifying this vision for its national audiences. Although Dayan and Katz point to examples of media events organized by nonestablishment entities, the massive ceremonial attention given over to civil rights organizations is remarkable.[46] For a few significant hours, the agenda of a grassroots movement for the empowerment of the disenfranchised and oppressed took over the airways, with TV reporters serving largely as masters of ceremony, sharing in the celebration of consensus.

Dayan and Katz provide three basic typologies of media events: contest, conquest, and coronation. The march on Washington was scripted largely as a conquest—the celebration of a charismatic hero struggling against huge odds to bring about significant change. This script emphasizes the primacy of the individualized hero much more than we see in March on Washington coverage, although Dayan and Katz's typology allows for "collective protagonists."[47]

In popular memory, of course, the march has become inextricably linked to the figure of Martin Luther King as hero and to King's "dream" of a world remade. Today, the march is remembered mostly as being about King, with the 250,000 marchers serving largely as audience or backdrop for his charismatic address. This was not how the networks covered the march on August 28. King was not the star of the show: the marchers were the "collective protagonists" along with all the speakers up on the podium, including King. King was in no way privileged. Reporters and commentators did not anticipate his speech or engage in any suspense-building discussion about King's place in the schedule of events. In this particular version of the "conquest" script, the multitudes accompanying their leaders into the potentially hostile arena were as significant, if not more so, than any charismatic leader. Together with King and the other speakers on the podium at the Lincoln Memorial, they all enacted a script of battle-tested (peaceful) warriors making their pilgrimage to the seat of national power and, against all odds, using the force of their numbers and their collective charismatic quality both to change the world and also to provide a vision of what that changed world would look like.

The March as News: CBS's Prime Time Coverage

By early evening, Bayard Rustin's organizing genius had managed to ensure that the quarter of a million marchers who arrived in the nation's capital that morning were safely on their way back home. NBC and ABC went back to their regular schedule of prime-time programming. CBS, however, found itself in a fortuitous position that evening. Its prime-time documentary series *CBS Reports* aired each week in the 1962–63 season on Wednesdays at 7:30, so a special report on the march fit quite nicely into its programming mix. The series, while highly acclaimed, had certainly never been a ratings winner. It typically pulled a 5.1 to 10 rating with a share of the audience between 15 to 20 percent. (Top-rated shows in this era pulled ratings of 25 to 31 with 40 to 56 shares).[48] On Wednesday night, CBS's special report on the march did particularly well against its rivals: it drew a 12 rating and a 23.2 share, compared with ABC's *Wagon Train* with a 12.9 rating and 25 share, and NBC's *The Virginian* with a 13 rating and 25.1 share.[49]

How did the CBS news team frame and package the march as a news story in the three hours after the event had concluded a little after 4:00 in the afternoon? The broadcast employed a number of frames that we saw in the live broadcast, including most prominently the "black and white together" theme. From narration by anchorman Walter Cronkite to remarks from commentator Eric Sevareid, to interviews with a sympathetic congressman, to the myriad images showcased, the broadcast emphasized over and over again that whites were fully participant and engaged in the event.

In the broadcast's opening shots of the massive crowd, the cameras quickly cut in to closer views, singling out images that included both black and white marchers, and ended on a group of white women dressed like prosperous housewives, one with a big baby carriage.[50] Cronkite's narration emphasized the images: "They called it the March on Washington for Jobs and Freedom. They came from all over, American Negroes *and* whites."

The "black and white together" frame was particularly evident in a segment on organizing for the march. CBS took a news crew to Cincinnati in the days before the march to record how one community drummed up support for the event. Cronkite described how a consortium of Negro groups came together to work on the organizing. Visuals showed black women in an office operating adding machines; leaflets coming off a mimeograph machine; envelopes being sealed. Then Cronkite continued, "For the first time in Cincinnati, whites were joining the civil rights campaign." The segment then shifted to a city street where organizers were selling buttons to raise funds for the march. The camera focused particularly on an attractive, young, white woman, probably a college student, persistently and cheerfully attempting to sell her buttons. She pursued a black man walking past the camera and out of frame. The camera panned over to him as she followed him. With lights and camera on him, he smiled somewhat embarrassingly, gave the young woman some money, and allowed her to pin the button (which featured a white hand clasping a black hand), and then hastily moved on. The segment then cut to another white woman pinning a button on a small black child. The camera panned up to the child's father who spoke to the camera about how they had waited long enough and not wanting his children to experience the same difficulties he had. The segment ended with the man in close-up.

This sequence suggests that whites were not merely "joining" the efforts but were actively engaged in mobilizing and organizing. The white women appeared to be bestowing equality (or the promise of it) on the reluctant Negro man and the small child. The white women were the active agents; the Negroes served mostly as the beneficiaries of their idealistic and energetic labors.

Another sequence of the Cincinnati segment also emphasized the actions of whites over those of Negroes. Illustrating the role played by area churches, the segment juxtaposed two clergymen—one black, one white—addressing their congregations about why they should participate in the upcoming march. The sequence began with the black clergyman presented in a highly respectful low angle tilt as he responded to a poll result suggesting that many felt the civil rights movement was moving too fast. "I ask: too fast for whom?" he preached in sonorous tones. "You cannot afford to stay home and watch the March on Washington on television." The sequence cut to shots of parishioners looking prosperous in their Sunday best, listening intently, and then cut to a much longer segment at a white Methodist church. In similar shot set ups, viewers saw the white parishioners framed against the church's stained glass windows, listening (in a long-duration shot) to the white minister. "I dislike the thought of carrying placards, conducting demonstrations, and making a march on Washington." In these opening remarks (at least these words were the first the news special chose to begin with), the minister appeared to both acknowledge and concur with the perspectives of much of the news coverage about civil rights activity leading up to the march. Coming from a white figure of authority and respectability, these comments appeared to validate the framing of the civil rights news story to date. However, as the sermon continued, the minister undercut this theme of unease and dislike of demonstration and showed both his parishioners and the television audience how and why the ideological frame of coverage had changed: "But I find myself growing desperate in my search to find some way to identity with the Negro and his needs." The minister pointed out that Jesus, in a similar situation, would have made a public declaration, even if it meant public disorder, and referred to Jesus clearing the temple of moneychangers. As a Christian, he instructed his listeners, he had to go against "the grain of my personal comfort," and while he would rather not go to jail or engage in a demonstration, "as a Christian, I have no option."

This privileging of the white minister over the black one and the choice made to excerpt this section of the white minister's sermon spoke directly to the majority white viewers of the program. Demonstrations and protest activity may have been ill advised in the past, but the situation now was different. Whites were now involved. Note the white minister's reference to wanting to "identify" with the Negro. Here was an invitation to adopt the subject positioning of the suffering and protesting Negro, to adopt his standpoint: to become like him.[51] In becoming like him, however, the demonstrating that previously connoted violence and disorder when attached only to black bodies now connoted Christ-like qualities when white bodies (especially middle-aged, middle-class, Midwestern ones) were engaging in the same behavior. The news special's privileging of the white minister invited white audiences to identify with him and thereby make the protesting and demonstrating they viewed that day not only unthreatening but normal and appropriate.

The news special also had to find some other ways to deal with the violence frame that had so dominated coverage leading up to the march. Cronkite referred to the violence issue a number of times—only to dismiss it, reassure his audience that there had been no violence, and emphasize over and over "the picnic-y, holiday spirit" of the crowd and its "good humor." The threat of violence now came not from the massive throngs of protesting black bodies but rather from George Lincoln Rockwell and his Arlington, Virginia–based American Nazi Party, which attempted to conduct a counterdemonstration.

The repeated reference to the march as a "picnic" or a "church social" served to reassure viewers and comfort them about what they were seeing. Eric Sevareid's commentary about the march at the end of the broadcast reiterated both the non-violence frame and the black-and-white-together frame to further sooth viewers:

> The March *in*, not *on*, Washington was precisely what its leaders called for. It was orderly, but not subservient. Proud, but not arrogant. Outspoken, but not raucous. It had all the combined elements of a political rally, a revival meeting, and a 4th of July picnic. This was the biggest gathering of American Negroes in their three hundred years in this country. But at times today there seemed to be almost as many whites as Negroes in the crowd. . . . This meeting was evident [*sic*] that the Negro cause is becoming a general and universal cause.

There were not "almost as many whites as Negroes in the crowd." But that was how it looked on television. Sevareid, working from the CBS headquarters in New York, commented not on the actual march but rather on its televisual representation. Editorial comment thus echoed the network-produced images.

The program could not, however, merely celebrate the fact of the march; some form of "legitimate controversy" had to be introduced at some point. So, working with the already-established frame of congressional response, the special report reasserted its journalistic objectivity by questioning the political and legislative ramifications of the march.

Cronkite pointed out that "the immediate purpose of the March on Washington was political" and then questioned whether the march worked as a means to support passage of the Kennedy administration's civil rights bill. He introduced Capital Hill correspondent Robert Pierpoint, who interviewed two "knowledgeable members of Congress." One of the two was Strom Thurmond, the staunch segregationist Dixiecrat from South Carolina. In response to Pierpoint's question of whether the march would help Negroes attain their goals, Thurmond insisted that Negroes had as many rights and opportunities in the United States as any other people. He questioned where else they would have so many houses, refrigerators, and dishwashers. Declaring the civil rights bill to be unconstitutional, Thurmond affirmed that the march, even with a million participants, would not change the vote of a single congressman. Pierpoint then turned to Senator Philip Hart, Democrat from Michigan. Reemphasizing the "black and white together" theme, Hart said, "This is a march of all Americans. It isn't a Negro march alone." However, like Thurmond, he also suggested the march would not sway congressional votes but rather would raise awareness that Americans did not practice what they preached around the world.

With two otherwise opposed Senators both suggesting the march would not affect the congressional process, Pierpoint could comfortably reassert a news frame that disparaged the political efficacy of mass protest over trust in elected officials. In his standup, Pierpoint informed viewers that Congress was not paying attention to the march. His evidence: only a half dozen speeches from the floor even referred to what was going on at the Mall. Pierpoint emphasized that almost all in Congress "agreed on one essential point: the march itself would not influence many, if any, congressmen's votes. Only the reaction of the voters at home to the march would do that—and they have yet to be heard from." This comment threw the onus onto television viewers to examine their own responses and do the right thing—and that did not mean to join the movement and get personally involved in protest activity and direct action, but rather to contact their congressmen and urge them to vote appropriately.

Even after the networks expended huge resources, time, personnel, and revenue to cover an example of political protest activity, newsmen reverted to a position that disparaged, questioned, and minimized the significance of that activity. CBS News found itself in a contradictory position: all of its news decisions suggested that the march had enormous political implications, and yet when correspondents engaged it on the familiar turf of the legislative battleground, they insisted on asserting more conservative notions of how democracy functions, and so mass movements, demonstrations, and marching in the streets had no obvious place in the equation.

If the march's ultimate purpose was political, then the speeches delivered at the Lincoln Memorial were crucial. The CBS special report devoted a significant amount of its broadcast hour to long excerpts of speeches—remarkably long in this pre–sound-bite era. CBS News's choices of which speeches to present to evening viewers (its daytime coverage broadcast all speeches in their entirety) and which to omit provide telling and surprising insights into the judgment of the news team in their packaging of the march in its immediate aftermath.

CBS cut this section together to give viewers the illusion that they were seeing the actual lineup of speakers. The segment opened with A. Philip Randolph and then the first and last female leader to speak, Daisy Bates, pledging support on behalf of all the women. CBS then cut the speech of the white representative of the National Council of Churches. But the most notable omission was the speaker who followed and who, next to King, is considered to have given the most powerful and memorable speech of the day: John Lewis, chairman of SNCC. Lewis's speech was by far the most "militant" and confrontational.[52] It was supposed to have been even more militant with lines like: "We will march through the South, through the heart of Dixie, the way Sherman did. We shall pursue our own scorched earth policy and burn Jim Crow to the ground nonviolently."[53] This rhetoric so alarmed the white churchmen, especially the Catholic Archbishop of Washington, who had agreed to give an invocation at the Lincoln Memorial, that they threatened to pull out of the march if Lewis did not tone it down. Even the moderated version of Lewis's speech contained forceful indictments against the Kennedy administration and the Democratic Party. Speaking for SNCC, he admitted to supporting the president's civil rights bill only with "great reservation."[54] He then proceeded to itemize all the ways in which the bill would not protect or help black citizens. Calling for "revolution" more than once, he indicted both Democrats and Republicans for their lack of principle or concern for the plight of African Americans. According to one civil rights historian, "When he finished, the 250,000 people listening cheered louder than they had for anyone all day. On the speaker's platform, every black speaker rushed up to Lewis to shake his hand and pound him on the back. Every white speaker stayed seated and stared into the distance."[55] If Lewis had provided the "emotional high point of the day" to that moment, why did CBS decide not to air even an excerpt of the speech?[56] His speech was certainly more dramatic and newsworthy than that of UAW's Walter Reuther, which received significant airtime.

Lewis's speech was more important within the context of civil rights politics and the ongoing struggle between SNCC and the SCLC, but this struggle and the discourse circulated by Lewis did not fit the ideological frame CBS had constructed for the march. The political purpose of the march, as the CBS news team believed or at least asserted through its coverage, was to influence passage of the civil rights bill. Lewis's speech muddied the frame, made things inconveniently complicated. His rhetoric also threatened to undermine the construction of protesting black bodies as essentially unthreatening, noble, and peaceful. Despite his inherent newsworthiness, Lewis threw discordant and undigestable noise into the proceedings. The best way to deal with this, apparently, was to ignore him.

More amenable to the news frame was the NAACP's Roy Wilkins, who was shown joshing a bit with the crowd: "I told them you would be here. They didn't believe me because you always make up your mind at the last minute."[57] His speech, while not completely uncritical of the limitations of the civil rights bill, displayed none of Lewis's firepower. But as head of the nation's oldest and most well known Negro lobbying organization whose legal arm had succeeded in convincing the Supreme Court to rule against school segregation, Wilkins fit the bill of an inherently newsworthy spokesman. Even though his speech was largely unmemorable, CBS excerpted large portions of it.

Framing King: Editing "I Have a Dream"

The final speech of the day obviously belonged to Martin Luther King. While every other speaker was strictly bound to speak no more than seven minutes, King ended up commanding the podium for fifteen. As was the case with most of the other speeches, prime-time viewers witnessed only a portion of King's address. But in one of the most remarkable journalistic gaffes in television news history, CBS presented its nighttime audience with the "wrong" part of King's historic speech.[58]

Many people probably assume that King's speech began with the words "I have a dream." King actually spoke from a prepared text for about ten minutes before that phrase first rang out through the Mall. News reporters and editors would have been familiar with the first portion of the speech, as a draft had been released to the press before the march. The "I have a dream" section, however, was not prepared ahead of time and had not been written down. King launched into his peroration extemporaneously, borrowing from set pieces that he had delivered frequently at mass meetings over the past year or so.[59] As Drew Hansen notes in his book-length study of the speech, the first part of the speech "made the familiar arguments of national politics."[60] King referred to the Emancipation Proclamation, signed by Lincoln exactly one hundred years earlier and its still unfulfilled promise of freedom for American Negroes. Using the metaphor of a promissory note and bad check, he explained why the marchers were assembling in Washington that day: "We refuse to believe that there are insufficient funds in the great vaults of opportunity of this nation. And so we've come to cash this check—a check that will give us upon demand the riches of freedom and the security of justice."[61] He then went on to answer the question posed to civil rights activists, "When will you be satisfied?" and then launched into poetic oratory about why the Negro could not be satisfied: because of police brutality, segregation in interstate travel, housing barriers, voting restrictions, and the injustices of racism. Hansen notes, "There was nothing particularly unusual about the substance of the first ten minutes of King's speech. He had opened with the argument from American ideals used by most progressive politicians of the era. Then he warned of continued civil rights demonstrations until the movement's demands were met—the same message John Lewis had delivered more effectively earlier in the afternoon. . . . [T]here had not been anything extraordinary about the substance of what he was saying."[62]

Because this portion of the speech contained nothing unusual, because it hit all the familiar themes that newsmen had heard before, and because it spoke to the politics of the occasion, the first part of the speech fit neatly into the political frame that CBS News had constructed for its evening coverage. And it helped that reporters had a prerelease version of the speech to use in crafting their instant analysis. During the live daytime coverage, Roger Mudd summed up his sense of the most significant portion of King's speech. It came from the first part in which King warned Americans that there would be no business as usual, meaning no respite from demonstrations and protest, until Negroes' civil rights were granted.[63] Mudd said nothing about the second half of the speech. Perhaps in his exhausted and sweat-drained state, he did not even really hear it but relied instead on the advance copy he undoubtedly received. In their sum-ups at the end of the evening broadcast, both Cronkite and Sevareid also pointed out King's warning from the first part of the speech.

In excerpting from King's address, the evening news special gave viewers generous selections from the speech's first half. Then they heard King urge his listeners:

> Go back to Mississippi; go back to Alabama; go back to South Carolina; go back to Georgia; go back to Louisiana; go back to the slums and ghettos of our Northern cities; knowing that somehow this situation can and will be changed. Let us not wallow in the valley of despair.
>
> I say to you today, my friends: so even though we face the difficulties of today and tomorrow, I still have a dream. It is a dream deeply rooted in the American dream. I have a dream that one day this nation will rise up and live out the true meaning of its creed: We hold these truths to be self-evident, that all men are created equal.

At this point, the broadcast cut to a shot of the massive statue of Lincoln, zooming in closer to Lincoln's stone face, and then cut back to the studio and Cronkite who briefly talked about how the march effectively shut down the city of Washington. There was no return to King's speech or any commentary about it. Left on the cutting room floor were King's now familiar words about dreaming of an America where his children would be judged by the content of their character rather than the color of their skin; his vision of allowing freedom to ring from every village and hamlet; and his final invocation of the old Negro spiritual: "Free at last, free at last, thank God Almighty, we are free at last." Prime time viewers of CBS's coverage, if they relied solely on the news special to provide them with news about the march, would have had no inkling about the majestic and stirring words King spoke that day.

How could CBS, in the immediate aftermath of the march, miss the core of what many consider to be among the most important speeches of the twentieth century? How could the news team have so misjudged the important portion of that address?

Part of the answer must be the sheer unfamiliarity with the "I have a dream" part of the address. When King launched forth into this oration, he was no longer giving a speech, he was preaching; he was giving a sermon. Of course everyone, news reporters and the general public, understood that King was a clergyman. But as far as the news media was concerned, King was primarily a political leader. He commanded a political movement and met regularly with White House and other elected officials. He was the recipient of a Nobel Peace Prize and increasingly, since the Montgomery bus boycott of 1955–56, was the "go to" person for quotes, responses, and guest appearances by the press, both print and broadcast. So in the news arena, King was only secondarily a religious leader. According to Hansen, at the time of the march, "King's oratorical ability was, for the most part, unknown outside of the black church and the civil rights movement."[64] Outside the movement, most Americans had never heard King deliver a sermon. When King left his prepared address, he left behind the persona most familiar to media audiences and he put on his preacher persona. Suddenly, "he no longer sounded like President Kennedy, John Lewis, or any other orator of the era. He sounded like Isaiah, the great visionary prophet of ancient Israel."[65]

The "I have a dream" address did not respond to current political realities faced by Negroes, nor did it put forth a political platform about how to change those realities. King left the world of the political and soared into the realm of visionary prophecy. He provided a glimpse into the redeemed America. Hansen notes that no political figures in this period spoke in these visionary tones about what America might look like after the elimination of segregation and racial discrimination. King provided something quite new to the discourse of race relations.[66] Also significant is the use of Biblical language. What were news reporters to make of this?

> I have a dream that one day every valley shall be exalted and every hill and mountain shall be made low, the rough places will be made plain, and the crooked places will be made straight and the glory of the Lord shall be revealed, and all flesh shall see it together.[67]

This prophetic, Biblical discourse did not fit any news frames that reporters in 1963 would have known what to do with. But this part of the speech was more stirring, dramatic, and captivating than what came before. The marchers punctuated King's flights of oratory with huge cheers. The sheer drama of it all made for great television. But that, to a somewhat lesser extent, was the same for John Lewis's speech. Clearly, dramatic visuals and sound were not the criteria used by CBS News in putting together this news special. It would take some time before CBS understood the import of "I have a dream." It would take some time before King would be so inextricably linked to visionary discourse.[68] By the end of the year, when CBS ran its year-end news special surveying the major news events of 1963, the news section had rectified its news gaffe. In its segment on the March on Washington, the special included Mahalia Jackson singing and Martin Luther King at the podium at the Lincoln Memorial. The only portion of his speech excerpted this time was "I have a dream."[69]

Response to the Television Coverage

Coverage about the march in the African American press in the aftermath of August 28 was voluminous and rhapsodic. Reporters, editorialists, and letter writers also took note of television's role in disseminating images of the march.

The *Pittsburgh Courier,* a nationally distributed weekly paper, was particularly enthusiastic about how television covered the event:

> And lest we forget . . . a BIG BOW in the direction of the radio and television industry. Theirs was truly a job for the ages. Knowing that the eyes of the civilized world were on them, they gave the entire day a dignity in keeping with the serious solemnity of the affair itself.
>
> They could have "panned" shots which could have been embarrassing to the people who conceived the March . . . and to the nation itself. But time and again they pin-pointed the raw drama, the stark reality of the affair. They showed Dr. King in the forefront, with the statue of Abraham Lincoln in the background.
>
> They "caught" in all its magnificence the intense and poignant expressions of those for whom the March meant so much. They could have done otherwise . . . but didn't.
>
> America and the American Negro was projected in a light which will forever remain as a credit to our country.[70]

The editorial displayed a significant sensitivity to the question of Negro representation, a concern that manifested itself over and over again among African American viewers and commentators during the civil rights era. Implicit in the editorial is a general distrust of the media in portraying African Americans with dignity and seriousness. In noting that "they could have done otherwise," the editorial gestures to a long history of images that showed blacks disrespectfully, in unflattering ways, or in a manner deemed harmful to the race. The TV coverage of the March on Washington was so notable because it did not fit the repertoire of imagery that blacks may have expected. The editorial displays a somewhat surprised sense of gratitude that television did not fall back on the predictable and undignified or embarrassing set of images that may have been more familiar.

This sensitivity—and a self-consciousness about white viewers and how they read images of blacks—was evident in a letter from an NAACP local official to Roy Wilkins in the aftermath of the march. Noting how thrilled everyone was with the pictures and news stories, the writer observed, "Some white people were probably surprised to hear and see such fine Negro speakers and to learn that Negroes could conduct a great program so perfectly. I heard [one] newsman say that they could not understand how the leaders held the people under such control. The March shows we can unite when we wish."[71]

There was some criticism in the black press. A *Courier* columnist complained about the framing of the coverage around questions of congressional response, pointing out how that limited a proper understanding of the march's significance:

> By and large the TV men who tried to report and interpret [the March on Washington] for America did a conscientious job but were handicapped by the double burden of their whiteness and their profession. Nothing has contributed more to the shallowness of America's thinking than the shallowness of most of her news "analysts."

For instance, there was the way they clung to the question: "What effect do you think the March will have on the civil rights bill before Congress?"

Only blithering idiots and Thurmonds looked upon the March as an attempt to browbeat Congress.

The columnist argued that the march was so much larger than Congress; it was a demonstration of Negroes' determination to claim all their rights and claim them now.

A reporter for the *Chicago Defender* took issue with the framing of the march as a "picnic": "The demonstration has been described as resembling a 'church picnic,' but many of the Chicagoans disagreed. They stood for hours in the sun, hardly able to move because of the throng. 'It was a sober, dignified assembly,' stated one. 'The people who went did so for freedom's sake and they did not have time for frivolity or foolishness.'"[72]

While the festive, picnic trope used by the CBS news team may have functioned to render it unthreatening to white audiences, for some African Americans the trope only robbed the march of its dignity, high seriousness, and import.

A letter writer to the *Baltimore Afro-American* found particularly notable, not the representation of African Americans in television coverage, but rather the representation of congressional Dixiecrats:

> The three Southern senators seen on TV expressing their opinion of the affair clearly showed how skillfully and careless[ly] they can handle the truth and well established fact that when it comes to the question of civil rights they are like snakes in the grass . . . The image of the 'Ugly American' can be seen in these men who insult the intelligence of people at home and abroad by outright misstatement of facts and conditions about colored living in their respective states. . . . They may run but they can't hide from public opinion now that the world, over TV, has seen just what they have always stood for. . . .[73]

Whether television footage accurately represented the marchers and their purpose may have been up for debate, yet—at least according to this and other viewers—television did a particularly fine job of accurately portraying Southern segregationist leaders. Many of the responses noted specifically the significance of the international coverage the march received. Reports in the African American press repeatedly noted the march's coverage by Telstar around the globe. The *Courier* editorial paired the portrayal of black marchers with a more generalized portrayal of America that would be beamed around the world. Likewise, the true image of white racists would be available to the global audience. For these commentators, the respectful portrayal of African Americans in TV footage had international implications for the ways the United States was to be perceived and understood by the global audience. The March on Washington and its televising thus brought the civil rights movement firmly into the arena of global politics. It was imperative that the images broadcast supported the movement.

Conclusion

In the aftermath of the March on Washington, the *New York Times'* influential television critic Jack Gould observed, "If the Negro for years has suffered one dominant handicap, it has been in communicating and dramatizing his lot. Not to the integrationists, not to the unyieldingly prejudiced, but [to] the indifferent white millions for whom integration or segregation was of scant personal concern. The sociologist of tomorrow may find that it was television more than anything else that finally penetrated this huge camp of the uncommitted."[74] With respect to the march in particular, he argued that it had to be seen in order to be understood: "Its eloquence could not be the same in only frozen word or stilled picture."[75]

The civil rights movement had a number of events and campaigns that played particularly well to the TV cameras: the Little Rock high school desegregation confrontation, and the riots at Ole Miss, Birmingham, and, as we will see in the next chapter, the Selma voting rights campaign. Unlike any of the other significant moments in the struggle for racial equality, however, the March on Washington required the specificity of television.

The Birmingham campaign played well to television, of course, once Bull Connor loosed the dogs and fire hoses and once King agreed to fill the streets and consequently the jails with schoolchildren.[76] At that point, the confrontation provided the morally eligible Manichean polarization between obviously good versus obviously evil forces that television news could narrate with ease. However, even though Birmingham was a significant TV news story and even though much of the SCLC's strategy involved playing to TV cameras and schedules (such as arranging marches and confrontations to conclude before 2:00, when network news crews would need to get their film ready for the evening broadcast), the news medium that mattered the most in this situation was not television.

Birmingham achieved its greatest power and its political and public opinion influence through photojournalism.[77] Still images of dogs lunging at Negro youths and high-pressure water drilling into the backs of cowering demonstrators—these forms of media representations caused more outrage than the television images of the same events. On television these images were chaotic, rapid paced, often difficult to see. By stopping the action to show the exact moment a dog sunk its teeth into a victim or to show in clinical detail the precise force of the fusillade of water pounding into a human body, viewers could experience the viciousness of Southern segregationist violence up close. Television coverage could merely supplement photojournalism in this instance. The March on Washington, however, as Gould argued, achieved its cultural and political impact because of television. Photojournalism and newspaper reporting performed the supplementary roles here.

Less than a year following the March on Washington, the Civil Rights Act of 1964 passed into law under the signature of the new president, Lyndon Johnson.

Commentators may debate whether John F. Kennedy could have achieved that landmark accomplishment or whether Johnson could so quickly and so uncompromisingly have done so were he not riding the nation's grief over Kennedy's assassination and thus the murdered president's unfulfilled mandate. Did television coverage ease the road to passage? Probably. By presenting viewers a "peek into racial utopia" with unthreatening visions of black and white Americans united, network television assuaged its audiences' fears about what civil rights legislation, integration, and equal rights would look like. Civil rights organizers cannily put together an event that would play beautifully to television cameras. Even the jumble on the speakers' podium may merely have reinforced the earnest authenticity of the moment, or as King eloquently put it, "the fierce urgency of now." The March on Washington provided a perfect synergy between civil rights organizers and network news personnel, both wanting to tell a similar story about the promise of racial equality. Two years later, they would come together again to tell a story about voting equality. In that case, network television's presence was indispensable to the passage of another landmark civil rights bill.

CHAPTER 5

Selma in the "Glaring Light of Television"

Network television in the 1960s had no more powerful lineup than Sunday night. CBS's perennial favorite, *The Ed Sullivan Show;* NBC's *Walt Disney's Wonderful World of Color;* and the powerhouse western, *Bonanza,* were all among the Nielsen's top twenty-five most-watched shows. ABC countered the consistently number-one rated *Bonanza* with its popular *ABC Sunday Night Movie.* No other night of prime-time entertainment drew larger audiences.

On Sunday, March 7, at 9:00 PM, about one third of all American households tuned in to *Bonanza,* as they did every week. But ABC lured approximately 48 million viewers to its premier telecast of the 1961 Academy Award-winning Stanley Kramer film, *Judgment at Nuremberg.*[1] Many viewers may have been drawn to the film's star-studded cast. Others may have been attracted by the subject matter: Spencer Tracy played an American judge asked to weigh on the culpability of four German judges and their role in the Holocaust. The film explored questions of guilt among "ordinary Germans" instead of the well-known Nazi leaders associated with the Nuremberg War Crimes Tribunal. Featuring actual newsreel footage from the concentration camps, ABC's massive audience would have to grapple with the depths of human beings' inhumanity to those deemed inferior and "other."

The mammoth three-and-a-half-hour broadcast had barely begun before the network's news division broke into the movie with a special report from Selma, Alabama. TV viewers would have been at least generally aware of the voting rights demonstrations that had been ongoing in this small Black Belt city fifty miles from the Alabama capital, Montgomery. Since the beginning of January, Martin Luther King and the SCLC had been coordinating almost daily marches to the Dallas County Courthouse with increasing numbers of disenfranchised black citizens from Selma and surrounding area. Network news provided frequent and, at times, nightly coverage of the standoffs between potential registrants and Selma's increasingly volatile county sheriff, Jim Clark.

ABC scooped its two more-established news rivals with its breaking report. For fifteen minutes, ABC viewers saw Clark's posse and Alabama troopers outfitted with gas masks and truncheons beat, gas, and brutalize a procession of black demonstrators who had crossed over the Edmund Pettus Bridge with the intention of marching to Montgomery to protest their disenfranchisement to Governor George Wallace. After this dramatic news report, ABC returned its viewers to the motion picture about German culpability in the brutalization and mass murder of Europe's Jews.

Two years earlier the networks had turned over a significant chunk of daytime television to the civil rights movement, broadcasting the March on Washington as a "media event." The movement needed network television as an ally in making its campaigns and demands a national political crisis requiring federal intervention. Attention from television cameras, far more than that of even national print media, provided the crucial ingredient for successful campaigns and demonstrations.

Yet even the SCLC's most media-savvy organizers could not have planned, predicted, or envisioned what happened on the Edmund Pettus Bridge that Sunday. The March on Washington coverage had seemed as good as it could get: respectful, ceremonial, and extended attention. The March 7 coverage of what came to be known as "Bloody Sunday," however, had the unprecedented attributes of vast viewing numbers. Nightly news viewership could never rival the numbers drawn to prime-time entertainment, and the prestigious prime-time documentary programs drew very modest audiences. Because ABC broke into an already highly rated entertainment program, the "Bloody Sunday" report garnered an otherwise unheard of number of viewers all at one time and all in one place. The civil rights movement found itself in as choice a place in prime time as the movement could have dreamed of.

The political significance of the televised screening of the violence on the Edmund Pettus Bridge is not in much doubt. Most historians of the civil rights movement acknowledge the profound impact that the televising of the confrontation had on the ultimate success of the Selma campaign and the quick passage of the Voting Rights Act five months later.[2] The Pettus Bridge confrontation may have been a point of maximum visibility for the campaign as a national news event, but in order to really understand how and why the Selma campaign succeeded as it did, we need to examine its representation on television news as an ongoing, nightly news phenomenon. How did network news frame the Selma story both before and after Bloody Sunday? How did network news represent the players, the issues, the confrontations, the political stakes, and the national significance of what was going on in this formerly sleepy Southern town?

This chapter will analyze one news program, *The CBS Evening News with Walter Cronkite*, and its coverage of Selma from the beginnings of the campaign in January 1965 to its triumphant conclusion in Montgomery at the end of March.

Inaugurated two years earlier, by 1965 CBS's and NBC's popular half hour evening news shows were already institutions. ABC may have "scooped" them with its "Bloody Sunday" report, but that network would not launch its own half hour news show until 1967.

In gauging the impact of televising the Selma campaign, close textual analysis tells us part of the story. David Garrow has examined how press coverage of Selma, both print and television, influenced legislators and the Johnson administration in pushing forward voting rights legislation. He argues that legislators were particularly moved by photographic representations of Bloody Sunday.[3] But what about ordinary citizens? And in particular, what about white Southerners? Those in Alabama found themselves, yet again, in the eye of the civil rights hurricane in early 1965 with the news media, television in particular, trained on them. How did they respond to the "glaring light of television" when their taken-for-granted world of racial hierarchies and sensibilities appeared before the entire country for televised examination?

Setting the Stage for Televised Confrontation

In 1964, Congress passed the Civil Rights Act. And although David Brinkley had confidently predicted that Congress would not see another civil rights bill "because there will not be much left to pass laws about," he was quickly proved wrong.[4] The Civil Rights Act, with its focus on outlawing discrimination in public facilities, employment, and government, and in requiring the dismantling of Jim Crow statutes in the South, did very little to address the wholesale disenfranchisement of African Americans in many parts of the Deep South. Young organizers affiliated with SNCC had attempted to register black Mississippians during Freedom Summer in 1964 and then dealt with the disillusionment of seeing the Democratic National Convention refuse to seat the Mississippi Freedom Democratic Party at the 1964 presidential nominating convention. That activity garnered a significant amount of media attention, especially when, early on, two Northern white volunteers were murdered along with a local black activist.

SNCC workers had also been in Selma with no media spotlight since 1963 working with the local Dallas County Voters League (DCVL) to push for black voter registration. Dallas County had fifteen thousand registered voters in the early 1960s; only 156 of them were black and only fourteen of them had been added to the rolls since 1954.[5] Considering that African Americans made up half the area's population, the systematic nature of the disenfranchisement was pretty obvious. On January 2, 1965, the DCVL invited Martin Luther King to speak in Selma and help kick start the local campaign there.

The SCLC had been casting about for a proper venue for its next major national campaign. Since Birmingham and the March on Washington, King and the SCLC found themselves a bit eclipsed by the youngsters of SNCC, and the

SNCC activists were not entirely thrilled to see the more hierarchical, top-down, leader-oriented organization come to town and take over from its grassroots organizing efforts. During the Selma campaign, major tensions and conflicts existed among SNCC, the DCVL, and the SCLC over the voting rights campaign. The Dallas County Voters League wanted to improve local voting conditions, while the SCLC wanted to use Selma as a stage set for a national campaign.[6] And the SNCC youths chafed at the SCLC's autocratic approach to decision making. Television news coverage would be blind to these internal tensions.

Selma was not an ideal staging ground for what the SCLC wanted to do in its plans for a national campaign around voting rights. A small, relatively isolated town, it did not meet the organization's "strategic requirements." According to Andrew Young, SCLC's executive director, "[W]e were leery of organizing in small towns far from media and airports."[7] Selma also did not have a reputation as an exceptionally racist community. The city's white voters had just elected a new mayor, Joe Smitherman, a young businessman who, although a segregationist like all Alabama politicians, had campaigned not on segregation but on bringing new industry to Selma and revitalizing its economic base.[8] Smitherman had also just appointed Wilson Baker as the new public safety director with full police authority over the city. Moderate and operating by the book, Baker had taught criminology at the University of Alabama. He was as far from the Bull Connor school of Southern lawman as one could find anywhere in Alabama. Neither Smitherman nor Baker fit the script that the SCLC needed to cast if it hoped for a Birmingham-style confrontation likely to capture the attention of the news cameras.

Selma did, however, have Dallas County sheriff James G. Clark. Clark could have come straight out of central casting. He often sported a white crash helmet, a swagger stick, and had at his disposal a motley crew of amateur lawmen. "Clark's posse," like their boss, paraded around in white crash helmets and openly brandished billy clubs. Like Bull Connor, Clark had a well-established history of hotheadedness and violence toward local black residents.

Smitherman and Baker fully understood the SCLC's game plan and attempted to minimize Clark and his posse's ability to create a violent scene. Clark had no enforcement jurisdiction within the city of Selma; however, he did control the Dallas County Courthouse, which was downtown, along with the steps leading up to the building. The sidewalk in front and everything else in town fell under Baker's control. Throughout the campaign Baker, Clark, and the voting rights demonstrators and allies enacted a tortuous dance on this highly contested territory with demonstrators occasionally goading Clark on his turf, with Baker trying to stop them from getting to Clark or to stop Clark from getting at the demonstrators. The standoffs and periodic clashes made for increasingly exciting and compelling television drama.

The Selma campaign began officially with King's instructing his supporters at Brown Chapel, the movement's chief gathering point a few blocks east of the courthouse, that in order to get the ballot, "we must be ready to march; we must be willing to go to jail by the thousands."[9] The campaign ended three months later on March 25 in Montgomery on the steps of the state capitol, where King addressed twenty-five thousand marchers and millions of TV viewers watching live coverage. During the intervening three months, national media (and eventually international media) set up shop on the streets of Selma. CBS news teams began regular reporting in January. By March, the media crush was massive, and Selma led the Cronkite broadcast most evenings.[10]

CBS News Covers Selma: Before "Bloody Sunday"

Coverage of the Selma campaign in its early days mirrored some of the themes and approaches used by prime-time documentaries in their civil rights stories.[11] Just as news reporters brought legally mandated desegregation into the "sphere of consensus," to use broadcast scholar Dan Hallin's schema, and exhibited few qualms about displaying support for the goal of school integration and equal rights, when covering Selma, CBS reporters felt no need to place the matter of voting rights into the "sphere of legitimate controversy."[12]

The question of demonstrations was a different matter. Selma news coverage on the Cronkite program did not give viewers individualized black worthy victims like David Robertson, the Cornell University graduate student deemed illiterate by a Mississippi registrar and thus ineligible for the franchise in Mississippi. Selma voting rights activists and marchers were invariably silenced and represented only as massed bodies. In one news report after another from January through early March, CBS news audiences would see them marching down the street, lined up at the courthouse, or walking in smaller groups on the sidewalk. The adults typically presented themselves in dignified poses, often in business attire, always restrained. While some marchers were shown in more humble dress, such as women in headscarves, they tended to be the exception. News correspondents typically narrated footage such as this neutrally or with hints of approval.

In a January 26 report as the camera tracked down the quiet line of mostly elderly men and women, some obviously poor, CBS's Lou Wood commented, "It was probably the quietest day since Martin Luther King began his voter registration drive in Selma a week ago." Wood obviously considered the silence, orderliness, and discipline good news. Over a zoom-out to an extremely long line of police cars, Wood noted that there were fifty state troopers standing by "in case of trouble, but there were no incidents." Reports like this, while narratively uninteresting, presented the preferred situation: black aspiring voters playing by the rules imposed on them by law enforcement about where and when they could present themselves at the courthouse, with law enforcement merely overseeing the situation. As long as blacks were docile but dignified bodies, and as long as Clark and his posse behaved like keepers of the peace, news reports tended to construct the situation as admirable progress.

But when black bodies appeared unruly and unpredictable, news reporters became more critical. A January 25 report opened by noting how "calmly" the day began as we see a line of potential registrants, mostly women, lined up on the courthouse steps. However, the camera kept focusing on one very heavyset woman standing in stocking feet, zooming in to her feet and panning over to where her shoes lay on the next step. The reporter noted that both sides appeared to be complying with a newly mandated federal court order for the processing of registrants meant to speed up the procedure. Panning down a line of mostly well-dressed women, the camera focused on the shoe-less woman, then held on her in close-up as she looked around, notably shifty-eyed. Later in the report, the correspondent informed viewers that "a heavy set Negro woman was scuffling with Sheriff Clark and three of his deputies." We get a jostled and obstructed view of the woman on the ground being handcuffed as numerous photographers and cameramen surround the action, cutting to a bizarre extreme close-up of the woman. She was either smiling or grimacing; it was hard to tell which. In a wider shot the deputies inelegantly rolled her over and lifted her up. The report shifted to Clark, shaking and out of breath, claiming that the woman, Annie Lee Cooper, whom he admitted hitting, had taken him by surprise. Off screen a reporter asked, "Is that why you arrested her—striking an officer?" Still in close-up, Clark smiled and laughed: "Ask stupid questions. She knocked hell out of me." He went on to claim that he had heard an obscene word, turned, and then Annie Lee Cooper knocked him in the eye. After a quick cut to the line of would-be registrants lined up on the sidewalk, Clark continued, "We were trying to get the line orderly. They were all over the place." Clark's comments were balanced with Martin Luther King's answering a question about whether he felt the federal order was being complied with. He responded that there was a limited effort to comply, but he noted the prospective registrants' "subtle hostility" was the result of "the brutal activities we saw this morning."

Clark received far more screen time than King. Annie Lee Cooper never spoke. The report's representational strategies clearly marked her as deviant, whereas Clark appeared validated in his description of the incident. No reporter challenged his remarks or asked for context.[13] King's comments about "brutal activities" were vague at best. Viewers could easily come away from this report convinced that Clark and his posse and the majority of would-be registrants were working together to speed up registration, but that a put-upon Clark had to grapple with unstable and violent blacks who deserved the law enforcement treatment they got.

Print news coverage of the incident was more ambiguous. Both the *New York Times* and the *Washington Post* described the confrontation, reporting that Cooper struck Clark and was then wrestled to the ground by his deputies. Clark then billy-clubbed the flailing and kicking Cooper. The accompanying photo that ran on the *Times'* front page and the *Post's* second showed Cooper pinned on the ground with two deputies on either side of her putting on handcuffs.[14] A grimacing Clark crouches over her gripping a billy club with both hands. He is either about to bring it down on Cooper's head or is pulling it out of her hand. To a casual viewer, it looks more like the former. Without the anchoring function of the news text, the photo's composition tells a story of police brutality: a prone woman being aggressively manhandled and beaten by an overwhelming police force. Even though the newspapers both noted that Cooper had acted violently toward Clark, the news photo emphasized white violence, and the picture's rapid dissemination meant "the movement salvaged a victory from the incident."[15] CBS News coverage provided no such victory.

As the marches to the Courthouse continued in the following weeks, CBS news reports maintained a mostly neutral stance with its generally respectful treatment of adult participants, but an early February report suggests some discomfort with younger marchers.[16] The first part of the report focused mostly on following a small group of well-dressed and dignified-looking black men as they walked down the sidewalk to the courthouse. Some pass solemnly very close to the camera but completely ignore its presence. In contrast to these adults, we

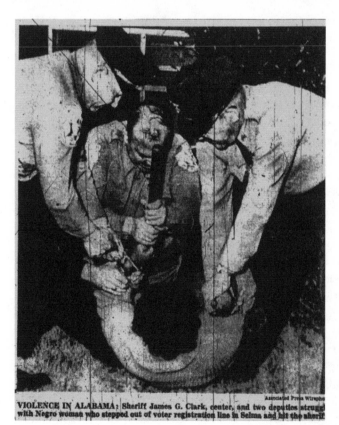

VIOLENCE IN ALABAMA: Sheriff James G. Clark, center, and two deputies struggle with Negro woman who stepped out of voter registration line in Selma and hit the sheriff

Sheriff Jim Clark and Annie Lee Cooper struggle on the front page of the *New York Times*. The confrontation looked much different on the CBS *Evening News*.

then follow an active group of teens gathered on the sidewalk, talking, moving about, smiling. Wood narrates, "Next it was the youngsters' turn. At least five hundred of them had played hooky again today to join the protest." Wood notes that when the "youngsters" got their orders to move from Brown Chapel, some went through backyards and back alleys and some got bunched up. "For a while Baker had his hands full as arrests were going on." We see a shot of a group of kids, some grinning pointedly at the camera, some craning their necks. Wood implies that the young marchers were not serious but rather engaged in high jinks and antics to get out of school. They did not present disciplined bodies that moved where they were supposed to and maintained the fiction that TV news cameras were not everywhere around them. The report redeemed these presumably frivolous marchers—who, of course, were too young to register to vote anyway—with the final shot. After the kids had been arrested, they were driven to the armory. The camera slowly zooms out to show viewers hundreds of young people standing behind a high chain link fence. Youthful horseplay now gave way to excessive punishment.

Although the CBS news reports frequently framed its Selma dispatches around the activities of the movement's marchers and demonstrators, the rank and file marchers were never considered worthy of being interviewed. Night after night in January and February, viewers would see activists and would-be voters, but CBS's correspondents never sought to discover their individual reasons and rationales for participating. Only King was deemed worthy to speak. Even King's various deputies and SCLC leaders such as Ralph Abernathy or Andrew Young were rarely called upon to provide comment. When King was away from Selma (which was frequently) or in jail, no other black representative took his place as spokesperson for the movement. On the white segregationist side, reporters would go to Clark or Baker, or to Smitherman or George Wallace. The voting rights movement had King or nobody. This was particularly problematic, since King did not speak for all constituencies in the movement; certainly, he did not speak for SNCC. On the other hand, by always going to King, television reporters portrayed a movement that was more unified, more leader oriented, and more moderate than was necessarily the case in 1965. The elevation of King as *the* spokesperson for the entire movement made the Selma campaign definitely more potentially palatable to white viewers, at least those outside the South.

The lack of attention to the diversity within the movement and the focus on King as the only face of the black freedom struggle wreaked havoc with CBS's attempt to accurately report Malcolm X's visit to Selma on February 4. Nelson Benton began by noting the "uneasy quiet" of the day as people hung around the church rather than marching. According to Benton, they listened to their leaders "and even to an uninvited guest"—Malcolm X, of course. Malcolm had come to Alabama specifically to speak at Tuskegee Institute about seventy-five miles from Selma, but members of SNCC had also extended an invitation for him to speak at Brown Chapel.[17] Yet considering how CBS had framed the Selma campaign, acknowledging or even recognizing that some segments of the campaign were not hostile to Malcolm would have introduced too much complexity and confusion into the picture. For much of the white media, even in 1965 after his break from the Nation of Islam, Malcolm represented black violence and hatred of whites. He was "the hate that hate produced."[18] In the white media, King and Malcolm functioned as binary opposites: nonviolent vs. violent; integrationist vs. separatist; potentially one of us vs. totally other. Benton's report on Malcolm's Selma visit played to all these distinctions.

We first see a shot of Malcolm after Benton notes that King's staff was wary of Malcolm's presence (illustrated ironically with a shot of the Brown Chapel sign reading "Visitors Welcome"). He is shown in classic "code of the villain" pose: extreme close-up, cut off at the forehead.[19] King, by comparison, was usually presented in full or medium shot or medium close-up, surrounded by support- ers, SCLC personnel, and, invariably, many news reporters, cameramen, and photographers. King was thus typically shown in some sort of context. Malcolm, in contrast, is thoroughly isolated in his extreme close-up. And the very tight framing makes him look ominous, dangerous, threatening. The report then cuts to a shot of reporters and a cameraman wielding a large 16mm camera, then back to Malcolm in a less tight close-up. He spoke at some length about how people would do well to listen to King and give him what he asked for, and fast. He emphasized that what King asked for—the ballot—was right and was going to be gotten one way or the other. To a reporter's question, Malcolm answered, "I don't believe in any kind of nonviolence," but then clarified, "I believe it is right to be nonviolent with people who are nonviolent, but when you are dealing with an enemy that doesn't know what nonviolence is, you're wasting your time."

During the entire report, Malcolm's only audience was news reporters. He was never pictured with voting rights activists or any Selma blacks, nor was any portion of his speech inside Brown Chapel shown. Malcolm's isolation from the movement was then contrasted to Coretta Scott King, whom Benton introduced as "one guest who definitely *was* invited." She is shown inside Brown Chapel giving a speech supporting the Selma activists by noting that she was from Ala- bama, too. The report cuts to her audience listening attentively. Scott King was thus part of the community, part of the movement, and emphatically belonged there. Malcolm's rather conciliatory speech delivered to the same audience did not merit inclusion in the report because it might suggest he had some legitimate reason to be there and some legitimate connection to the movement. Ironically, given the way the report juxtaposed Malcolm and Coretta Scott King, Malcolm had approached Scott King after his speech and, according to Taylor Branch, told her "that he had hoped to visit her husband [still in Selma's jail] and assure him that he meant to aid rather than hinder his cause, but he had to rush off to a conference in London."[20] A little over two weeks later, Malcolm was dead, assassinated by members of the Nation of Islam. The potential rapprochement between the two black leaders to which the news media had been blind, could now never blossom.

As the Selma campaign continued into February, some of its momentum seemed to peter out. On February 8, viewers saw a "good news" story about a King-led march of over a thousand people to the courthouse for one of Dallas County's two days of open voter registration testing. The reporter gushed that it was "the biggest and most peaceful demonstration yet." More peaceful and uneventful days like this, no matter how large the turnout, and the news media would likely pack up their crews as they had in Albany, Georgia, and leave town assuming a stable situation when, in fact, by taking national attention away from the struggle, their absence would assure victory for the status quo.

CBS News's next dispatch from the Alabama Black Belt four days later could not have been more different from the good news story about peaceful demonstrating. In fact, the February 19 report was unlike anything seen before in the network's reporting on the civil rights story. The report opens with correspondent Robert Plante sitting in a bare studio looking very grim. Rather than reporting from the scene, he spoke from the network's affiliate facilities in Montgomery. The unusual set up signaled something quite out of the ordinary. The story Plante covered was indeed out of the ordinary.

Civil rights activists had decided to shift the struggle to neighboring Perry County and the little rural town of Marion to protest the jailing of an SCLC voting rights organizer working there. Activists had decided to proceed with a night march even though nighttime demonstrations were inherently more dangerous both to marchers and to newsmen. On the one hand, the darkness helped hide white violence and, on the other hand, the darkness made news camera lights an easier target for whites who blamed those cameras for all their region's racial troubles. As it turned out, both marchers and newsmen ended up victims of Alabama trooper and white vigilante brutality. NBC's Selma correspondent Richard Valeriani was clubbed in the head with an ax handle. He delivered his report the next day from his hospital bed with a bandaged head and slurred speech.[21] Other newsmen suffered lesser injuries but had their equipment destroyed. Scores of marchers were beaten. One of them, Jimmie Lee Jackson, was shot in the stomach as he attempted to protect his mother from being beaten by Alabama troopers. Eight days later he was dead: the campaign's first martyr.

Plante began his report noting that a hundred troopers waded into a group of four hundred marchers and attempted to disperse them while brandishing clubs. Said Plante: "We were among the few newsmen who arrived early enough before the troopers began holding off the press. We returned to stay in one spot on the sidewalk across the street from the church. White bystanders harassed us with homemade clubs, cursing us, and blaming the press as the cause of the demonstration. Camera lenses were sprayed with paint. CBS cameraman Bernie

Nudelman wiped the paint from his lens and shot this film before we were forced to turn off our floodlights."

Extraordinary is Plante's self-reflexive reference to his own newsgathering activity. Even though the presence of news cameras was always part and parcel of the story, news reporters insistently ignored their own presence and its impact on the activities they recorded. This silencing may have reflected professional codes of journalistic objectivity: reporters and camera crews were there to observe disinterestedly and recount the event; they were never to be involved with the event or considered to be influencing it. In the case of civil rights demonstrations, this was obviously an agreed-upon fiction that news organizations and civil rights activists pursued together. White segregationists emphatically did not wish to participate in this particular fiction. In the Selma campaign, however, especially following Bloody Sunday, the massive presence of cameras and journalists presented an uncomfortable evasiveness in the television news coverage. The sheer mass of news personnel often threatened to crowd out whatever event or activity TV news reporters were documenting, especially if King was in the footage. CBS news reports could make reference to anything and everything going on in the footage, except the crowd of newsmen.

This silence about what was so manifestly present in so much of the televised coverage may have been an attempt by this still-new journalistic institution to behave like other, more established journalistic entities. But print journalists had an easier time ignoring the presence of their peers, since photojournalists whose work accompanied the written reports typically attempted to frame their shots to not include other photographers. For instance, TV coverage of Clark's confrontation with Annie Lee Cooper showed lots of press surrounding the scene; the famous photograph that splashed onto the nation's newspapers did not. Television journalism had to deal with the more unpredictable nature of moving pictures that could not necessarily be artfully framed. Plante's report is so noteworthy because in this particular instance, the news apparatus could not efface itself. And, in order to explain why newsmen were being attacked, Plante also had to give voice to the segregationist critique of the journalist–demonstrator relationship.

The footage that Plante showed to viewers was murky at best. We see an image of the church that was both the embarkation point for the march and where marchers attempted to flee to safety from the trooper and vigilante violence. However, viewers could not really see anything in the footage. Then we hear a voice in a Southern drawl order, "Pull that light out! Cut it out! Keep it out!" The murky image goes dark.

The Marion film was not "good footage."[22] It was not clear and legible; it did not give viewers a sense of visual mastery of a scene. By the standards of professional journalism, this was really quite unusable. The only reason to show it was as evidence of the violence directed at newsmen. It also functions as "crisis coverage," Mary Ann Doane's terminology to describe moments when "the formal markers of the political process . . . unravel . . . before our eyes: the loss of the camera's control of the image is one of the things that tells the audience that political control, too, is up for grabs."[23] Along with CBS cameraman Bernie Nudelman's "loss of camera control" at Marion, the report showed a loss of control over the fiction of neutrality, disinterestedness, and objectivity. Newsmen's outrage at being the recipient of segregationist violence extended to outrage at the violence inflicted on the activists.

When Plante returns after showing the footage, he describes the bludgeoning of Valeriani: "As four police and state troopers watched, a television reporter was clubbed with an ax handle." Plante suddenly looks down at his notes as if attempting to control his emotions. He then looks up and reports the shooting of Jackson and the injuring of other Negroes. He ends the report saying, "Later last night a reporter called the sheriff's office to ask what had happened. A deputy sheriff told him, 'It was a small incident. One Negro fell down.'" Plante stared into the camera with what looked like barely contained outrage.[24]

Jackson's death mobilized the civil rights community in Selma, which quickly developed a plan to march from Selma to Montgomery to protest his death in the cause of voting rights. Hastily planned, the organizers likely did not expect to get far outside of Selma before being turned back. King returned to Atlanta to attend to his largely neglected pastoral responsibilities at his church, assuming, according to Selma campaign historian Charles Fager, "that the march would be a cakewalk which would be stopped without either violence or much public impact, and that he could just as well spend the day resting at home and preparing himself for the second try, which would probably be more eventful."[25] SNCC, after fractious debate, decided not to participate in or sanction the march as an organization but allowed individual members to do so if they wished.[26] An isolated John Lewis, his chairmanship of the organization now tenuous, ended up leading the March 7 procession along with SCLC's Hosea Williams. What happened that overcast afternoon nobody in either organization could have predicted.

Reporting Bloody Sunday

ABC may have been first to air with its film of the confrontation at the Edmund Pettus Bridge, but CBS and NBC followed later that evening. Nelson Benton's report for CBS, lasting three minutes and fifteen seconds, aired on both the Sunday night and Monday morning news.[27] How did CBS package Bloody Sunday for its viewers?

Charles Kuralt, who anchored the Monday news program, insisted on framing the event as a confrontation between Governor Wallace and Dr. King, even though neither one had been anywhere close to the Pettus Bridge. Insisting on a news frame of leaders and elected officials over grassroots activists, Kuralt sat in front of two large photos of Wallace and King. Describing them as "two determined men," he said, "Yesterday their determination turned the streets of Alabama into a battleground as Wallace's state troopers broke up a march ordered by King."[28] Set up this way, the marchers were little more than passive dupes for King's grudge match with Wallace, while the troopers and Clark's posse were little more than tools for the Governor. Kuralt's framing denied any agency to the actors on the bridge: they were only stand-ins for the real political players.

Benton begins his narration not with any explanation or identification of the actors we actually see in the footage, but rather with the one we do not see: King. Benton tells viewers that King was absent in order to plan a legal campaign against Wallace's ban on the planned march to Montgomery. Although not exactly correct, this was probably the line that SCLC staffers gave reporters. By beginning the report this way, Benton both excuses King's absence and metaphorically inserts King into the action. King may not have been visible in the footage, but Kuralt and Benton's commentary insisted on King's presence nonetheless in order for the march to be politically meaningful.

Benton goes on to note that the six hundred who marched "made little headway towards the state capitol some fifty miles to the east. They barely left Selma. They marched in small groups through the city of Selma and were not stopped." We then see a shot of the first group of marchers appearing at the crest of the bridge. The images of the confrontation that unfold shortly thereafter borrow some representational strategies from the Hollywood western and its iconic shoot-out sequences between hero and villain on Main Street. We start with footage from one of Benton's two cameramen positioned to the side of the standoff at the foot of the Pettus Bridge as the marchers stand in single-line formation. Panning over to the Alabama troopers arrayed before them down the street, we then hear the order to disperse, and the camera continues to pan back and forth between the two adversaries. Benton explains that the marchers were given two minutes to return to their homes. "They didn't." We then hear, "Troopers, advance toward the group." Benton's cameraman cuts in to a closer shot of the marchers and then pans over to the troopers as they begin their advance. Cutting in closer, the troopers plow over the marchers and we see people going down and being pushed backward. On the soundtrack the screaming begins.

At this point in the coverage, we have very good film by the standards of television journalism—and very good television, more generally. Benton's cameraman gives viewers a ringside seat with no visual obstructions. According to a later interview with Benton, "[T]he first camera crew had gone on ahead, guy named Bernie Nudelman, waved us over to where he was and said, 'Al Lingo says get right over here, and we'll have a ringside seat.' . . . And we shot and no one prevented us from shooting."[29] This situation was different from what had happened to Nudelman in Marion. Along with the visual clarity, the mise-en-scène echoing the western shootout gave viewers moral clarity as well. The familiar visual composition cued

Bloody Sunday: among the most politically consequential television newsfilm in American history. Sheriff Clark's posse and police violently plow over peaceful marchers at the Edmund Pettus Bridge.

viewers to construct an appropriate narrative: bad guys vs. good guys. Cutting to a wide shot, marchers go down and others try to run. The camera follows the panicked scramble and then zooms in on a couple of downed marchers lying on a grassy area next to the sidewalk. We then zoom out as troopers mounted on horseback begin their attack. Benton returns with his narration, matter-of-factly describing the mounted advance.

At this point, the footage takes on more of the quality of "crisis coverage" as Benton's camera teams no longer have quite the optimal view of the violent proceedings. The soundtrack carries more signifiers of brutality as we hear constant screams but cannot visually locate their origin. We also hear explosions of tear gas. The footage shows an image further back toward the bridge, which is becoming obstructed by the tear gas. In the middle distance, a crowd of troopers, partially hidden by a car, is beating with billy clubs. We cannot quite see the victims. Suddenly a woman runs out of the melee. The camera pans with her, then pans back to the cloud of tear gas and troopers. A quick cut shows a tear gas canister being kicked by a trooper.

The footage at the beginning of the confrontation was disturbing because it so clearly showed white brutality. This subsequent footage was disturbing for what it did not show. Viewers had to imagine, with the audio assistance of disembodied shrieks and screams, what was going on behind the car and inside the clouds of tear gas. Rather than a Hollywood western, viewers were now watching a horror film.

Final shots showed crumpled bodies by the sidewalk and a dazed young woman with a cloth to her mouth. The final shot frames a small group of troopers slowly and casually strolling away from the camera with gas masks dangling at their

A horror film at the Edmund Pettus Bridge: tear gas obstructs TV viewers' ability to see the carnage on the bridge as marchers attempt to flee the police brutality.

sides. In voice-over, Benton reports, "Scores of marchers were treated for tear gas burns, open wounds, and broken bones. One hospital treated forty people."

Although the "Bloody Sunday" footage suggested both the Hollywood western and the horror film in its representational strategies for depicting a violent confrontation, ultimately the power of the footage is grounded in melodrama. Linda Williams has argued that this narrative form is "the fundamental mode by which American mass culture has 'talked to itself' about the enduring moral dilemma of race."[30] Melodrama is premised on narratives of stark moral clarity with clearly drawn forces of good and evil providing a "moral legibility" in a secular world bereft of the theology of the Sacred that in pre-Enlightenment times grounded Western societies' sense of ultimate reality. Melodrama requires the suffering and brutalization of the virtuous hero or heroine in order to make manifest the ultimate triumph of Virtue.[31] In the American melodramatic imagination, the suffering black (typically male) body has a long genealogy that Williams traces from Harriet Beecher Stowe's Uncle Tom. In the civil rights era, we can trace this genealogy to the tortured dead body of Emmett Till, whose pulverized face Till's mother insisted be displayed in an open casket in order to make graphically visible the horrors of the Southern racial system.[32] Martin Luther King seemed to speak the discourse of the melodramatic imagination when he invoked the redemptive value of unmerited suffering as a key rationale for nonviolent protest in the face of violent response. By suffering in a highly visible way at the hands of Southern segregationists and racists, the movement presented the American audience with a drama requiring the ultimate triumph of virtue which, within the melodramatic storyline, was clearly and unambiguously signified in the figure of the suffering black body. The confrontation on the Pettus Bridge could not be morally more clear or its meaning more obvious. It fit into a genealogy deeply sedimented in the American cultural imagination.

Network television's news coverage of Bloody Sunday and, to a much lesser extent, stories in newspapers like the *Washington Post* and the *New York Times*, galvanized viewers and elected officials. In Washington, a dozen speeches on the floor of the Congress specifically linked Governor Wallace to Hitler and Clark's posse to Nazi storm troopers.[33] Garrow notes that congressional speakers "seemed to be saying that televised film coverage of Selma had had a more intense impact upon them than had still photographs or written reports."[34] Television news—the ABC broadcast with its juxtaposing *Judgment at Nuremberg* with the Selma footage in particular—had a direct effect on how Bloody Sunday was being made sense of in its immediate aftermath.[35] King, still in Atlanta, hastily sent out a call to clergy of all faiths to join him in Selma on Tuesday for a second march to Montgomery.

The news coverage, along with King's call, also galvanized ordinary Americans. George B. Leonard, an editor at *Look* magazine, repeatedly linked the Holocaust and the situation of American Negroes and the requirement of citizens to activate their moral conscience to intervene. But he also emphasized the importance of television news coverage in mobilizing that intervention:

> We were in our living room in San Francisco watching the 6 P.M. news. I was not aware that at the same moment people all up and down the West Coast were feeling what my wife and I felt, that at various times all over the country that day and up past 11 P.M. Pacific Time that night hundreds of these people would drop whatever they were doing; that some of them would leave home without changing clothes, borrow money, overdraw their checking accounts, board planes, buses, trains, cars . . . that these people, mostly unknown to each other, would move for a single purpose, to place themselves alongside the Negroes they had watched on television.[36]

Like George Leonard, hundreds of outraged citizens traveled by whatever means available in order to attend the march, which received heavy coverage by a growing phalanx of print and broadcast reporters.

CBS had to insert King metaphorically into the Sunday march. On Tuesday, however, the news team had a much easier task centering their coverage on him. By doing so, they inevitably simplified the situation. The march had been barred from proceeding to Montgomery pending a decision by the U.S. District Court Judge Frank Johnson in Montgomery. King was loath to defy a federal court since the movement had always viewed the federal bench as sympathetic, and Judge Johnson was considered moderate and fair minded. In conference with CORE and SNCC, King initially agreed to ignore the march ban, particularly considering the massive numbers of clergy and other citizens streaming hourly into town to walk in the march. But when the Johnson White House heard of King's decision, it worked frantically to head off a confrontation. In the end, King bowed to presidential pressure. After leading twenty-five hundred marchers to the very spot where the smaller group had been gassed and clubbed two days earlier, King knelt and led the marchers in prayer. Then, by prior agreement, he turned the march around and led the throng back, peacefully, to Brown Chapel. "Turn around Tuesday," as it came to be called in movement circles, led to significant anger and frustration with King's leadership of the Selma campaign.

CBS News's Tuesday night coverage of the march, not surprisingly, remained oblivious to the nuances and complexities around the aborted march. The piece is significant for the CBS camera crew's tortuous attempts to construct visuals that framed King at the center of the proceedings, rendering the twenty-five hundred other marchers little more than extras. Although the reporter describes the march as composed of "Negroes from Selma and white clergy from all over the country," the footage individualized no one but King. With the crush of other reporters, along with still and moving camera operators, CBS's cameraman had a great deal of difficulty keeping King in frame. Frequently we see a bobbling, shaking frame. At one point a still camera gets in the way. Often the view of King gets obstructed. As the marchers reach the line of Alabama troopers and are commanded, "Stop; stand where you are; this march will not continue," the CBS film loses focus, becomes hazy and jumpy. As King requests the opportunity to kneel and pray, we see another hazy image as though the cameraman was filming into the sun. During the prayer, we lose all access to King's visual image. The cameraman zooms in closer, presumably trying to find King, but ends up framing only another reporter. The image does take in Andrew Young somewhat away from the praying group with armed crossed, clearly not in prayer. The cameraman zooms in on him, but there is no voice-over identifying him or discussing his actions. Apparently, Young was keeping an eye out for possible attacks on King. As the group rises and turns around, the camera zooms out to take in a fuller image. With King again center framed, he and the lead marchers pass through a veritable gauntlet of press.

This part of the report is notable because it departs from standard CBS news-reporting style. During the aborted confrontation, there is no voice-over narration from the reporter. The report takes on a cinema-verité quality, drawing attention to its ragged, badly framed, visually substandard film footage. The lack of narration and the verité look gives a feeling of liveness, immediacy, and lack of mediation. There is a rawness to the film that deviates from standards of professionally constructed, composed, and edited news reports with the reporter's narration used to provide clarity. And, as we have seen before, when the reporter does narrate, he is silent about one of the overwhelming features of the footage: the sheer crush of press. The visual fact of immense media presence at Selma and on the march to Montgomery, which finally would get underway on March 21, could never be acknowledged even as that presence was so glaringly evident in shot after shot and report after report. Frequently, as the Selma campaign continued, CBS viewers would be seeing "not good" images and obscured views because other reporters and cameras got in the way.

Covering Selma's Martyrs: Jackson, Reeb, and Liuzzo

Shortly after the "turn around Tuesday" march, one of the white clergymen who had journeyed to Selma in response to King's call suffered a vicious beating by white attackers. Rev. James Reeb, a Unitarian minister from Boston, lay in a coma for a few days before succumbing to his massive head wounds and becoming the Selma campaign's second martyr. There would be a third at the end of the campaign: Viola Liuzzo, a white housewife from Detroit, murdered by four Klansmen as she ferried marchers back to Selma after the completion of the march to Montgomery. The sustained and individualizing coverage given these martyrs stands in stark contrast to the minimal coverage given to the campaign's first martyr, Jimmie Lee Jackson, an African American.

CBS News focused attention on Jackson only twice. First, in Bill Plante's reporting on Marion, Jackson's shooting was mentioned in passing, although his name was not. Plante was more intent on reporting violence to newsmen. On March 3, Plante covered Jackson's funeral at Brown Chapel. Although the coverage was respectful and solemn, with an opening shot of a banner over the Chapel reading "Racism killed our brother," Plante went on to refer to the 26-year-old as a "farm boy" as well as "deacon of his church, mason, and activist." The "boy" reference was unfortunate. Over shots of Jackson's casket and a procession of young men and boys, Plante describes the reports about Jackson's mortal wounding, noting that "others said he'd turned on someone who had just clubbed his mother on the side of the head." The subtle suggestion of Jackson's potentially violent response was then balanced with a dignified zoom in on the grief-filled face of Jackson's mother. At no time were Jackson's mother or other family members interviewed, nor were any witnesses interviewed about his shooting. His case merited no further coverage.

In Reeb's case, by contrast, *The Evening News* spotlighted an interview with the two white clergymen who had been with Reeb when he was attacked coming out of a black-owned café. One gave an extensive description of the attack. The reporter then asked the men their view about the racial situation, thereby giving them the privilege to analyze the circumstances from the movement point of view usually afforded only to King. The next day, March 11, Reeb was dead, and CBS News provided an interview with Rev. Reeb's widow. The broadcast also included a long report on a prayer vigil for Reeb that occurred before he passed away.

The Liuzzo murder received the most sustained and poignant coverage of all, in part because, with the climactic completion of the march in Montgomery, the Selma campaign as a narrative had largely come to an end. The Liuzzo case supplied a tragic coda and new story line to keep reporters going. Eric Sevareid, who provided regular commentaries about news events, noted with palpable outrage that Southern courts tended to allow white murderers of civil rights activists to go unpunished. He observed, "This week in Montgomery, placards were carried through the streets saying, 'Be a man, join the Klan.' The killings that the manly men are implicated took place at night, generally from behind. The victims, now including a mother of five, were unarmed and unsuspecting." Sevareid's commentaries were privileged moments in the Cronkite broadcast. Here, the day after twenty-five thousand people converged on the city, along with hundreds of marchers who had made the four-day trek down Highway 80, Sevareid did not devote his commentary on the significance of the completed march, nor on King's soaring oratory, nor on the march's effect on voting rights legislation. Apparently, it was more important to focus on the appalling novelty of a white woman's murder.

Liuzzo's death received more attention than either Jackson's or Reeb's to a large extent because of gender. CBS played up the melodramatic elements of the story in a way not evident in its coverage of Reeb. Although the news broadcast provided an interview with Reeb's widow, it did not emphasize elements of pathos. In the same broadcast containing Sevareid's commentary, viewers also saw a story from the Liuzzo home. It opened with a shot of the exterior of the house and a reporter describing, "The peaceful Liuzzo home was thrown into shock, disbelief, and sorrow by shattering news of Mrs. Liuzzo's murder." Cutting to the home's interior, viewers saw close-up shots of framed portraits of the Liuzzo children on the wall. Liuzzo was thus metonymically constructed as a homemaker and as a mother, not as an activist. Her house and her children were the only aspects of her life represented. But then to heighten the pathos of the family melodrama even more, the report showed a grief-stricken Mr. Liuzzo impulsively placing a call to George Wallace's office.

This focus on heightened emotion and the privatized sphere was somewhat unusual in this era of television news. News reports tended to emphasize public actors and their discourse and actions in the public arena. Because Viola Liuzzo had been constructed first and foremost as a wife and mother, the news reports about her tended to deemphasize her actions in the public sphere and consigned her to a traditional and more familiar place.

The perhaps predictable focus on whites within the movement extended not just to the dead. Along with the large number of clergy who heeded King's call, many white college students made the trek to Selma. A March 19 report gave voice to these young white activists while at the same time marginalizing and trivializing them.[37] Over a shot of new arrivals disembarking from a bus, including one priest and, behind him, a smiling, college-age female, Bill Plante frames the report by posing the question he will subsequently ask twice again: "Are the college students coming to Selma to protest instead of going to Florida to lounge on the beach and litter the streets with beer cans?" A male student from San Francisco State tells Plante his group had decided it was time for them to come.

PLANTE: Is this in lieu of another trip you might take on your spring vacation?
STUDENT: No, it's in lieu of classes.

Next the smiling female from the bus gets the spring break question and parries it thus: "No, it certainly is not. We have a lot of work to make up at school."

The images and answers of the two students help undercut Plante's trivializing frame. But, more significant, the activists are given the opportunity to voice their motivation, a privilege never given to any of the black activists and marchers during the Cronkite news coverage of the Selma story. Perhaps their motivation was seen as self-evident. Perhaps reporters, by relying on King as spokesman for the movement, felt that the movement's rank and file did not need to be given voice since their presumed leader was given ample opportunity to speak. Perhaps the motivations of Northern, white college students who were not personally implicated in black voting rights were more open to journalistic scrutiny. Nevertheless, the coverage gives us visible but silenced black actors whose voices are seemingly not deemed worthy of being heard; their visual representation is all that matters. They are spoken by their images. The whites, on the other hand, have to speak because their images cannot speak for them. They need to be explained. But by explaining them and allowing them to explain themselves, the news coverage bestows on them a significance and importance out of keeping with their actual role within the Selma campaign.

Perhaps the most important white person throwing his considerable support behind the Selma campaign whom CBS News profiled was President Johnson. On March 15, Johnson delivered a historic address to a joint session of Congress about Selma and announced his voting rights bill. Johnson, unlike his immediate predecessor in the White House, was not known for stirring oratory, but the address Johnson delivered that night is considered one of the great American speeches of the twentieth century. As was standard, all three networks carried the speech live in prime time. Along with congressmen, senators, Supreme Court justices, and members of his cabinet, Johnson spoke to approximately 70 million Americans that night.[38] One of those television viewers was Martin Luther King, whose eyes welled with tears as he watched Johnson throw the entire power of the presidency behind King's cause.[39]

The following evening Cronkite's broadcast found a stirring way to link together the President's speech and the day's activities in Selma. Reporter Nelson Benton described a memorial march for Rev. Reeb, giving viewers close shots of King and a white priest on the steps of the Dallas County Courthouse and wider shots of the large assemblage surrounding the building. Then, suddenly, the report cut back to Johnson and the portion of his speech that brought tears to King's eyes and that remain the most well-known phrases in the address: "Their cause must be our cause, too . . . and we *shall* overcome."

Cutting back to the assemblage at the courthouse, we clearly hear them singing "We Shall Overcome." The report holds on a wide shot of the singing marchers for a long take with no further narration from Benton. The blending of the president's use of the movement's signature phrase with that of the Selma marchers effectively knits Johnson into the demonstration. The president seems almost to lead the singing of the freedom song. The editing of this report through both image and sound emphasizes that the Selma campaign, like the March on Washington before it, was fully within the journalistic sphere of consensus. By juxtaposing the Johnson address with the Selma marchers, CBS News seemed to be suggesting that the two were one. Johnson's support, however, was far more emphatic and emotionally resonant than Kennedy's had been for the 1963 event. By speaking the words "we shall overcome," Johnson, the white Southerner from Texas, had joined the movement along with all the other whites from around the country who had descended on Selma over the past week.

Marching to Montgomery

With such a stunning and ringing endorsement from the White House, the coverage of the Selma-to-Montgomery march almost inevitably took on the character of a ceremonial media event, much like the March on Washington. Immediate pre-march coverage focused largely on the procedural issues around the march, which would proceed over five days with marchers camping out on land donated by cooperating local black farmers. Federalized National Guardsmen would provide protection along the fifty-mile stretch. On days two, three, and four of the march, only three hundred marchers would be permitted to participate because Route 80 turned into a much narrower two-lane highway.

The question of who would be included in the three hundred turned into another story that put whites at the center. Murray Fromson's report of March 19 focused on a contentious discussion Andrew Young had with marchers about who of the thousands who participated in the Selma campaign could continue on in the second, third, and fourth days of the march. We see film of Young responding to a marcher suggesting that all the whites go back. Young counters that white people are their protectors and points to the surrounding National Guard, arguing this federal force would not be there if only Negroes were marching. But he goes on to emphasize, "This is not a black movement. This is not a Negro problem." The camera zooms in to a close-up. "This is America's problem. And white people are as much responsible for it and carry as much of the burden for it as we do. So it's important for some white people to be with us." We hear clapping and then we pan over to a group of white marchers.

The privileging of Young's discourse (the only voice we hear from any march participant) centers white people as crucial to the movement. By choosing to include this particular exchange, CBS News reverted back to the "black and white together" theme we saw as central to the consensus strategy in the March on Washington coverage. And if CBS gave viewers white mothers pushing baby carriages as one of its consensus images of that march, newsmen had a particularly compelling image of whiteness to serve up to viewers of the Montgomery march.

Besides King and Young, the only other individualizing image we see of a Selma-to-Montgomery marcher is white Michigan participant, Jim Letherer. Letherer, who was never named or apparently interviewed in the *Evening News* coverage, was an amputee who hobbled on two crutches. He was one of the three hundred. The news report shot Letherer from a number of angles, zooming in on him, panning behind him, focusing on his one leg from the rear.

The case of Jim Letherer, whose image shows up over and over again in the Montgomery march coverage, suggests not only the work done by CBS in wanting to privilege white marchers and a "black and white together" consensual vision of racial harmony; more important, Letherer's recurring image indicates the work done by the SCLC and the movement in choreographing its media images. The Letherer image suggests the extent of the movement's media savvy and visual sophistication. It understood the concept "photo opportunity" almost two decades before that phrase and that concept came into general semantic circulation. We can get a fascinating glimpse into the elaborate "photo op" dance between the CBS news crew and the movement by examining not only the network's coverage for March 25, the fourth day of the march, but also the raw footage that the news team had to work with. Looking at both helps us to see the choices CBS News made of the visuals that the movement provided. And we see images very carefully orchestrated to have maximum semiotic power.

The Cronkite broadcast began its report on the march's penultimate day with footage replete with signifiers of "Americana" and the Revolutionary War. Jim Letherer is flanked on one side by a young, attractive white man hoisting a large American flag; on Letherer's other side, a black man also hoists a flag. Right beside him another black man plays "Yankee Doodle Dandy" on a flute. The report gives viewers a close-up of the flutist, a close-up of Letherer's one leg, a close-up of the white flag holder, then a whip pan over to the black flag holder. On the reel of raw footage, it is clear that Letherer and company are far out in front of the march, well positioned to be filmed and photographed. The raw footage also shows numerous newsmen in front of them. As Letherer moves past the news crew we can hear off screen a voice, probably the CBS cameraman, saying "thank you." Obviously there was nothing random or accidental about this arrangement of marchers and props. The iconography of crutches, flutist, and flag carrier was semiotically rich in connoting patriotism and in linking the black freedom movement to another freedom movement circa 1776. Somebody must have grouped these marchers together and strategically placed them in front of the march for maximum photographic visibility. In instances like this, the movement appeared quite willing and able to stage-manage its representation to the media, television in particular. Movement organizers understood the semiotic power of the televisual image long before most other political actors did.[40] Reporter Robert Plante's only attempt to undercut the built-in meanings of this proto-photo op is his observation that "Yankee Doodle" might be "rubbing it in" to some Alabama residents.

In the aired report, Plante noted that the restriction to three hundred marchers no longer applied. He illustrated the influx of more marchers by focusing on a busload of black middle school or high school students. The raw footage contains a lot of scenes from inside the bus, as excited school kids sing and clap to freedom songs. The news team had a problem, however. The kids kept acknowledging the camera, pointing to it, looking straight at it, and in general refusing to pretend they were not being filmed. In the aired film, the team managed to find a section of footage in which the kids did not acknowledge the camera. Here again, television news attempts to efface itself. The march to Montgomery may have turned into a consensual media event, but CBS did not want to acknowledge its crucial and enabling presence.

March organizers and participants, at least the adult ones, also appeared to understand the needs for consensual images that would help the news media— television in particular—to construct pleasing representations. Marchers did not carry placards or signs. Rather, many carried flags. The CBS camera crew seemed

Photo op: a carefully constructed arrangement of Selma-to-Montgomery marchers. One-legged Jim Letherer is always privileged in the newsfilm.

particularly intent on framing shots with flags. The raw footage is filled with such shots. In the aired report, as Plante comments on the anticipation of marchers for the next day's climax, we see what looks like a march of flags rather than a march of people.

Continuing the focus on the significance of whites in the movement, the raw footage contains some shots of the camera crew panning and tracking marchers resting or getting water. In general, whenever the cameraman zooms in to frame an individual, that person often tends to be white, typically a young, white female. In the aired report, we see footage of the marchers and then cut in to a close shot of an elderly white woman wearing a headscarf.

Not surprisingly, the only voice, other than Plante's, that viewers heard in the report belonged to Martin Luther King. We see King in an uncharacteristically jocular and informal pose. In shirt sleeves, white cap, and smiling broadly, King exults with marchers: "When we go across the city line tomorrow, we'll have a new song to sing: 'We *have* overcome.'" Marchers clap. "'We *were* not afraid.'"

Plante ends the report illustrated with a flag-festooned stream of marchers, that "tonight's entertainers and speakers will drive home once again the point that they want their freedom and they want it now." Tellingly, the emphasis is not on the specifics of voting rights, but on the more generic and more "Americana" ideals of freedom. Thus, the "photo op" that opened the report—and that the movement choreographed to encourage reporters to frame the march in patriotically American ways—fully paid off.

Viewers Respond: The Black Press

As a television event, the Selma campaign was a roaring success for the civil rights movement. Commentary in the African American press acknowledged this success and praised the medium in tones similar to remarks about the televising of the March on Washington. Discussion in Alabama papers, both editorial remarks and letters from ordinary white Alabamians, provides a stark contrast that is not surprising. While these white viewers and critics were highly conscious of television and the mediating function of the television camera and of the news media more generally, the African American press by contrast highlighted television's role only rarely.

One of the few direct references to television coverage in the black press came from the *Pittsburgh Courier's* "Video Vignettes" columnist Hazel Garland, who said, "Through the medium of the electronic tube, viewers were able to see for themselves the brutal treatment accorded the peaceful marchers seeking to dramatize the plight of the Alabama Negro who wanted merely to secure his constitutional rights. . . . So when someone says teevee isn't serving a great purpose, one should only remember the splendid coverage given such events."[41]

For Garland, television functioned as a mirror, providing direct, unfiltered, unmediated engagement with the situation faced by blacks struggling in the South. Television news provided the truth, unadorned. Therefore, it did not present representational problems for African Americans, unlike other forms of mass media that had historically circulated stereotypes and demeaning images of black people. When mass media constructed objectionable images such as the early film industry did with *The Birth of a Nation,* the early radio industry with *Amos 'n' Andy,* and early entertainment television with *Beulah* and *Amos 'n' Andy* again, the black press and civil rights groups like the NAACP rose up in protest. For much of the twentieth century, the question of black representation in mass media would be an important one for black civil rights organizations. Media imagery of the civil rights movement appeared to provide African Americans with the novel experience of black representations that did not fit previous patterns. With the media not disseminating problematic imagery, the apparatus did not require discussion, attention, or criticism. For the most part, the media apparatus disappeared, and only its content remained—content that during this brief period seemed empowering.

Commentary that did exist tended to focus on the representation of Southern figures of segregation such as Clark and Wallace and what those images revealed to the world. A *Courier* editorial reflected on the culmination of the march to Montgomery and images television viewers saw of Wallace and the Alabama capitol building: "He speaks like a tried and true American. Yet television showed that this self-styled 'American' doesn't even fly the American flag over the State Capitol of Alabama! Instead, TV pictures showed a Confederate flag and the state flag of Alabama flapping in the breeze."[42] Again, the televisual apparatus functioned as a mirror to reflect the truth about, in this case, Governor Wallace's inherent lack of patriotism and fealty to the nation. Undoubtedly, the television images that emphasized the absence of a U.S. flag atop the Alabama capitol were juxtaposed to shots of the plethora of U.S. flags toted by march participants.[43]

One mild critique about the nature of television coverage made it into *Ebony*'s coverage of the march to Montgomery: the incessant focus on King.

> To give the pilgrimage a worldwide impact, hordes of photographers, writers and TV leg men converged near the front line jotting down notes on every twist of the mouth or wrinkle of the forehead of leader King. A TV truck slowly wended its way up the highway recording almost every step of the elite marchers.
>
> With attention focused on the leaders, the real beauty and meaning of the people's army went almost unnoticed. Who were these non-descript marchers? Why would they undertake such a strenuous journey?[44]

Unlike CBS News, which never undertook to answer those questions, *Ebony* went on to highlight the comments of these non-elite participants.

White Alabamians Respond

While many African Americans looked at television news coverage of the civil rights campaigns and saw a mirror reflecting truth and reality, many white Alabamians may have felt that the TV news mirror belonged in a carnival fun house. Their frequently resistant and oppositional readings provide clues to help us understand the profound shock and dislocation that results when a society's naturalized common sense begins to unravel. For white Southerners, the status of "reality" became alarmingly unstable.

Jason Sokol, in his study of ordinary white Southerners during the civil rights era, points out whites' views of blacks and of the racial order constituted a carefully elaborated myth and worldview that the civil rights movement traumatically shattered. In examining white Georgians' response to the Albany movement, Sokol points out:

> White convictions about local blacks, "outside agitators," and civil rights formed a definable worldview and buttressed a way of life. This worldview possessed a certain logic (circular though it may have been) and interpretation of history (inwardly consistent if grossly distorted). If a Jim Crow defender could establish that no past problems existed between whites and blacks, several conclusions followed: civil rights demonstrators were unnecessary, people from outside Albany devised them, and the local blacks wanted no part. . . . The health of this social order depended upon the white belief that it was tolerable—even pleasant—for everyone.
>   . . . If one claim stood, the others seemed instantly legitimate. If whites were the best friends of the blacks, surely good race relations prevailed. If Albany blacks were happy with segregation, they were grateful to the whites who powered that system—and they felt victimized by the outsiders in their towns. . . . If blacks were in fact unhappy, then whites' entire worldview would be false, and they might have to admit that, for blacks, their city was more purgatory than paradise.[45]

Television news in particular, and mass media more generally, served an important role in undermining this internally consistent worldview. The response by white Alabamians in the white heat of the media spotlight on Selma gives us a glimpse of what, at its very beginnings, would be a long and fraught process of fundamental change for white Southerners.

How did white Alabamians react to the construction of "reality" provided by television news? The initial response was blunt denial. Numerous respondents in the letters section of the *Selma Times-Journal* (the section grew significantly as the crisis developed) focused on the media image of their town and lambasted the media for not having the "true facts" about Selma and its race and voting situation.

One of the first television programs to generate the ire of Selma whites was not even a news show but rather *The Tonight Show Starring Johnny Carson*. One

Selma resident sent the *Times-Journal* a copy of a letter he had sent to Carson chiding him for incorrectly stating that a Selma resident had attacked Martin Luther King recently. He insisted that the perpetrator was not from Selma and that he had been immediately arrested and jailed.[46] "We are not a bunch of hoodlums—our streets are safe at night—and we are making a tremendous effort to maintain law and order under extremely trying circumstances."[47] A few days later, the local Jaycees also weighed in with their protest to Carson. "The privilege of having the opportunity to rebut untrue and harmful publicity, on a popular national TV show, is not afforded to all people in our great nation," they noted, and went on to argue that Carson needed to relate the truth, not half-truths.[48] Another letter writer fumed at the national media's depiction of Selma's "racial image" and in particular its characterization of Sheriff Clark and his posse. "We in Dallas County can 'face the fact' since we have the true facts no matter what outside newspapers and the television news media concoct to write about."[49] The *Times-Journal* also voiced its ire about the depiction of voter registration processes in Dallas County: "You won't hear it on the national TV newscasts or see it in headlines in the nation's press, but we think that these facts about the Selma situation ought to be known." The newspaper referred to a press release from the Dallas County registrars that "will have a hard time catching up with the image of this Alabama city already created by the reporting of events during these past couple of weeks."[50]

This insistence that Selmians and Alabamians possessed the "true facts" while the national media disseminated distortions, errors, and outright lies was an understandable response by white Southerners seeing their previously unexamined worldview profoundly questioned. Latching onto clear errors such as Johnny Carson's helped white Selmians hold on to a vision of their town as one in which good race relations prevailed and racist violence (and concomitantly race protest) came only from outsiders.

The "true facts" response strategy, however, quickly gave way to another, more powerful discursive means to counteract the media coverage: it was all a vast publicity stunt. The *Times-Journal* reprinted editorials from a number of other Alabama papers that explained the situation this way for their readers. According to the *Dothan Eagle*, "The cunningly calculated and federally sanctioned torment of Selma and Dallas County is the biggest, cruelest, and most unjust publicity stunt staged in a long time and for television in particular."[51] The *Troy Messenger* fulminated, "Martin Luther King is experiencing in Selma another hour of manipulated triumph thanks to television, simpering writers, assorted agitators and carpetbaggers, hybrid congressmen from Washington, the courts, and no less a personage than President Johnson himself."[52]

These editorialists were not wrong in recognizing the importance of the Selma campaign as a televisual event requiring the attention of the cameras. King and the SCLC needed the oxygen of national media "publicity." Selmians and Alabama residents were employing a certain level of truth about the situation to uphold their otherwise threatened segregationist worldview. But in this discourse, King and his followers wanted publicity only for the sake of publicity.

A letter writer to the *Birmingham News* made sense of the presence of clergy who descended on Selma after Bloody Sunday this way: "Are the clapping, singing ministers and nuns now massing in Selma sincere? To ask an absurd question like that is to answer it. Remove the video and newspaper coverage and watch the Wallace-denouncing Bible wavers beat a hasty retreat."[53] The media literacy of these respondents and their understanding about television's role in disseminating the protests and marches could go no further than that. Thus a high school student saw King as "a publicity hungry man that is using other people, of both races, to satisfy his desire."[54] Similarly, a *Times-Journal* editorial asserted that King's purpose in coming to Selma and prolonging his stay was "to use Selma and its captive actors, both Negro and white, to present a nationally televised tragicomic drama for which the price of admission to well-meaning but misinformed spectators is a donation to the M.L.K. charity and some influence peddling among the liberal membership of the Congress."[55]

So, the entire Selma campaign ultimately boiled down to a devious King wanting to feather his nest both financially and politically, and using television to accomplish that goal. Clergy from outside the state were there only to see their faces on the TV news or in newspaper photos. Voting rights had to be evacuated from consideration—since white Alabamians had the "true facts" on their side that any "qualified" black voter could exercise the franchise, as long as they were patient and followed the rules. By focusing so intently on the role played by television and the national media, these respondents used their media literacy to block any attention or acknowledgment of the message of street demonstrations. In this case, the media, indeed, *was* the message.

With the Bloody Sunday confrontation and the murder of Rev. Reeb a few days later, Alabamians had diminished recourse to the "it's all just publicity" strategy. In fact, the brutal turn in the Selma campaign (Jimmie Lee Jackson's murder was largely ignored in the white press) caused a significant amount of soul searching among both letter writers and editorialists, suggesting a crack in the segregationist hegemony. One young respondent from Auburn, Alabama, adopted the "Nazi storm trooper" reading strategy:

> I have just witnessed on television the new sequel to Adolf Hitler's brown shirts. They were George Wallace's blue shirts. The scene in Alabama looked like scenes on old newsreels of Germany in the 1930s that I am too young to have known. . . .
>
> What is happening to my beloved state? Are we attempting to establish the Fourth Reich? Have Alabamians become so engrossed in our efforts to lure in business, to sit in front of television, to attend church services that we fail to see passion surge forward and dominate reason?[56]

Another Auburn resident was similarly moved by the television coverage: "We deserve the reaction which the rest of the nation has shown to those television scenes because all of us are to some degree responsible, but we are not all that bad! Brave newspapers have helped reform deplorable conditions: let us hope you can do the same for Alabama."[57]

The letter writer referred to the *Birmingham News*'s remarkable page-one editorial condemning the state-sponsored violence at the Pettus Bridge. The editorial was noteworthy because the paper's editorial stance was otherwise staunchly conservative. Provocatively titled, "Alabama—Look in the Mirror," the editorial declared, "You do NOT need to strike unarmed, non-resisting people with clubs, whips or anything else to move them back. So we now had not only new violence by the individual, vicious hoodlum [Reeb's killers]—the nation now has pictures of state police literally attacking unarmed citizens who happened to be Negro." The editorial unequivocally backed black voting rights, acknowledging, "We believe many whites in Alabama really do not believe Negroes should vote." The editorial thus ripped away the discursive smokescreen used by many segregationists who said they supported "qualified voters." The *News* would have none of that. Using typography to grab readers' shirt collars, the editorial proclaimed, "NEGROES ARE CITIZENS."[58]

However, many Alabamians did not appear willing or able to confront the images of Bloody Sunday and their aftermath with new thinking. A Selma woman asked a series of questions that suggested the coverage might have shaken her worldview a tad. "We walk around and wonder what is going on. We pick up a newspaper and read how brutal we are. We turn on the television and see what a group of people say we are. But who has made us this way, or are we really this way?"[59] Perhaps the questions were too uncomfortable to explore more deeply because the letter writer went on to circulate the familiar knee-jerk charges that King and the civil rights movement played into the hands of the communists and that blacks really only wanted intermarriage.

A recurring strategy employed by Alabamians attempting to make sense of the Selma violence was to deny that this violence said anything about uniquely Southern race relations. A Ragland woman professed to have been sickened by Reeb's murder, but then pointed out the eleven women strangled in Boston, the thirteen gangland killings, and six attempted murders there.[60] Another letter writer asked, "A few months ago when all the race riots were gong on in New York and other Northern cities, why didn't the big wheels in Washington discuss it like they are the Alabama demonstrations? . . . If this same incident [Bloody Sunday] had happened in any other state than Alabama or Mississippi, it probably wouldn't have even made the headlines."[61] Another respondent suggested a double standard in coverage of violence in the North versus violence in the South: "When is a murder really murder? When is a dead man actually dead? According to the national news media ... the answer to these questions apparently has to be qualified as to the geographic location of the death and whether or not it was directly or indirectly associated with the civil rights drive."[62] She went on to point out the murder of a young man on a New York City subway and the mortal wounding of a young woman in the city's suburbs left to cry for help unaided for almost an hour.

The *Birmingham News,* in particular, assisted readers in making this reading strategy by regularly including on its front pages news briefs about murder and mayhem (often with a racial component) happening in Northern cities. However, this sectionalist approach wasn't limited to readers of the *News.* Its usefulness was obvious in assisting many white Alabamians in deflecting the suggestion that the South's racial caste system depended ultimately on white violence. Such an acknowledgment would, as Sokol points out, fundamentally undermine the interlocking assumptions that girded the white Southern worldview. So the violence attending the Selma campaign was really no different in character from the urban violence in New York or Boston. The only distinction was the national news media's appetite for the Southern version.

The Alabama print media in general assisted its readers in their media consciousness. The *Birmingham News* reprinted an editorial cartoon depicting a white businessman labeled "The Sensible South" holding a report titled "Progress in Commerce, Industry, Race Relations" while a slovenly hillbilly labeled "Racist Politics" stands in front of him, gesturing rudely to a big television camera whose lens is carefully trained on him. The cartoon asks, "Who Speaks For The South?"[63] According to the cartoon, television was interested only in the antics of extremist riff-raff, although network news reporters often went out of their way to focus on white moderates even when doing so, such as in the James Meredith story, distorted the actual situation on the ground.

While CBS News managed to be almost willfully blind to the massive media presence during the second (aborted) march to the Edmund Pettus Bridge, the *Selma Times-Journal* felt no similar shyness about reporting on the reporting. A page-one photo showed an overhead view of demonstrators marching down a city street. The caption explained it this way: "With scores of cameramen and newsmen in the forefront, civil rights demonstrators set out this afternoon for Montgomery."[64] The following day, Selma readers faced another page-one photo of the march. This time the photo framed a news cameraman centered in the shot with other photographers clearly positioned in the foreground. Civil rights marchers were visible encountering a line of state troopers in the photo's mid-background. The caption, describing the scene as a "historic confrontation," alerted readers that "an estimated 150 newsmen from across the United States and several foreign countries documented the historic moment."[65] A front-page story in the *Birmingham News* about Bloody Sunday and the planned second march emphasized the national media coverage that the violence on the Pettus

Who Speaks For The South?

—Eric, *Atlanta Journal*

Originally published in the *Atlanta Journal* and reprinted in the *Birmingham News.*

Bridge received, noting that NBC's *Today Show* had that morning carried film about the breakup of the march.[66]

A week after Bloody Sunday, the *Montgomery Advertiser*'s political reporter, Bob Ingram, attempted to uncover what was supposed to have happened that day and how the original plan had gone awry. Ingram's investigative report focused heavily on exonerating Wallace and placing blame on the head of Alabama State Highway Patrol and the public safety director. It also emphasized the crucial role of television coverage—both what was seen by viewers, including the governor, and what was not seen:

> First, a fact. Wallace was infuriated at what happened. First reports from the scene via radio had indicated only a mild pushing match and the governor was not displeased. But when he saw the TV film he could see—as anybody with walking around sense could see—that something bad wrong had happened.
>
> It was not nearly so horrifyingly tragic as the Birmingham church bombing

that snuffed out the lives of four children, but in this instance here was some-thing which could be seen. The cameras were there, they were grinding and by nightfall millions of people in America and around the world had seen the rush of the troopers, the exploding canisters and the swinging clubs. . . .

Later, new developments came to light that eased Wallace's mind to some extent. The rock and brick throwing done later in the afternoon by some of the non-violent demonstrators took a great deal of luster off the cries of police brutality. Of course there were no TV cameras around to record the rocks and bricks.[67]

Ingram pointed out a little-discussed truth about the Bloody Sunday melee. The actual degree of brutality the marchers encountered was rather mild compared to the forms of violence routinely visited upon blacks in the Deep South—whether the murder of the four little girls at Birmingham's Sixteenth Street Baptist Church that Ingram referred to, or the killing of Jimmie Lee Jackson that, as we have seen, garnered very little media attention, or the innumerable lynchings and bombings that for decades had been a normalized form of terrorism against the black population. As civil rights historian Adam Fairclough has pointed out, "The propaganda value of violence depended more on the quality of the confrontation and the press's ability to report it than on the seriousness of the violence itself. Snarling dogs, gushing fire hoses, and club-wielding troopers had more impact than murders and bombings if reporters and film crews were present. . . . SCLC sought to evoke *dramatic* violence rather than *deadly* violence."[68]

Ingram understood the SCLC media strategy quite well. Bloody Sunday was a disaster for Wallace and for white Alabama because of how the selected images looked on television rather than because of the inherent viciousness of the vio-lence. The enactment of even relatively mild violence, as long as it was captured on film—and captured with both visual and moral clarity—could only be a victory for the civil rights movement and a disaster for its opponents. The news media had also constructed their script in such a way that images of rock throwing marchers would not fit. (In fact, the rock throwing that troopers and posse men encountered came mostly from residents of the housing project adjacent to Brown Chapel, not marchers.)[69] Ingram seems to suggest that the television story of Bloody Sunday might have been quite different if these compensating visuals had been available. Perhaps, but the melodramatic power of the Pettus Bridge footage makes it hard to imagine the television news industry subverting that power with such complicat-ing matters. Television news tended to want to keep the story simple. The story of Selma that day was white violence on black worthy victims.

The march to Montgomery and its immediate run-up whipped up a new level of anxiety and consternation among Alabamians who worried about the image of their state disseminated to the world by the news media. When the campaign stayed in Selma, the media spotlight stayed there too, for the most part. Once marchers left the Edmund Pettus Bridge behind them and wended their way down Highway 80, the media spotlight would widen to the state more generally.

Some Alabamians tried to mollify themselves by asserting a negative television image of the marchers rather than any negative image of their state and its white power structure. One Plattville resident railed against the "phony clerics" and the "obscenities which go on in the streets as night falls, which fail to reach the public thru mass media, yet have been witnessed by law abiding citizens, both in Selma and Montgomery."[70] In the midst of the march, a Montgomery woman wrote, "How disgusting it has become to turn on the TV set and see groups of Negroes marching and chanting, too impatient to wait for the results of legislation being processed to further their 'rights,' too ignorant to realize that prejudice does not disappear in a day." An ex-pat Alabamian fumed similarly: "Yesterday I witnessed on nationwide television coverage the sickening demonstration in Montgomery by a group of thoughtless, careless and foolish people protesting the current right-to-vote demonstrations in Selma."[71] The staunchly conservative *Montgomery Advertiser* bolstered this line of thinking about the march and the marchers in an editorial in which it counseled Alabamians to stay away from the march, which it compared to Reconstruction "occupiers." The editorial zeroed in on the national media and its role in this spectacle: "Not even the incompetent northern newspapers and the tube can indefinitely prevent the folly of this bizarre procession from being understood by the American people, nor keep from oozing out the character of the demonstrators and their coarse conduct."[72]

While network television coverage presented the marchers as uniformly positive, even heroic, and grounded in images of conspicuous patriotism, white Alabamians had to read those images in aggressively oppositional ways. Where the news media attempted to circulate representations of dignity and moral and ethical purity cleansed of political considerations, white Alabamians saw that coverage with its images of American flags and marchers playing "Yankee Doodle" evoking not the Revolutionary War but rather the "War of Northern Aggression" and its calamitous aftermath. White Alabamians tried to convince themselves that their reading strategy of the televised marchers was accurate. If only their understanding of the civil rights participants would be embraced by viewers in other parts of the country, then their besieged positions might not be as hopeless and things could get back to some semblance of normalcy. Or as the Montgomery woman who found the televised marchers "disgusting" concluded in her letter: "Soon the agitators will find other places to take their misery: the uncombed white followers will grow bored and seek other causes which they have not the intelligence to understand nor the compassion to care, until the T.V. cameras turn to subjects more newsworthy. Then Alabama will be left at last to finish the work that was begun before the endless, pointless demonstrations slowed down (not helped) the advancement of the Negro in Alabama."[73]

The letter writer expressed a residual position of the white Southern worldview that assumed whites were Negroes' best friends and would, as they always had done, ensure that "their Negroes" would be well taken care of.[74] The *Birmingham News*, however, saw the change blowin' in the wind. Another quite remarkable front-page special editorial in the paper's Sunday edition following completion of the Montgomery march suggested as much to its readers. It merits quoting at length:

> Three weeks ago Alabama state troopers stomped through a mass of unarmed Negroes in Selma and clubbed them. The nation saw it on TV.
>
> Since then, despite Montgomery's good efforts to keep peace there, almost in the shadow of the Capitol building itself mounted possemen and troopers again clubbed demonstrators. The nation saw that on its TV.
>
> Since then, the Rev. James Reeb and two other white ministers were beaten as they peaceably walked Selma streets. Reeb died and the widow and his body went home from Alabama in one of the airplanes of the President of the United States. The nation saw that on TV.
>
> Since then, there came a march that the governor of Alabama said our state couldn't afford to protect and so, because Alabama didn't handle its own peace-keeping, the President of the United States federalized our own men and hauled in more from Fort Bragg and Fort Hood and saw to it that the peace was kept in Alabama during that march. The people of the nation saw that on TV, too.
>
> Since then, however, troops were barracked and Alabama had keeping the peace on its hands exclusively again—and a white Detroit woman was gunned down as she drove an automobile down Highway 80. The people of the nation didn't see the gunning, but they saw the car doors agape with blood on them, all of it on their living room TVs. . . .
>
> Talk about "outside agitators" all you want. Talk about keeping complaints in the courts which people of course should do. Talk about Communist fronts or killing on the New York subways—talk about all of that as people have end-lessly been doing in an increased bitterness—but that's not what the people of the United States are talking about. They're talking about Alabama in terms of all those things they've seen on TV—and about what've read, fully reported by an army of special correspondents encamped in newsmaker-Alabama for weeks.
>
> And this is Alabama's problem RIGHT NOW. . . .
>
> The closed-door, the slick domination of a TV screen to spell out Alabama alibis isn't accomplishing a thing. It's making Alabama look further ridiculous. Glib words do not match the national image of Alabama in terms of a dead mother of five sprawled across the steering wheel of a car out of control.[75]

For the *News*'s editorialist, it was clear that the "glaring light of television" required the state to act. Because the nation saw it on TV, painful change was necessary and unavoidable. The *News* articulated a not particularly welcomed but nevertheless emergent post–Jim Crow common sense about where the South had to go. And television served as the prod. So, finally, the Alabama newspaper declared what civil rights organizers could only hint at and what television reporters and producers had to ignore: the absolute centrality of television to the Selma campaign, the march to Montgomery, and the ultimate reconstruction of race relations and race power in the Deep South.

Coda: Watts

On Christmas evening, 1965, CBS News presented its annual news special surveying the events of the previous twelve months. Not surprisingly, the Selma campaign loomed large in the coverage, along with the new ground war in Vietnam.[76] The first half of the news special focused largely on the war; the second half largely on race. But rather than connect the significance of the Selma story primarily to the swift passage of the Voting Rights Act, at the close of the year CBS News inextricably yoked Selma to a very different sort of racial uprising in a very different place.

Host Charles Collingwood began by informing viewers that although 1965 was the year of the voting rights bill, "just as a reminder that the civil rights revolution isn't over yet, it was also the year of the riots in Watts, California." Discursively, Collingwood insisted on placing the Watts turmoil within the bounds of the civil rights movement, even though the Watts conflagration was unorganized, had no clear political goal and no political leadership. And, most significant was that, unlike the organized Southern movement that was philosophically and strategically grounded in nonviolence, Watts, of course, was all about violent rage and destruction.

The turmoil began August 11, four days after President Johnson had signed into law the Voting Rights Act, providing the victorious culmination to the Selma campaign. By the time the rioting had run its course five days later, thirty-four people were dead, a thousand suffered injuries, and a twenty-square-mile area lay in devastation, burned and looted. Approximately thirty-five thousand people actively participated in the rioting against sixteen thousand National Guardsman and Los Angeles law enforcement.[77] Television played a significant role in the turmoil and was castigated (especially local television) for fueling and prolonging the rioting. In fact, the McCone Commission, which the governor of California appointed to investigate the riots, recommended that the press (television in particular) either be banned from areas of rioting or at least that the press withhold "voluntarily . . . news of racial flare-ups until the danger of increasing tension has passed. . . . [H]elter-skelter coverage without feeling for the total community interest cannot be tolerated in the future."[78]

The implementation of such policies during the Southern civil rights campaigns would have snuffed out the Selma campaign almost immediately. And just as TV news cameras and reporters were targets of attacks in Selma and other Southern flashpoints such as the University of Mississippi, so they were in Watts as well.

However, this time it was black demonstrators inflicting the violence. ABC-TV reporter Ray Fahrenkopf was stripped, beaten, and robbed, his car overturned and torched by black rioters.[79] In reporting on the Southern struggle, white seg-regationist violence against newsmen tended to align reporters with black dem-onstrators. In Watts, black violence against reporters only aided in throwing their sympathies toward largely white law enforcement and in demonizing black demonstrators.

The causes of the Watts uprising had much to do with the black community's anger toward a militaristic police force and to a sense of hopelessness in the midst of rhetoric about hope, advancement, and progress for the race coming from the Southern civil rights movement and increasingly from the White House with its new War on Poverty and Great Society programs. The rising tide seemed to be doing nothing to lift the proverbial boats in the inner city of Los Angeles.

CBS News and its end-of-year special was not much interested in exploring causes. It lavishly displayed the spectacle of violence and destruction that made for fabulous visual images. It ignored the voices and perspectives of Watts's black demonstrators just as CBS coverage had ignored the more "worthy" black march-ers in Selma. But in the Watts case, the news coverage seemed preoccupied with the sheer strangeness, otherness, and excessiveness of black looting bodies. Selma blacks were silenced and noble; Watts blacks were silenced and deviant. For in-stance, over a reporter's description of "widespread looting in broad daylight," we see shots of women and children: one woman holds what looks like a baby mattress. The reporter continues, "You'd see happy, laughing looters toting off furniture, clothing, even outboard motors." We see a shot of a black male lugging this very item. The improbability of an impoverished Watts resident needing such a thing served to heighten the senselessness and mindlessness of the riots. There could not possibly be a rationale for any of this chaos.

In a wrap-up at the end, CBS reporter Bill Stout comments, "And there amidst the palm trees and bungalows of California is as a real measure of Negro tempera-ment as the rallies, marches, and voting drives of the South." In order to make racialized sense of Watts, it had to be constructed as the dark "Other" to Selma. Stout noted with approval the positive changes in the South, from black voter registration, which would inevitably influence the 1966 elections, to the fact that an all-white jury in Alabama recently convicted a white man for murdering a Negro. The Negro "temperament" that compelled these changes was compre-hensible to the white newsman. It was logical and had concrete and beneficial results that could only strengthen American democracy and the justice system. However, when Stout looked west and metaphorically North, the Negro tempera-ment became opaque and frightening. He declared, "We must face the ugly truth that there is a whole generation of Negroes ridden with hate: hate for all whites, hate even for those Negroes considered too light, too soft, or too successful." In apocalyptic terms, Stout concludes that the challenge must be met, or "we may indeed see an America so torn by hate and violence that it could destroy itself from within."

Watts provided network news with no worthy black victims, no melodramatic heroes whose very bodies, through their brutalization, signified virtue and moral purity. There was no redeeming storyline of inevitable progress in Watts. The coverage did, however, introduce a new representational figure into the American racial imagination, albeit one grounded in the familiar "brutal black buck" stereotype dating back to Reconstruction. This new figure, the angry, violence-prone ghetto black, would become an increasingly familiar folk devil in the American visual and mental landscape. This folk devil would frequently haunt television's black imagery and its reception in the post-Watts era.

Yet the medium could have pursued a different representational strategy in portraying urban ghetto dwellers. In the next chapter, we will see a pre-Watts angry ghetto male portrayed by James Earl Jones that in both its production and reception strategies attempted to knit the figure into the Southern nonviolent movement even as the setting was Harlem. But, on the other hand, the portrayal also portended what was to follow in the ghetto uprisings even as it did not provide a prototype for future media representations of the angry ghetto black as coverage of the Watts riot did. After Watts, Americans, especially white Americans, would have a visual repertoire on which to draw in order to represent "ghetto blacks." Increasingly, that new repertoire would crowd out the other televisual images we have examined so far. And, as we will see when we get to *Julia* in 1968, network television's celebrated but controversial attempt to bring blacks fully into prime time, even the attempt to give viewers a black representation that embodied all the ideals and goals of the integrationist civil rights movement, the specter of the rioting black body kept erupting onto the scene.

PART 2

Civil Rights in
Prime-Time Entertainment

CHAPTER 6

Bringing "Urgent Issues" to the Vast Wasteland

East Side/West Side

In May 1961, the National Association of Broadcasters, the powerful trade group for American commercial television and radio broadcasters, held its annual meeting in Washington, D.C. As was customary, the NAB invited the new head of the FCC to address them. The recently appointed chairman, Newton Minow, was a lawyer and former aide to Adlai Stevenson with little broadcast law experience but plenty of passion for television. A quintessential Kennedy "New Frontiersman," Minow was smart, idealistic, and confident that government, including its regulatory powers, could improve the lives of Americans. He hoped to prove it in his speech that night.

As they sat in the audience, network executives were feeling fairly self-satisfied. In the aftermath of the quiz-show scandal of the late 1950s, the networks had begun beefing up their news and public-affairs programming, along with providing a number of highly touted and publicized special programs, all in the name of "public service.[1] The three networks' signature prime-time documentary series, *CBS Reports* and *Eyewitness,* NBC's *White Paper,* and ABC's *Bell and Howell Close Up!* all of which had recently aired reports on the civil rights story, had been on the air for at least a year or more. If the vast majority of prime time constituted westerns, family sitcoms, some variety shows, more westerns, some detective shows, and yet more westerns—practically none of which dealt with socially relevant issues of the day—broadcasters nevertheless had reason to feel that they were meeting their public interest commitments.

Minow took the stage and walked into history by famously labelling network television "a vast wasteland." He railed against "a procession of game shows, formula comedies about totally unbelievable families, blood and thunder, mayhem, violence, sadism, murder, western bad men, western good men, private eyes, gangsters, more violence, and cartoons. And endlessly commercials—many screaming, cajoling, and offending." He challenged network executives to do better and held the stick of license revocation over broadcasters' heads if they did not take their "trust accounting with [their] beneficiaries" more seriously.

Minow echoed the criticisms of many cultural critics who had held high hopes for the new medium and who now despaired at the perceived nose dive in quality programming.[2] The early 1950s now seemed a "Golden Age" with its live anthology dramas as critics conveniently forgot the controversies around less-high-flown shows such as *Amos 'n' Andy* and *Beulah,* along with the "ethnic" sitcoms that were no more distinguished than the sitcoms Minow castigated in his speech.

Response to Minow's speech was fulsome in its praise from most cultural commentators. Even network executives felt compelled to acknowledge the criticism, although CBS's head, Frank Stanton, declared that Minow's charges were a bit out of date as far as his network was concerned and did not reflect CBS's recent self-improvements. ABC's chief, attempting to butter up Minow, proclaimed that, unlike its more powerful rivals, his network, like Minow himself, "reflected the New Frontier in television."[3] Nevertheless, in the wake of Minow's speech and the new more interventionist regulatory regime sweeping into Washington with the new Kennedy administration, the networks began to rethink programming more assiduously. News and long-form documentary shows increasingly received more resources and space on the national air, which had significant repercussions for the civil rights movement. But the networks also began to experiment with new approaches to entertainment programming, and this would also have ramifications for the visibility of civil rights.

In turning our attention now from news and documentary to the core of network broadcasting's business—entertainment programming—we will see much continuity in theme and preoccupation with what we have traced already. However, entertainment programming had to confront an even harder challenge in soothing its presumed white audiences about race relations. Ratings and audience share were on the line here in a way they were not for the networks' news divisions.

The networks pursued a variety of formulas in prime-time entertainment to narrate a new world of race relations and representations of black and white, some successful, some less so. All dialogued self-consciously with the ongoing societal changes sparked by the black empowerment movement. In varied ways, all negotiated the trope of the "worthy" black civil rights subject. All attempted to give white viewers black protagonists they presumably could be comfortable with. The "black and white together" theme, with the figure of whiteness front and center, took interesting twists and turns. In some key ways, entertainment television, however, could not tell the same story that news television did, particularly with respect to setting and the sectional divide convulsing the country. But the next two chapters show that even though neither of these examples of "equal time" television took place in the Jim Crow South, some viewers insisted on making sense of these shows' racial themes as if they were located below the Mason-Dixon line.

The New Frontier Comes to Prime Time

With "vast wasteland" ringing in their ears, each of the three networks began over the next couple years to inaugurate a new form of programming that television historian Mary Ann Watson has dubbed "New Frontier character dramas."[4]

Lawyer shows like *The Defenders* (CBS 1961–65), doctor shows like *Ben Casey* (ABC 1961–66) and *Dr. Kildare* (NBC 1961–66), classroom dramas like *Mr. Novak* (NBC 1963–65), and the social work series *East Side/West Side* (CBS 1963–64) all grappled with contemporary social-problem topics. They provided networks a way to deflect at least some of the criticism levelled at them from commentators and FCC commissioners about the mindlessness of their programming fare. But perhaps more important, the New Frontier programs were significant popular culture sites for mediating Kennedy-era liberalism and social engagement. Watson argues that these series echoed the "service to society" ideals of the Kennedy years, especially the optimism that concerned professionals and institutions could ameliorate, if not solve, problems like poverty, racism, and juvenile delinquency.

CBS's *East Side/West Side* was not one of the era's most successful social problem dramas, but it was certainly the most audacious, controversial, and daring. It was one of the first prime-time shows to feature an African American in a continuing role, with Cicely Tyson as an assistant to the show's protagonist, social worker Neil Brock, played by George C. Scott. Like other dramas of its type, episodes of *East Side/West Side* dealt with issues like juvenile crime, urban renewal, prostitution, and the death penalty. However, the show's greatest significance—and its greatest controversy—rested on its handling of episodes about race. *East Side/West Side* brought issues of racism, black rage, white guilt, and liberal responses to them all into prime-time entertainment with unprecedented urgency and directness. Even as network television relied mostly on its news divisions to tell viewers about race and the ongoing black civil rights struggle, *East Side/West Side,* in the entertainment division, provides us with clues about how programmers and audiences grappled with significant changes in race relations outside the perhaps "safer" arena of news.

In this chapter, we explore how *East Side/West Side,* at the levels of production, text, and reception among viewers and critics, manifested tensions associated with white liberalism of the period—especially the challenges to race relations from the civil rights movement. The show provides a revealing case study of how educated, middle-class whites used a piece of popular culture to begin an often painful process of working through the meanings of fundamental social change. The series' two high-profile episodes on race issues brought to maximum discursive visibility a cultural preoccupation with the place of African Americans in American society and the appropriate response by white liberals.

"Entertainment" versus "Urgent Issues"

East Side/West Side was not an easy show to get onto network television. Produced for CBS by David Susskind's Talent Associates–Paramount, Ltd., the project appeared out of step with the programming strategy of the network. CBS had a winning prime-time schedule filled with unsophisticated, rural-oriented, "hayseed" shows. *The Beverly Hillbillies* (1962–71) and *The Andy Griffith Show* (1960–68), both comedies extolling the virtues of country living and lore, exemplified the pattern of entertainment programming more and more associated with the network. Not coincidentally, the relocated Southern Clampett family never had to put their racial sensibilities on display for their urbane Beverly Hills associates. North Carolina's idyllic Mayberry either had no black population to speak of, or the town practiced such rigid segregation that its white townsfolk managed never to see a Negro.

The Susskind project, on the other hand, took place on the mean (and multiethnic) streets of New York City—and unlike most television shows in that era of burgeoning telefilms, the series was entirely shot on location in the metropolis.[5] Focused on the cases taken on by an angry crusader for social justice—social worker Neil Brock, who worked for an independent welfare agency, the Community Welfare Service (CWS)—the show dealt with the problems of urban America. These were a world away from the warm-hearted dilemmas faced by the gentle folk of Mayberry. The CWS was located in a slum neighborhood, and many of Brock's clients suffered from the vicissitudes of poverty and social neglect.

Network head James Aubrey was unimpressed. He loathed the show and wanted the CWS relocated to Park Avenue. Aubrey declared, "They've got just as big social problems on Park Avenue and that's where I want the goddamn show to be."[6] Susskind managed to prevail.

Narratively and thematically, the show owed more to the era of live anthology dramas with their frequently urban locations and social-problem themes. Susskind himself had begun his television career as a producer of respected anthology series. However, in the new world of "escapist" television fare so successful with Nielsen families and with sponsors wanting "happy people with happy problems" sandwiched between their advertisements, *East Side/West Side* not only was not escapist, as far as the network was concerned, it was not even entertainment.

Memos from CBS executives reveal a semiotic struggle over the definition of "entertainment" when the material concerned the "urgent issues" of the times. From the network's point of view, explorations of such issues were best left to news and documentary programming where "an objective and dispassionate approach is possible." During the show's development, CBS's Director of Program Development Lawrence White argued that examinations of proposed story ideas about "fall out shelters, the Birch Society, sympathy picketing, negro [sic] ghettos, etc., etc., is certainly out of the show's domain. The dramatized treatment of important current social and political questions must, for impact, take either an editorial point of view or endorse solutions, which automatically seems to eliminate the objective view."[7]

Uncritically buying into the myth of journalistic objectivity, White set up a binary between news and drama. Fictional narratives dealing with topical issues inherently lacked the appropriate mechanisms that journalism persumably possessed to maintain a (politically safe) proper distance. White's concerns about objectivity were likely grounded in a fear of alienating potential viewers who might disagree with the social-change agenda implicit in a series about social work and the amelioration of urban problems. The network stance also suggests the philosophy behind the "escapist" programming CBS was perfecting. If the news, public affairs, and documentary division of the network could now handle such topics, then the entertainment section should avoid them entirely—as shows like *Mr. Ed* (a show about a talking horse) appeared to do—in order to properly separate the two areas of network operation.

CBS also had problems with *East Side/West Side* because, by focusing on *social* issues, narratives did not concentrate with appropriate emphasis on the problems of individual characters with whom audiences could identify. White argued, "[Y]ou must understand that the problem of the individual based on an emotional need which finds some relief, some understanding and some compassion from the character of Neil Brock is the true subject matter of our series. . . . His commitment must always be to the human—to the individual—to hope." By committing to the individual, however, the narrative would be unable to commit to a program of social change and political activism. Individual problems needing Brock's assistance would thus not have a fundamental social or economic basis.

The network seemed particularly concerned about the "tone" of the program: it had an "over-grim documentary feel." And while unhappy endings may have been acceptable for such reality-based material, the network expressed concerns that this fictional project lacked humor. White argued to CBS programming head Michael Dann: "We all know that what makes life bearable for the inhabitants of the jungle that many parts of our world have become; what makes people live with poverty and lack of hope is the God-given ability to laugh at oneself, to hear the laughter of children in the worst tenement."[8] White's Pollyanna view suggests a strategy the network wanted the show's producers to use in order to defuse whatever incendiary material they were encountering. Presumably, tenement problems of poverty and economic distress could somehow be mitigated if viewers could be convinced that poor people still had a wealth of laughter at their disposal.[9]

East Side/West Side producers attempted to negotiate with CBS over this issue. While not backing away from the "urgent issues," they assured Lawrence White that scripts with a lighter, more comic tone had been commissioned, including a love story involving Neil Brock.[10] However, writers and producers for the show engaged in a certain amount of self-censorship over the types of "urgent issues" they would endeavour to examine. One project involved police brutality in Harlem. CBS countered by suggesting a story about an individual "sick cop" whose singular sadistic tendencies ruined an otherwise perfect neighborhood. The project's scriptwriter, along with George C. Scott, refused to entertain CBS's proposal. To David Susskind the writer argued, "I felt that approach was a whitewash of police brutality after weeks of research in Harlem and the Lower East Side with social workers."[11] He recommended dropping the story idea as just too "hot" a topic.

Despite the network's reservations about the entertainment values of *East Side/ West Side*, and despite poor responses from test audiences who reportedly found the pilot too "harsh" and "severe," the series went ahead more or less as Susskind, Scott, and Talent Associates wanted it.[12] However, in publicity materials, the production company tried to negotiate a preferred reading of the series that emphasized CBS's definition of entertainment. In a press release to television editors at eighteen hundred newspapers, Talent Associates declared: "[T]elevision should reflect reality and 'East Side/West Side' does just that but within a framework of showmanship and entertainment. We want the viewer to be absorbed, involved, entertained and informed—all by the same program! . . . The subject matter in 'East Side/West Side' is unusually varied. Some of the programs are actually comedies because life even at its most corrosive level is sometimes that or it could not be lived at all."[13]

The debates over the entertainment value of this television project indicate anxiety about prime time as a venue for narratives with a social conscience. How should mass-distributed fictional texts interact with a newly activist political and social climate? The early 1960s witnessed an interventionist liberalism in Washington, bolstered by optimism that both government and private social welfare organizations could eradicate systemic social ills. Grassroots movements agitating for fundamental social change, like the civil rights campaigns, were further transforming the political culture of the nation. Yet American network television, which came of age in the more politically quiescent 1950s, when McCarthyist red scares discouraged questioning of the status quo, had a more complicated time coming to grips with the new sentiment blowin' in the wind.

Despite protestations about journalistic objectivity, we have seen how network news provided largely sympathetic coverage to the civil rights movement. We have seen how the networks provided almost celebratory coverage of the 1963 March on Washington and the 1965 Selma-to-Montgomery march. More generally, we have seen how network news tended to position the overarching goals of the movement where they aligned with those of the White House into a sphere of consensus. Additionally, the networks complied with the Kennedy administration, providing often-fawning coverage of the telegenic chief executive.[14] But unlike the entertainment segment of the network, the news division was not fundamentally concerned with maximizing audience share but rather was more occupied with satisfying the newly activated FCC around issues of public service.

In fictional programming, however, the networks took a somewhat contradictory approach to programming in the early 1960s. Vincent Brook has noted how the trade press ballyhooed a "Minowization" of entertainment television with significant minimizing of violent programming and an increase in shows (such as the New Frontier character dramas) that emphasized "social consciousness."[15] Nevertheless, there were limits to what the networks could embrace. *East Side/*

West Side ended up marking where those limits lay. Industry critics of "Minowiza-tion" also castigated the new forms of programming that responded to the FCC chairman's challenge as "generally antiseptic, somewhat didactic, slightly dull, offensive to no one and above all else 'justifiable.' The words 'entertainment' or 'pleasure' are seldom, if ever, mentioned. Like Latin and spinach, these shows are supposed to be good for you."[16]

Fans of the show also participated in the debate over the issue of what "enter-tainment" meant. *East Side/West Side*'s travails with the ratings system encouraged a number of obviously educated viewers to construct mass/elite arguments about the television industry and its audience. One viewer, a PhD from Roosevelt, New Jersey, condemned the show's cancellation and CBS as a broadcast network "for a complete disregard of responsibility towards a good many of its viewers and towards the use of TV as a medium for cultural enhancement and intellectual enlightenment. I simply do not think that it is fair to lower TV standards to the lowest common denominator who may be some poor, ignorant, bigoted person in some section of the country."[17] Letters like this one constructed television as a battlefield where the debased political and intellectual capabilities of the masses destroyed the promise of the medium. Escapist entertainment television was something the "stupid masses" enjoyed—and inflicted on the more discriminat-ing minority. A viewer in Dallas noted, "Since you have no hillbillies, no glamor, no pies in the face, and no stupid fathers, your show is almost foredoomed to be way down in the ratings." A married couple from Utica, New York, warned, "If our television viewing is to be dictated by either economic groups or bigots, you may be assured that this family in addition to many others will de-plug the black box and terminate our interest in television broadcasting."

Over and over again, these viewers represented themselves as a discriminating minority able to appreciate the value of a series like *East Side/West Side*. They took pains to geographically locate the dumb, bigoted masses whose tastes they felt were adversely influencing programming: "entertainment" was being defined by dumb Southerners. Mail coming to the Susskind show displayed Northeast, Midwest, or Southern California addresses, mostly from urban areas; further, these viewers either implicitly or explicitly imagined the dumb masses and their reactionary politics as nonurban and from the South. A viewer from New York City fumed, "Frankly, I am just fed up with TV catering to the southern group that is against humanity & humans." Such views neatly located bigotry and ignorance away from the letter writer's locale.

The first phases of the civil rights movement and its coverage on television may have encouraged viewers to think about racism and reactionary politics as a Southern problem. The early 1960s saw little attention paid to miseries of ghetto life and poverty in Northern and West Coast cities. That poverty was mostly hidden until the explosion of urban black riots that began with the 1965 Watts uprising in Los Angeles. Poverty and discrimination that did exist in the North were, presumably, being dealt with by the interventionist liberalism that *East Side/West Side* championed. But the South, at least from the perspective of some Northerners, was something else. Northern liberals constructed a Southern "other" to shoulder the responsibility for debased popular culture and debased politics.[18]

Although *East Side/West Side* was noteworthy for its handling of various contemporary social welfare problems, it is remembered mostly for the unprecedented way it dealt with Northern, urban race relations. On November 4, 1963, and December 2, 1963, the series aired two highly publicized, much discussed, and hotly debated episodes.[19] Both dealt with housing and racism, one about a Harlem couple trapped in deadly and soul-destroying conditions, the other about white suburbia and the turmoil of integration, Northern-style. Following the March on Washington, the episodes came at a key moment as far as the relationship between television and the civil rights campaigns was concerned. The two shows also bookended another landmark television moment: the assassination of President Kennedy and the resulting four days of continuous coverage of that national trauma.

East Side/West Side debuted less than a month after the March on Washington, which the networks presented as a paean of racial integration peacefully achieved. The show's first race episode aired three months after the march and only two months after four black schoolgirls were massacred in a Ku Klux Klan bombing of the Sixteenth Street Baptist Church in Birmingham. Increasingly, Americans, north and south, found their previously naturalized notions about race questioned through their television viewing. As the case of white Alabamians showed, the process could be very painful and disorienting. Televised images of black struggle shocked many into rethinking what America stood for, especially when it came to the rights of black people. The shocking quality of the images, such as those from Selma, impelled numerous Northern whites—mostly idealistic college students—into actively joining civil rights campaigns. However, most viewers did not end up going down South to participate in voter registration campaigns, "freedom schools," or other such activism. Nevertheless, the searing quality of the images challenged spectators to react in some way to what they were seeing night after night. This period in broadcast history is significant not only because viewers found themselves inundated with journalistic representations of the social change struggle but also because they were being confronted, albeit less frequently, with fictional representations of the same struggle. The *East Side/West Side* episodes may not have been seen by as many viewers as the news coverage of civil rights activity, but they functioned in a similar way: they forced viewers (in often painful ways) to confront racism and their own implications within that system.

In the following sections, along with textual analysis of these two famed episodes, we examine how viewers negotiated meanings around racism, liberal responses, and white guilt within a context of heightened intensity about those issues—heightened largely by television coverage. The reading strategies viewers adopted in relation to these two shows provide useful clues about how numerous white Americans in the North were coming to grips with the shocks of racial social transformations that so many experienced via their television sets. Press commentary and the response of *East Side/West Side* viewers suggest a complex set of negotiations as white viewers found themselves having to grapple with the no-longer-invisible struggles of African Americans within a white social system. Like the white Alabamians we have already discussed, *East Side/West Side*'s viewers had to confront the crumbling of a previously naturalized worldview that had not included black people as subjects.

"Who Do You Kill?"

"Gritty realism" does not begin to describe this remarkable example of television drama.[20] Focused almost entirely on a ghetto-imprisoned young couple, Joe and Ruth, and their baby, who is fatally bitten by a rat, George C. Scott's Brock is mostly superfluous and commands little screen time.

James Earl Jones plays Joe as gloweringly angry with pent-up violence just barely under control. Joe is a study in emasculation. He cannot find work that is not servile and has to rely on Ruth as the family's breadwinner while he handles the domestic duties. His dialogue is filled with expressions of nihilism and despair. Ruth, on the other hand, is a figure of hope and optimism against the odds.

In one scene as they stroll Harlem's streets, they come across the neighborhood reverend (who looks remarkably like Martin Luther King) nailing up a sign about a protest meeting. Joe rails against the garbage that does not get picked up, the condemned buildings, the firetraps, the lack of good jobs, but he is disdainful of the possibilities of protest. An associate of the reverend informs Joe, "There's a wind blowing through this country, young man, from Birmingham to Washington." Joe dismisses this with: "The only wind I hear is the flappin' of tongues." As Joe turns away, Ruth exclaims that she thinks it is a good idea and that she will come to the meeting. Thus, Ruth's optimism includes the utility of protest. While the location is very obviously the urban North, with the episode's insistence on displaying the actual streets of Harlem in all their poverty and neglect, we keep getting signifiers of the Southern civil rights campaigns—from the King-like reverend to references about Birmingham and the March on Washington.

The signifiers of the civil rights movement continue in a later scene after the baby has been bitten by the rat and lies in the hospital in intensive care. Ruth, accompanied by Jane Foster (Cicely Tyson), Neil Brock, and Freida Hechlinger, the head of the CWS, sit in a church for a protest meeting about the incident. The white protagonists sit surrounded by blacks singing "We Shall Overcome." For viewers who watched the March on Washington coverage a few short months earlier, this image could not help but echo the "black and white together" images

Bringing the
Southern civil rights
movement to Har-
lem: the reverend
who looks very
much like Martin
Luther King Jr.

so insistently conveyed in that media event. The reverend talks about "nonviolent" determination as the community's weapons—along with dignity and laughter. He declares, "Violence betrays our cause," when Joe abruptly breaks into the meeting: the signifier of potential black violence.

Joe, as a figure of black rage, would become more familiar to television viewers in a few years. In 1963, Americans would likely associate the alternative to King and nonviolent protest with Malcolm X and the Black Muslims. But Joe is too nihilistic, apolitical, and isolated to call to mind Malcolm and his movement. However, after the riots in Harlem the following summer and then more famously in Watts in the summer of 1965, the angry ghetto black would become a familiar image to Americans for the rest of the decade. Network television— prime-time entertainment in particular—would have to find ways to negotiate with this figure. In many ways, Joe served as a portent of what was to come, as white America would eventually have to turn its eyes away from the Jim Crow

Black and white
together: Brock and
Hechlinger attend
a Harlem protest
meeting and sing
"We Shall Over-
come" with black
residents.

South to the urban-ghetto North. However, in 1963, a drama about precisely the conditions that would lead to summer after summer of urban rioting in the years ahead had only a limited representational repertoire of "blackness" upon which to draw. And when it came to representations of black protest and politics, that repertoire invariably evoked the Southern campaign.

The episode did, however, do a superlative job in displaying the abysmal conditions of ghetto living. Joe and Ruth live in a tiny, cramped, one-room hovel with the baby's area marked off with sheets attached to a clothesline. But even as the episode is unstinting in showing the deplorable way the little family must live, Joe and Ruth are never reduced to their living conditions. Even with Joe's rage and hopelessness, James Earl Jones, with his deep baritone voice and stately demeanour, always depicts Joe with dignity. Similarly, Diana Sands's Ruth is never brought low by her surroundings. Her apartment may be decrepit, but she is always well dressed, well coifed, and well spoken. In this way, like the Southern "civil rights subjects" network news presented its viewers, Joe and Ruth are, likewise, worthy black victims deserving of white liberal attention.

The episode's crisis occurs when the baby is bitten by a rat as she lays sleeping in her crib behind the sheets. The narrative has already alluded to the infestation of rodents by providing shots of the walls and ceilings with broken plaster through which we can hear rats scurrying. As the baby screams and Ruth shrieks, Joe bundles the infant up and runs into the nightmarish Harlem streets, trying in vain to hail a cab. None will stop for him, further emphasizing his lack of power and control.

Only at this point does our hero, Neil Brock, enter the narrative, but Brock and his colleagues are mostly ineffectual as they try to find work for Joe, support Ruth, and encourage both to attend the reverend's protest meeting. Joe is predictably hostile to Brock, and the two engage in a confrontation in the doorway of the decrepit apartment. Jane tries to stand up for Brock, explaining that not every white man is his enemy, but she receives a fusillade of Joe's rage: "What do you

"Worthy black victims": Joe and Ruth are never reduced to their deplorable living conditions. They are dignified, well spoken, and loving.

Black rage: Joe
confronts Brock,
"I don't want you
here, man!"

know about white men? I work for Mr. Charlie every day of my life—just livin'."
Then pacing in between Jane and Brock, he delivers the line that got quoted over
and over again in reviews: "The white man stick a knife in my back. Another white
man pull it out and stick on a bandage. You think I'm gonna kiss his hand!" Ruth
encourages them to leave as Joe looks about to lose control of his rage, especially
as Jane counsels him to have a little hope.

This representation of black anger against whites was quite remarkable for
television and, frankly, for any form of popular culture. What makes it even more
remarkable is that the episode went to considerable lengths to contextualize and
explain that anger. Not only is it situated within the relentlessly realist mise-en-
scène of the ghetto milieu that director Tom Gries manages to make palpable
in cinema-verité visual style, but Joe's rage is further contextualized through the
attention the narrative pays to discriminatory employment practices that keep
blacks out of nonmenial jobs. We see Brock's colleagues visit a union official to
see about getting Joe into an apprentice program. But even when Jane and Frieda
show Joe's trade school certificate, the official merely hems and haws. They discover that only six Negroes work in the union official's outfit, all in maintenance.

The episode's denouement, such as it is, is the child's funeral, which has been
held up because Ruth, who has emotionally fallen apart, has been resisting attending and thus fully acknowledging the death of her child. At the last moment,
she appears, and the grief-stricken couple embrace, thus supporting each other,
as they will need to do in order to go forward. Did Brock and the CWS help? It
does not appear so. Did the reverend, with his appeals to protest? The narrative
remains ambiguous, although Ruth comes to Joe, and the couple unites in the
reverend's church. Part of what makes this episode such a remarkable moment
in television history is its refusal to provide easy answers, a predictable narrative
trajectory, or a satisfying narrative closure.

The philosophical debates between the show's producers and CBS, evident during the series' initial stages, continued during the preproduction of this episode. Written by Talent Associates producer Arnold Perl, the script was supposed to be both a love story among the tenements and an exposé of appalling Harlem living conditions. CBS objected to the first draft script's "editorializing" and "tract"-like qualities, wanting a more universal love story of a young couple dealing with difficult circumstances. Larry White, speaking for the network, particularly objected to the "sermonizing" about slumlords, quotas, and overcrowded hospitals that he argued "vitiated" the drama. In a contentious meeting with scriptwriter Perl, White declared he disliked the background given to explain why Ruth withdrew after her baby's death. It was not needed, he argued: "It is universal." Perl countered that neither his nor White's child would ever be bitten by a rat in a slum. "When I added that this was the whole point of the show—that these were not people even as you and I, but an average Negro couple living and trying to make out in an average Harlem existence, he moved to another point."[21]

The network wanted an uplifting story only coincidentally about impoverished black ghetto dwellers. Harkening back to the distinction White made between drama and journalism, any narrative that incorporated material about documented social conditions somehow would no longer be effective drama. However, "universalizing" the story would, of course, make it politically safer. The universal human condition would be less likely to generate interventionist political movements or respond to historically specific mechanisms of social change.

The *Los Angeles Times* praised the show: "It was not a story of color but of the eternal struggle of man in an imperfect world."[22] This reading could be seen as unconsciously racist, since the specificity of African American struggles with poverty and racism were so aggressively denied. If this were a universally human story, then it could be a white story, too.

Another reviewer who disliked the episode castigated the show for *not* doing precisely what the *Los Angeles Times* critic thought the show did so well. This reviewer argued that the difficulties faced by the young black couple "are indigenous to poverty. They're problems that know no color barrier." She went on to explain that black performers had fared much better when they were "integrated" into storylines, such as on *The Nurses, The Defenders, The Fugitive, Ben Casey,* and *Mr. Novak* in "unostentatious" ways. "What's objectionable [in *East Side/West Side*] is the automatic raising of the racial question every time a Negro appears in a dramatic scene."[23] The reviewer seemed uncomfortable with any representations of black people that pointed to difference. As long as black images refrained from making whites uncomfortable by pointing to unresolved and contentious issues of race relations—as long as they "integrated" themselves into familiar narratives and representations—then all was fine.

Although reviewers appeared to be confused about whether the episode was unique to the African American experience of poverty or whether it was a universal story of struggle, the episode's director, Tom Gries, appeared incoherent on the issue. In an interview on the filming of the program, he argued that while the narrative was a "Negro story, native to Harlem," it could just as easily have been a story about white people, because it was so universal. Then, apparently thinking the matter over, he said, "No . . . I guess the story belongs to Harlem. Do you know Harlem? I didn't. Those people will all go to heaven because they live in hell now. We shot for three days at 118th St. and Lennox Ave. and I didn't believe it—I didn't believe people lived that way."[24]

The broadcasting of this episode generated a great deal of discussion and was preceded by an exceptional amount of publicity. Producer Susskind persuaded his good friend, New York Senator Jacob Javits, to view an advance copy of the episode and to praise it on the Senate floor.[25] Talent Associates also launched a word-of-mouth letter-writing campaign to a hundred "outstanding American leaders," including Martin Luther King. The leaders got a copy of the script and were asked to inform friends and members of their organizations about the upcoming broadcast. The story generated enough interest that almost all television critics were expected to write on the episode.[26] Ratings were generally quite good, drawing a 38 percent share of the television viewing audience.[27]

Two of CBS's Southern affiliates decided against broadcasting the episode. KSLA-TV in Shreveport, Louisiana, claimed the show had to be preempted for a televised debate among candidates for a local political race. The general manager of WAGA-TV in Atlanta found the show "too rough for prime-time television" and declared that "it would be detrimental to the cause of good race relations in Atlanta and surrounding areas."[28] Even though the drama had nothing to do with Southern race relations, these affiliates still felt their white racial sensibilities under attack.

The episode generated a relatively heavy amount of viewer mail.[29] Considering that viewers would also have been exposed to news stories and imagery about civil rights activity, it is no surprise that many linked the program's impact to the civil rights movement. A Massachusetts letter writer wrote that "the impact of the story was worth a million sit-downs or protest marches." A Pomona, California, viewer argued that "programs of this sort will do more to help our country solve this problem than all the pleading, marching, praying or legislation."[30] Although well-meaning, these responses suggest white viewers who were not entirely comfortable with black people protesting, marching, and agitating for civil rights. Network news programming, of course, also was not all that comfortable with Negro mass protest either. For some viewers, fictional representations may have felt less threatening, less confrontational, less demanding of immediate response.

Other viewers read the episode as part of a continuum of civil rights activity: the program bolstered and extended the political goals of the movement. A New Jersey fan wrote, "The program dramatically and graphically made believable and immediate the protests we have heard before only in speeches." Another viewer hoped the show would "lend impetus to the 'Freedom Now' movement to free all oppressed all over this land." Thus, rather than being a substitute for the direct-action practices of the movement, the *East Side/West Side* episode was itself a political intervention. Unsympathetic viewers opposed to civil rights also read the show as connected to civil rights politics. Another New Jersey viewer condemned the episode as "nauseous propaganda. . . . Even the 'reverend' was made up to look like that rabble-rouser, Martin Luther King."

Although this viewer's oppositional reading indicated an unwillingness to see herself implicated in Northern mechanisms of racism, many others found themselves compelled to examine their own whiteness and its accompanying privilege in relation to an oppressed black "other." A Weymouth, Massachusetts, mother wrote, "I am ashamed to be one of the so-called white Christians who have let such a situation exist. I feel guilty as I look around my clean suburban home and my small ones sleeping in clean beds." A priest in Fargo, North Dakota, wrote, "I was both angry and guilty. Angry because of the awful agony of the young couple. Guilty because as a white man I am partially responsible for anguish so rife and unnecessary and damaging." Many viewers were self-conscious about identifying themselves as white, and many engaged in similar bouts of liberal guilt. "Whiteness" for these viewers had become something that needed attention—"whiteness" had social and political consequences. Skin color was connected to power, and to distinctions. This fictional drama forced many of its viewers to recognize, perhaps for the first time, that as middle-class whites, they were caught up in power relations of race and privilege. The denaturalizing of that set of relations was clearly painful but potentially emancipatory.

Other viewers caught up in white liberal guilt expressed a degree of helplessness, in changing the system of race relations with which they were suddenly grappling. One woman pleaded, "Please someone let us know what we as citizens, better yet, as human beings who *care* about other human beings—what can we do to help. . . . Do we write the Mayor, our Congressman, our Senator? I feel helpless but I must help in some way." A woman in Scarborough, Ontario, asked, "Is there something a white Canadian can do to begin to help change things? Not patronizingly but sincerely. I can't think of anything specific and feel sick about the whole thing." A woman in Brooklyn wrote, "We were moved to write to you because in our sense of helplessness over the dramatic situation presented, this was the only positive step we, as viewers, could take."

The palpable agonizing these viewers expressed raises some perplexing questions. Clearly these white viewers were moved enough by the representations of black poverty, discrimination, and despair that they wanted to engage in some form of intervention for social change. Yet, at that very moment, an organized movement expressly committed to racial social justice was active and very visible. Although viewers made the connections between the civil rights movement and this program, they did not seem to make the further connection that if they

wanted to engage in ameliorating race relations, they needed to become politically active. As predominantly white Northerners (plus one non-American), it is
possible that these viewers understood civil rights activism as strictly a black, as
well as a Southern phenomenon. As such, this program about Northern, urban
poverty did not call to them to get politically involved, unlike viewers of some
news coverage about the Southern civil rights campaigns did, most notably the
footage of the beating of marchers at the Edmund Pettus Bridge in Selma that
galvanized so many Northerners to immediately head to Alabama. These prime-
time viewers may have been unable to conceive of themselves participating in
a social change movement. Their desire to do something got channelled into
writing letters to the show's producers. Supporting *East Side/West Side*, which
was already threatened with cancellation, became a substitute for involvement
with civil rights activity. Fandom for the series functioned as an alternative way
to express a nascent political position.

Although the program may not have created new white foot soldiers for the era's
civil rights campaigns, it did appear to encourage some profound soul searching
among viewers about their own internalized racism. One viewer who had grown
up on Chicago's South Side admitted that "even as a loving Christian, [I] have very
little love and understanding for my negro [*sic*] brother. But the picture last night
has opened my mind and heart to the negro and I can honestly say that I now
have a deeper insight to the terrific plight of the negro." Another Chicago family
used the show to engage in some painful self-exploration of the limits of their
own racial tolerance. The letter writer described family members being reduced
to tears. Their sixteen-year-old daughter asked why Negroes had to live like that:

> Finally, after going through the whole bit about the unfairness of our treat-
> ment of the negroes, [*sic*] she remarked, "Yes, but you wouldn't want them living
> next to you, would you?"
> Now, I had always thought that we—as a family—were unusually tolerant and
> understanding, but I realize now that our sterilized life in the suburbs has *and
> is* producing another generation of segregationists. No, maybe I wouldn't like to
> live next door to negroes, but how do I know? I never have tried. But, whether
> I like it or not, it is morally wrong that I even feel this antipathy towards them
> when I have had absolutely no socializing with them.

In the end, perhaps the show's most noteworthy achievement, based on clues
in these letters, was a contribution to consciousness-raising among whites. This
piece of fictional entertainment programming did much the same in forcing
white Americans to face the truth of racial injustice and inequality endemic in
their society. Prime-time series like *East Side/West Side*, along with news specials
and evening newscasts, worked to set a foundation of sympathy among many
white television viewers for the goals of a movement they engaged with only
via their TV sets.

Although none of these viewers seemed to have been ready to engage in any form of direct action in response to what they had seen in the program, such was not the case for a group of intrepid executives from Kinney Service Corporation. According to *Daily Variety,* the group decided to take a tour of Harlem to ascertain whether housing conditions were as bad as the episode suggested. Shocked at what they discovered, the businessmen decided to choose a block and clean it up—exterminate the vermin, paint buildings, and cart away garbage. Using their business clout, they prevailed over slumlords who wanted no outside interference with their property. After cleaning up the block, a passing policeman watching the cleanup told the group about an even filthier block up the street. The businessmen resolved to clean it up, without even bothering to contact the landlord.[31] The story is a perfect illustration of the can-do spirit animating the early days of the War on Poverty. The urban blight that Harlem represented could be fixed with enough good old determination and resolve.

"No Hiding Place"

East Side/West Side's other famous episode on race relations aired the week network television resumed its regular schedule after the four days of continuous coverage of the Kennedy assassination and funeral. Viewers could be assumed to be in a more sober, serious, and contemplative mood, and the episode certainly provided viewers no pleasant escapism from the emotional trauma of the preceeding days. Written by formerly blacklisted screenwriter Millard Lampell, the show provided a complex look at how a middle-class, white, suburban community in Long Island, and one liberal family in particular, reacts when unscrupulous real estate agents attempted to "block bust" their neighborhood.

The episode opens with a moving van entering Maple Garden, a prosperous Long Island suburb. A sign pointedly proclaims it "a friendly community." Annie Severson, with a very pronounced Southern accent, is on the phone to her husband, Chuck, at his office in the city. He has no identifiable accent. A car pulls up next to the moving van and a well-dressed Negro couple with a school-age daughter get out. We cut back to Annie at the window watching them; ominous chords play on the soundtrack. Annie's status as a Southerner sets up viewers to assume that she is racist and opposed to integration. Chuck is given dialogue in the opening scenes extolling his color blindness: "You know what I believe: people are people." He asks if she believes that. While she says yes, her demeanour suggests far more hesitation and lack of conviction. Thus, as the narrative begins, we have the Northerner who cheerfully embraces the goals of the civil rights movement, while the Southerner functions as the potentially problematic and untrustworthy obstacle. But *East Side/West Side* avoided predictable narratives and character types, so Annie's status as a Southern racist is undercut almost immediately.

Civil rights subjects: the Marsdens conform to all the markers of middle-class respectability and achievement.

When a real estate agent lands on the Severson's door encouraging them to sell their house now before "our dark brothers start pouring in," Chuck Severson angrily tells the agent he is not interested in selling, and then he and Annie end up at Brock's office. The social worker, an old friend of Chuck's, is able to offer more assistance to his fellow middle-class whites than he could to Joe and Ruth. Explaining the tactics of "blockbusting," whereby unscrupulous real estate agents attempt to panic whites into selling their homes at discounts to them so that the agents can turn around and sell the houses at premium prices to blacks desperate to leave bad inner-city neighborhoods for the promise of a better life in the suburbs, Brock tells the Seversons how they can combat the blockbusters. But he warns them it will be long, dirty, and heartbreaking—not a game for amateurs. They need to be in this to the finish. Brock's concern appears to be with regard to Annie and her level of commitment.

The Seversons host a neighborhood party to introduce the white residents to the black Marsdens, and we see awkward racial exchanges. Severson tells Mrs. Marsden about his love of jazz and that he's a "Miles Davis man" and then asks her who she "digs." Very coolly, she replies, "Bach. I dig Mozart, too. But mostly Bach."

Eventually, Annie Severson and Mrs. Marsden bond, and they do so over the signifiers of domesticity and traditional femininity, particularly food and cooking. But as the women begin to overcome their inherited assumptions of the other, the blockbusting threat continues. Notably, it is Annie who must make a decision about her level of activism and commitment to the cause. Because she is Southern, her embrace of integration and color blindness is subject to constant narrative doubt; however, on the other hand, Annie ends up the most activist character, determined to stay and fight the good fight. Chuck, meanwhile, wavers as he considers their shaky financial situation. The catalyst for Chuck's shift from

Mrs. Marsden and the white Southern Annie Severson bond over shared domesticity and traditional femininity.

the politics of color blindness is the second Negro who agrees to buy a house in the neighborhood. Brock and Annie devise a scheme whereby the panicked owner agrees to sell the house directly to a willing buyer without going through the blockbusters, thus preserving property values. The buyer, Mr. Adams, is black but quite unlike Mr. Marsden, an MIT-trained engineer. Mr. Adams is an older man who worked his way up from elevator operator to owner of a fleet of dump trucks. In an exchange with Brock, after the Seversons have met the man, we see the limits of Chuck's embrace of integration.

> BROCK: You wanted a white Negro and you got a black one.
> CHUCK: I'm telling you he isn't the type for this community.
> BROCK: What if he were white? What then? A rough, uneducated, decent sort of guy who made it the hard way. A guy who could never be your particular friend. Is that any reason for keeping him out of here? We have a different yardstick for measuring a Negro, don't we? If he went to Harvard; if he plays golf; if he looks like a Boston gentleman and talks like a Philadelphia lawyer, why fine, let him be . . . *brown*—only not too brown. [Turning to Annie] Your husband believes in equality . . . *but*. Mr. Adams was the *but*.

Chuck proceeds to request that the Marsdens ask Mr. Adams, whom they know, to cancel the deal. Mr. Marsden refuses, to which Chuck replies, "You ought to have a little understanding of our problem. After all, we've stuck our necks out, we've taken your side in this." Marsden retorts that Chuck has not done them any favors. "We have a right to live here. You say you believe in that right? Well, maybe we're doing you the favor. Giving you the chance to prove it."

First Annie had to prove her commitment to integration and color blindness, which the narrative has shown her as accomplishing. Chuck, who blithely affirmed his commitments verbally, is now in the very position he put Annie in earlier in the story. However, the narrative has made the issue harder for him—and, by extension, for the white viewers watching the episode. Chuck turns away and later confronts Brock, saying they have not got a chance against panicked selling. Brock kicks back, gut checking him about what he says he believes: "You haven't got a chance if you don't believe what you've been telling me all these years. You've got to make a personal decision." Telling him it doesn't matter what anyone else does, Brock yells and gesticulates on each word: "You—gotta—stop—playing—Larry Liberal and make up your mind!"

The episode does not show us Chuck making up his mind. Annie has; she proclaims to Chuck that she wants to stay, telling him that the battle is not "out there" in the neighborhood but rather inside, and they would take that battle with them wherever they might go. Caressing him, she tells him she loves him but does not know him. In the episode's final line of dialogue, Annie tells Chuck, "You're going to have to decide." Chuck thus becomes the stand-in for all seemingly broad-minded Northerners and urban sophisticates who may have watched television news coverage of the civil rights movement and expressed strong support. "No Hiding Place" revealed the dilemma in which the issues of racial equality, integration, and opportunity would be just as wrenching and dislocating for whites when those issues moved out of the Jim Crow South. The episode refused to make the issue easy; in fact, it emphatically made it hard.

As with the "Who Do You Kill?" episode, "No Hiding Place" garnered a significant amount of attention from both the press and viewers.[32] Viewer mail was mostly favorable; however, a significant minority of viewers displayed deep discomfort with the prospects of black people living in their midst.[33] White viewers may have responded with less conflict to the Harlem story because its concerns were spatially removed from their own lives, just as the TV news coverage of Southern desegregation was. They could feel bad for Joe and Ruth and wish to

"You've got to stop playing Larry Liberal!" Both Severson and viewers have to make up their minds.

No closure: we never discover what Chuck Severson decides to do.

"help" in some vague way, but they would never have to worry about the couple moving in next door. The December 4 show, however, hit many of the series' white, middle-class, suburban viewers literally where they lived. The drama called on white viewers in ways such that many would have little choice but to accept the positioning of themselves as "Larry Liberals" and face their own embedded anxieties and prejudices about the black "other." Like the Chicago family whose daughter forced the issue about integrated neighborhoods, "No Hiding Place" may have forced many viewers to grapple with the question of whether or not they were a new generation of segregationists.

One viewer, like the fictional family in the show, lived in a Long Island neighborhood that included a lone black family. Her response indicates how profound the impact of this episode could be: "Because of your programs, I find myself reexamining my own position toward integration. I am very indignant towards bigots when I watch a show like the "Rat Bite," but when I hear the fears and doubts expressed by "Chuck" in "No Hiding Place," I understand and sympathize with them. I haven't resolved any of my conflicts on this subject because of your series. I have become more aware of my own bigoted attitudes, which surprised me." This liberal and well-intentioned viewer appeared to understand that racism was not only the activities and discourses of grossly and hatefully intolerant rednecks and Southern segregationists. Racism had a more insidious and subtle form as well. And she saw herself implicated in this "gentler" version. However, by forcing this viewer to realize her own previously unexamined bigotry, the episode helped to create a potentially emancipatory experience. The viewer's nonracist racism was suddenly apparent to her. The discomfort it caused could encourage her to reexamine her assumptions and begin a process of personal change.

A number of other viewers who praised the show and mentioned their own support for integrated housing felt the need to mention, usually parenthetically ("by the way" or "incidentally" or "perhaps I should add") that they were white.

Such self-consciousness, which we will encounter somewhat differently in re-sponse to the 1968 black family sitcom, *Julia*, may indicate that these viewers saw the struggle for racial integration as essentially a black issue. They suddenly found themselves having to negotiate their own racialized subject positions within this terrain. Such self-consciousness could be potentially liberating because their own whiteness, previously naturalized as a nonposition (because invisible), was now visible to them. A number of these viewers indicated that they were actively working for integration in their own neighborhoods, suggesting that recognition of "the wages of whiteness" might be a first step to active engagement with civil rights activism.

Although the program may have had this potentially emancipatory effect on some viewers, others negotiated different readings. The drama's lack of closure and refusal to mandate a solution left viewers free to construct readings determined by their own social positioning and experiences. A white musician and published writer from Brooklyn wrote a long, narrative letter to David Susskind praising him for the episode and recounting her own experience of being blockbusted. She described a formerly clean, safe, beautifully appointed street where she could walk late at night after coming home from the Academy of Music. All of a sudden, her neighbor's house was sold and a "carload of Negroes" moved in: "Then the horror began. There is no other word for it. One by one the fine houses sold for two or three thousand dollars. Negroes moved in. Noise replaced peace and quiet. Prostitutes yelled from windows at night and were carted off by police kicking and screaming. No one was safe. Cockroaches became a torment. Relief tenants ruined the houses, leaving their front doors open night and day for the drinks. I had Negroes on both sides of me." Fearful of going out at night, and with the captain of police urging her to move, the letter writer made her decision: "So, I sold my lovely home with its black walnut woodwork, its high ceilings, spacious rooms, hundreds of paintings specially lighted, thousands of books. I had a splen-did library, many books out of print. I went about the house lovingly touching the walls and apologizing for deserting them. I knew it would be turned into a rooming house for Negroes and it was right away." The writer's class position as well as her whiteness put her at odds with her new neighbors. What is particularly noteworthy, however, is that this letter writer felt the episode justified her own opinions and attitudes. She praised the show, asserting that the people in the play should leave, as she was forced to do. Susskind and scriptwriter Millard Lampell may not have welcomed such a reading of their show, but the open-ended quality of the narrative and the fact that Lampell allowed no closure may have made such readings easily negotiable. No "Larry Liberal," this letter writer made her decision and managed to find support for it in that ambiguous ending.

Few viewers constructed such idiosyncratic readings. Many connected the show to their own efforts in promoting integration. A number of clergymen and laypeople involved in attempts to fight for integrated housing praised the episode as helpful in assisting the movement. Yet rather than emphasize the need for collective action and broad-based organizing to achieve these goals, many letters emphasized individual solutions. One in White Plains, New York, asserted, "While [the episode] left no questions answered, this is consistent with the realities because the questions can only be answered by each individual himself." A pastor in Xenia, Ohio, echoed this sentiment: "You left the decision there in the hands of the individual, and this is, of course, where the race crisis must ultimately be solved." As was the case with some of the viewers of "Who Do You Kill?" a number of white viewers here appeared reluctant to admit that integration and racial amelioration would require political and activist intervention. If solutions were ultimately in the hands of individuals, then a political movement (such as the civil rights movement) was not really necessary. Lampell's script, appealing to viewers as rational, liberal individuals who could make appropriate, individual decisions, may have privileged these readings. And if antiracist solutions were up to individuals, then racial bigotry was likewise a problem of individuals rather than a systemic condition related to whiteness.

Other viewers had a much more antagonistic reaction to the episode's portrayal of white bigotry. They appeared resentful and alarmed at having their whiteness and its powers held up to them as problematic. An anonymous "disgusted viewer" stated: "Instead of helping, you are just making it worse. You rile up the colored people against the whites everytime they see a show of this sort." Unwilling to confront their own bigotry, these viewers felt under siege. Integration and civil rights had nothing to do with ameliorating injustice to blacks but rather with punishing whites. These viewers rejected the invitation to see themselves as "Larry Liberals" who needed to make decisions about how they were implicated in racism. Instead, they saw reverse discrimination. A viewer from East St. Louis fumed, "It is amazing how all the negroes [*sic*] inadequacies can conveniently be blamed on the white race."

The African American press welcomed this unmasking of racism and the discomforts it caused. The *Pittsburgh Courier* praised the episode for emphasizing that Northern whites could no longer assume that racism was just a Southern problem. The columnist observed that "during the racial violence in Mississippi, Alabama, and other Southern states, Northern whites shook their heads sadly and pointed an accusing finger at the South. . . . Now the scene shifts to the North, and while we don't have segregationists like Barnett and Wallace defying the Federal government, the sentiments coming from many Northerners on the question of integrating are just as bitter."[34]

The *Courier* was correct in predicting that Northern whites would have a difficult time coming to terms with their own racism, as the letters about "No Hiding Place" make clear; however, some Northern viewers still insisted on believing that the problem was most acute in the South. A Chicago viewer asked, "Will this show be seen in the South—you must educate the *whole* country, not just the north."

A Great Neck, New York, viewer lamented, "I'm sure the program did not reach the areas where it would do the most good." She did add, however: "[W]e in the North are very much in need of programs of this type."

These viewers, like the ones who protested "dumb Southerners" dictating the kinds of debased entertainment fare available on television, indicate how geographically divided the nation remained over questions of race, entertainment, and what it meant to be an upstanding white American. However, white Southerners as well as Northern and Southern blacks, for the most part, did not join the discursive struggle offered by "No Hiding Place." Southerners may have had a difficult time finding the show on the airways because up to twenty-six CBS Southern affiliates dropped the series.[35]

The episode—and the series itself—also did not appear to generate a great deal of attention from blacks either. Little, if any, of Susskind's viewer mail appears to have come from black viewers. The African American press, likewise, paid only perfunctory attention to the series. The few articles in the *Courier* and *Chicago Defender* praised the series, but they focused mostly on the banning of *East Side/West Side* and other "integrated" series from some Southern television markets. One might assume that one of the first television series to feature both an integrated cast, along with highly publicized episodes about race relations, would have generated heavy interest from African American critics and television viewers. Although the lack of letters from blacks cannot serve as empirical evidence that blacks did not watch the series in significant numbers, the lack of much coverage in the black press is more suggestive.

The relative absence of interest indicates that *East Side/West Side* and the other New Frontier character dramas were addressing white audiences—especially liberal whites in Northern urban areas. "Who Do You Kill?" may have depicted an urban black reality, but the episode was constructed as a white problem to be solved by white liberals. "No Hiding Place" positioned white liberals at the center of the drama and asked them to choose how they wished to respond to the black presence. To some extent, the black characters in both these episodes functioned as objects of narrative action (or inaction, as the case may be) rather than as subjects. The black press may have had relatively little interest in the series, also, because the arenas of struggle for African Americans in 1963 were not focused, as they had been in the past and would be again in the future, on black representations in entertainment media. In 1951, before the advent of the civil rights movement, the appearance of *Amos 'n' Andy* on network television did function as a terrain of cultural and political struggle, especially for middle-class African Americans and the NAACP.[36] In the early 1960s, with civil rights activism receiving large amounts of mostly sympathetic media coverage from network news television and other mainstream media outlets, questions of black representation on entertainment television may have seemed less pressing in the struggle over positive images.

Conclusion

East Side/West Side consistently won its time slot in the Nielsen ratings, yet the series was never fully sponsored. Add to this problem the fear and the fact that numerous CBS Southern affiliates refused to carry the show. Despite respectable ratings, critical praise for the series, and numerous awards (including Emmys and a citation from B'nai Brith), the show's one-year run always operated under the cloud of imminent cancellation.

Inevitably perhaps, CBS cancelled the series. Whether it did so because of Southern-affiliate grumbling, or ratings, or sponsor problems, the network found itself with a politically unappealing series that seemed to serve up nothing but unwanted controversy. Rather than blame the network, many Northern white viewers blamed Southern racists for the show's demise. Susskind, perhaps attempting to defuse the geographical tension, admitted that the network could not sell two minutes of the show's airtime to advertisers, thus losing $84,000 a week on the series. The producer praised CBS for keeping the show on the air as long as it did, even as it lost a reported $2 million in the process.[37]

East Side/West Side became a terrain of struggle for mostly Northern, mostly white Americans trying to negotiate positions around race and around Kennedy-era liberalism. That Southern whites were mostly silent and that Northern whites so castigated them indicates how important the divide between the two halves of the country remained a century after the Civil War. That black Americans appeared not to have found the series of particular salience suggests that, during this moment at least, the politics of representation in popular culture was not at the top of many African Americans' list of important issues. That the network broadcasting this series appeared profoundly uncomfortable with the show suggests that television executives, after perfunctorily appeasing broadcast reformers like FCC head Newton Minow, wanted to go back to business as usual in the entertainment branch of their operations. Later in the decade, network television would find more politically palatable ways to bring questions of race to the small screen by constructing postintegration worlds were blacks fit in without problems into white worlds, such as *I Spy* (NBC, 1965–68) and *Julia* (NBC, 1968–71), which we turn to next. *East Side/West Side* presented a more troubling representation for viewers and for broadcasters. In the relatively optimistic climate of America in the early 1960s, a liberal-inflected program that did not provide answers and solutions may have been prescient but, alas, doomed to failure: "brilliant but cancelled."

CHAPTER 7

Is This What You Mean by Color TV?
Julia

"Annus horribilis" would be one way to label America in 1968. The country lurched through a series of calamities and shocks that suggested a wholesale rending of the sociopolitical fabric of the land. Early in the year, what remained of Americans' faith that victory was possible in Vietnam suffered a body blow as the North Vietnamese launched the Tet Offensive. Television viewers saw the U.S. embassy in Saigon briefly overrun by enemy troops; sometime later Walter Cronkite declared to his nightly news audience that the war was hopelessly stalemated. Shortly after that, President Johnson went on national television and stunned the nation by unexpectedly declaring he would not seek a second term.

On the civil rights and race relations front, the year was particularly traumatic. Martin Luther King and the SCLC were fundamentally adrift as their nonviolent approaches gave way to the more militantly confrontational politics of the Black Panther Party and a more aggressive Black Power–oriented SNCC. Armed "self-defense" appeared more relevant in the new racial arena post Watts. The slogans "Burn, baby, burn" and "Off the pigs" largely replaced "We shall overcome" in the media imagery of Negroes in revolt. The Panthers with their Afros, shades, and black leather jackets became antihero media darlings as representations of a most dangerous form of "cool."[1] In 1968, police clashed with the Panthers while one of the group's celebrity leaders, Huey Newton, was sentenced for murder. At Cornell University, armed black students sporting bandoliers occupied the administration building, while at Columbia, black and white students took over the campus protesting both the university's ties to war research as well as its racist land grab in Harlem.

King attempted to find a new, compelling campaign to shake the conscience of the nation as had Birmingham and Selma in what now seemed a lifetime ago. The Poor People's Campaign, a proposed march to Washington by an interracial movement of the poor to demand an economic bill of rights, preoccupied King until, in March, he agreed to put his support behind a strike by black sanitation workers in Memphis. He was back in Memphis on April 4 when shots rang out over the balcony of the Lorraine Motel where King stood. The champion of non-violent resistance had been violently blown away by a white racist. Within hours of the news, anguished and enraged black people took to the streets all over the country. Before the rage spent itself, forty-six people were dead, almost all black, twenty thousand were arrested, and 130,000 armed soldiers and members of the National Guard had been deployed.[2] Inner-city sections of numerous urban areas lay in smoldering ruin. Smoke from burned and looted buildings could be seen from the nation's capitol.

Later in the summer further blows to the body politic: Robert Kennedy, campaigning for the Democratic presidential nomination and a particular favorite of African American voters, was assassinated just after he declared victory in the California primary. Television viewers saw him lying glassy-eyed and near death on the floor of the Ambassador Hotel. At the end of the long, hot summer, the Democratic Party all but committed televised suicide during its convention in Chicago as Mayor Daley's police went on a rampage against antiwar demonstrators camped out in the city's parks, but also against anyone in the path of their billy clubs. They even clubbed Dan Rather as he broadcast from inside the convention amphitheater. By the fall, it seemed like the country had suffered through a nervous breakdown, much of it televised over and over again.

In the midst of all these shocks, particularly the calamities involving African Americans, many Americans saw an insurrectionary, if not potentially revolutionary, situation among the black population. However, into this tumultuous environment, NBC decided the time was right to introduce the first prime-time series to star an African American since *Amos 'n' Andy* and *Beulah* went off the air in the early 1950s.[3] *Julia* was the creation of writer-director Hal Kanter, a Hollywood liberal Democrat who had campaigned actively for antiwar presidential candidate Eugene McCarthy. Earlier in his career, he had written many episodes of the radio version of *The Beulah Show*; *Julia* may have helped Kanter to expiate the perceived sins of his work on that other representation of black womanhood. *Julia* starred Diahann Carroll whose image was as different from that of Ethel Waters, Louise Beavers, or Hattie McDaniel as one could hope for. Unlike the three rotund and mostly asexual Beulahs all well into middle age, Carroll exuded the sophisticated beauty and refined sexuality of a Lena Horne. Whereas Beulah's world revolved around her white employers, Julia appeared to be the epitome of the independent career woman. She worked as a nurse in an aerospace industry health clinic, a profession very far from the servile, domestic role previously associated with black women. Like Beulah, however, Julia had no husband: he had been killed in a helicopter crash in Vietnam. Unlike Beulah, however, Julia had a child: a precocious and adorable six-year-old son, Corey. *Julia*'s appearance on television at this particular moment almost begged to be read as "Not The Beulah Show."

NBC executives did not expect the show to succeed.[4] They scheduled it opposite the hugely successful *Red Skelton Show*, where it was expected to die a noble, dignified death, having demonstrated the network's desire to more fully break the prime-time color bar. Unexpectedly, the show garnered high ratings and lasted a respectable three years.[5]

Despite its success, or perhaps because of it, *Julia* generated great controversy. Considering the upheavals of the late 1960s around race as the black movement shifted North and into a more confrontational mode discomfiting to many whites, it almost could not avoid being a flashpoint for heated debate. Popular press articles written before the first episode even aired and continuing through the show's run castigated *Julia* for being extraordinarily out of touch with and silent to the realities of Negro life in the late 1960s. While large numbers lived in exploding ghettos so presciently depicted in *East Side/West Side*'s "Who Do You Kill?" episode, Julia and Corey Baker lived a luxury lifestyle improbable on a nurse's salary. While hostility and racial tension boiled, and the Kerner Commission Report on Civil Disorders described an America fast becoming two nations separate and unequal, tolerance and color blindness prevailed in *Julia*'s world.

Coming on the heels of the civil rights movement, the stakes for black representation, particularly on television—the medium that proved so crucial in bringing the black freedom struggle to the nation—were enormous. Phillip Brian Harper, writing about this period, has suggested that "televisual representation of black people has for so long served as a focus of debate [because] it is seen as having effects that extend beyond the domain of signs as such and into the realm of African Americans' material well-being."[6] It was assumed that better and more numerous representations on television would translate into improved objective living conditions for black people.[7] *Julia* in 1968—and *I Spy* before it in 1965, featuring a youthful and noncomic Bill Cosby co-starred with a white partner—gave viewers fully integrated, middle-class Negroes seeming to bear out the promise of Martin Luther King's vision of a color-blind society in which blacks had achieved true equality and freedom. Aspirational figures of "simulacral realism," Julia Baker and Alexander Scott were not meant to "tell it like it is" to white or black viewers. Gritty realist imagery in *East Side/West Side* with Joe and Ruth might do that job but would not provide the models of uplift and racial advancement that these "simulacral" figures might.[8] If Carroll's Julia and Cosby's Alexander Scott could achieve (and do so with the apparent approbation of white TV viewers), then the goals of the civil rights movement and the daily lives of black people in American society would be successful.

I Spy and *Julia* were both overt attempts by network television to respond to the civil rights movement and the revolution in race relations. The genesis of *Julia* as an answer to the movement is particularly instructive. Creator Hal Kanter attended a fundraising speech given by the NAACP's Roy Wilkins and decided he needed to do more than just write a check to the organization; he could use television to further the civil rights organization's larger goals. Christine Acham points out that Wilkins not so subtly disparaged nascent Black Power militancy in favor of the more gradualist approaches the mass media found more comfortable. "In saying that Wilkins inspired him, Kanter aligned his personal politics with the NAACP and not with groups that asserted a black power agenda."[9] And, not surprisingly, Kanter's prime-time handiwork emphatically displayed that political orientation.

But *Julia* is a far more complex and contentious phenomenon than this image of a Hollywood liberal's feel-good valentine to safe color blindness might suggest. This chapter will explore the diverse and often conflicted ways that both the show's producers as well as its audiences and critics struggled to make sense of the show—what it should be and how it should work—within the context of the nation's erupting racial unrest and rebellions.

Viewer mail sent to Kanter, along with script revisions for various episodes, reveal just how significantly *Julia* functioned as a site of social tension.[10] These tensions also show up over and over again in popular press articles and commentary. These documents help to reconstruct the contentious dialogue that took place among audiences, magazine critics, and the show's producer and writers. A key feature of this dialogue was a discursive struggle over what it meant to be black and what it meant to be white at the close of the 1960s. We have already seen manifestations of these struggles among white viewers of the race relations episodes of *East Side/West Side* and of Northern and Southern whites in the news and documentary coverage of the civil rights movement. With viewers of *Julia*, we hear from self-identifying black audiences whose voices have been largely mute so far since the historical record has provided us with only the perspectives and responses of the African American press in providing clues to reception strategies. As we will see, black viewers, white viewers, and mainstream press critics all made sense of the *Julia* in notably different and, at times, contradictory ways.

Producing Difference

Hal Kanter's script files show how he and his production team struggled to construct images of African Americans in the context of the civil rights movement. Particularly revealing is the file for a 1968 episode, "Take My Hand, I'm a Stranger in the Third Grade," which contains the initial six-page outline (the first working-out of the episode's storyline) and a thirty-six-page first-draft script (the first fleshing out of the story in dialogue form) written by Ben Gershman and Gene Boland; Boland was one of the series' four black writers.[11]

The story revolves around Corey's friend Bedelia Sanford, a black schoolmate who tries to win his affection by stealing toys for him. In the original storyline, Julia confronts Bedelia's mother who lives in a slum with numerous children. Flaring up at Julia's expressions of sympathy for her situation, Mrs. Sanford calls Julia "one of those uppitty [*sic*] high-class Colored ladies who thinks she's somebody because she went to college and has a profession. Well, says Mrs. S., she's got a profession too—she's on welfare." Hal Kanter underlined that final line and wrote in the margin next to it with emphatic underlining: "*No, sirs!*"

In the first-draft script, Mrs. Sanford has transformed into an upper-class black woman whose preoccupation with money making diverts her from attending to her daughter. When Julia accuses her of trying to buy Bedelia's love, Mrs. Sanford accuses Julia of "always tearing down our own," calling her a mediocre Negro who has attained all the status she will ever have. Julia retorts, "But that Gauguin print and that Botticelli and your *white maid* all rolled together isn't going to change the fact that you are a failure as a mother."

The adjustment of the Sanford's economic status upward indicates that Kanter and his writers were anxious about their depiction of black Americans. The characters were either demeaning ghetto stereotypes or upper-class "white Negroes," a term critics used to describe Julia. The stereotypical images of Negro life that most whites had previously taken for granted had, by the late 1960s, become, at least to *Julia's* creators, problematic constructs. As predominantly white creators of black characters, Kanter and his writing team wanted to avoid racist representations but appeared stumped in their attempt to come up with alternative images that were not merely mirror opposites. The repertoire of black images—in this case, particularly of black women—proved inadequate, and there was no new or expanded repertoire on which to draw.

Kanter's production team encountered a similar set of problems in an aired episode from early in the first season.[12] Julia, having landed her job at Astrospace Industries, needs to find a mother's helper to care for Corey during the day. Julia and Corey, both dressed very formally and properly, with markers of respectable middle-classness dripping off them, are seated in the interview room of an employment agency as the agency head, an African American man who also appears very formal and proper, introduces a series of black women for the Bakers to consider.

The first is costumed in a traditional mammy outfit with headscarf and shabby, slovenly clothing over an ample body. She collapses exhausted in the chair in front of Julia and Corey and speaking in shades of black dialect asks Julia if this is a "live-in job." When Julia says no, the mammy figure exclaims, "This ain't no live-in job? Ah wants me a live-in job. Ah gots three children of mah own that Ah'm tryin' to get away from. They frazzle mah nerves."

Cutting to a close two shot, Julia and Corey crinkle their noses at each other while the soundtrack plays a sour note before cutting to the next applicant: an overly exuberant, also portly "church lady" figure dressed as if in her Sunday finest. She opens her white-gloved arms wide for Corey, declaring, "He'll certainly do till the judge comes along. Come give Grace a great big hug."

Next we are treated to a quasi-black militant figure: a highly disaffected, hostile young woman with a small Afro. When Julia asks her why she left her last job, she mutters, "Didn't like the lady—she was white. Ain't that enough?" When Julia pointedly responds no, the quasi-militant complains say that she did not want to

Julia and son Corey
as impeccable civil
rights subjects.

wear a uniform: "I ain't no Aunt Jane." We cut to another crinkle-nosed shot of Julia and Corey.

All three of these characters play to the limited repertoire of representations of black women, marking "blackness" as inadequate and unpleasant. All are little more than familiar stereotypes. The final applicant, however, comes with no markers of "blackness." A part-time college student, the young woman literally bops and barrels into the room lugging her books. In rapid-fire stereotypical adolescent-speak, with head and body shifting and tilting, she rattles off information about herself, concluding " . . . and kids just knock me out!" To Julia's surprised but positive response, the girl exclaims with a snap of her fingers, " . . . you swing!" In the place of the markers of "blackness," this applicant is filled up with a bizarre compendium of signifiers of 1950s teen style, with a small dollop of squeaky-clean beatnik patter added in. Some viewers would express great difficulty with this character, particularly around the questions of what it now meant to be "black" or "white." For some she was just too white.

This assemblage of black females suggests a real crisis in representation. The successful applicant, and the one Julia, Corey, and viewers are supposed to favor, does not appear "black"; the other three, who are failures in the narrative, are in various ways "too black." All these representations are one-dimensional constructs of a white imagination. As with the Bedelia Sanford episode, this one also indicates how stumped Kanter and his writers were in their attempts to engage with questions of race difference, even in representing females, supposedly less fraught with cultural danger than representations of black men.

Julia also found another area of gender representation highly problematic. One might expect that a program dealing with a working woman's attempts to raise her child alone would open a space for questioning sexual inequality. Scenes from the series' first episode and pilot suggest this was not the case. Although the show

The "mammy"

The "church lady"

The "militant"

The teenager who doesn't seem "too black"

was often hyper–self-conscious about its portrayals of "prejudice," Kanter and his writers seemed blithely unconscious in their portrayal of women and sexism.

The second episode of the series includes the following scene between Julia and her future boss, Dr. Chegley.[13] Julia enters Chegley's office to be interviewed for a nurse's position. The doctor, with his back to Julia as she enters, examines an X-ray and, without looking at her, asks her to identify it. Julia replies that it is a chest X-ray. He then turns to face her and the following dialogue ensues:

CHEGLEY: You have a healthy looking chest. . . . I believe you're here to beg me for a job.

JULIA: I'm here at your invitation, Doctor, to be interviewed for a position as a nurse. I don't beg for anything.

CHEGLEY: I'll keep that in mind. Walk around.

JULIA: Beg your pardon?

CHEGLEY: You just said you don't beg for anything.

JULIA: That's just a figure of speech.

CHEGLEY: I'm interested in your figure without the speech. Move. Let me see if you can walk.

JULIA: I can. [*Walking*] I come from a long line of pedestrians.

CHEGLEY: Turn around. [*As she does*] You have a well-formed fantail. [*As she reacts*] That's Navy terminology. I spent thirty years in uniform. [*Then*] Do you wear a girdle?

JULIA: No, sir.

CHEGLEY: I do. I have a bad back. Now you can sit down.

The pilot, "Mama's Man," contains a similar scene.[14] Julia is to be interviewed by an Astrospace Industries manager who becomes very flustered when he sees her. He tells her that all her qualifications are in order, but that she is not what he expected. Julia asks whether she should have been younger or older, or "Should I have written at the top of that application—in big, bold, black letters, 'I'm a Negro?!'" That has nothing to do with it, he tells her. The problem is that she is too pretty. "When we employ nurses far less attractive than you, we find that we lose many man-hours. Malingerers, would-be Romeos, that sort of thing. In your case, you might provoke a complete work stoppage."

From a current perspective, these two scenes display examples of rather egregious sexism and sexual harassment. When the episodes aired, however, the women's movement was not yet a part of mainstream public consciousness. *Julia's* creators, therefore, did not yet have to contend with the oppositional voices of "women's liberation" and the feminist movement. On the other hand, the producers were quite concerned with the highly visible civil rights and black power movements, and they were well aware that representations of racial discrimination and harassment were now socially and politically unacceptable. These two episodes of *Julia* reveal a self-conscious understanding of that unacceptability; however, anxiety about that situation resulted in a displacement. Discrimination and harassment were shifted from racism onto sexism. Both job-interview scenes needed to relieve the anxiety created over Julia's difference. The writers could not allow her racial difference to function as an appropriate reason for the denial of a job or for demeaning banter, but there were no such political taboos in relation to her sexual difference.

Conflicted Reception: White Viewers Respond

Kanter's viewer mail, the majority coming from married women, provides a particularly rich case study of how *Julia's* audiences attempted to make sense of the program and how they grappled with racial difference and social change through their engagement with it.[15] At times, the statements in the letters echo those in the popular press; more frequently, both the reading strategies and the debates are different, suggesting the limits to press critics' agenda-setting abilities. Many of the letters include carbon-copy responses from Kanter, setting up a fascinating, often contentious dialogue between TV viewer and TV producer. Perhaps the most compelling characteristic of these letters is the remarkably conflicted, diverse, and contradictory responses among audience members. *Julia* viewers, black and white, fan and critic, certainly provide polysemic readings, but it was a polysemy bounded within the context of race and gender politics at a uniquely turbulent moment when a form of integrationist politics was being naturalized in the face of more threatening black-power challenges.

Many of the favorable letters written by white viewers display a marked self-consciousness about racial self-identification. White respondents of *East Side/West Side's* "Who Do You Kill?" did something similar. But *Julia* viewers did not have to grapple with feelings of white guilt since this program, unlike *East Side/*

West Side, did not challenge whites to take a position on racial injustice. "I am white, but I enjoy watching 'Julia,'" said one viewer.[16] "Our whole family from great grandmother down to my five year old, loved it," said another. "We just happen to be Caucasian." A third proclaimed, "As a 'white, middle-class Jewish' teacher, may I say that it is finally a pleasure to turn on the T.V. and see contemporary issues treated with honesty, humor, and sensitivity."[17]

The self-consciousness of many letter writers identifying themselves as whites may have been a response to the novelty of a black-centered program: it raised questions about traditional and previously unexamined definitions of racial identity and difference. One mother of two boys in Ohio struggled with this very issue in her letter: "Being a white person I hope this program helps all of us to understand each other. Maybe if my children watch this program they will also see the good side of Negro people [rather] than all the bad side they see on the news programs such as riots, sit-ins, etc. I know this program will help my two sons so when they grow up they won't be so prejudice [*sic*]."

Although the woman made some problematic distinctions between good black people and bad black people, she did grapple with racial difference. Definitions of what it meant to be white were becoming a tad uncertain. The crisis in race relations signified by "riots, sit-ins, etc." made Negroes visible, and their depiction had ceased to be a stable field. As representations of black people became increasingly contested, self-representations of whites likewise became unsettled. Some whites responded with self-consciousness. In the aftermath of the integrationist civil rights movement and in the midst of black-power activism, what it now meant to be white in America needed working through. Additionally, this viewer endowed the show with "extra special effects": the show's portrayal of black characters would have a palpable and positive impact on her two sons who would respond to Negroes in the non-TV world differently.

Other white viewers thought about race, perhaps paradoxically, by denying difference. A letter from an idealistic fifteen-year-old girl in Annandale, Virginia, affirmed, "Your new series has told me that at least SOME people have an idea of a peaceful and loving existence. So what if their skin pigmentation is different and their philosophies are a bit different than ours—*they are still people.*" A woman from Manhattan Beach, California, describing her race as Caucasian and her ancestry as Mexican, wrote, "I love the show. Keep up the good work. This way the world will realize that the Negro is just like everyone else, with feelings and habits as the Whites have." A mother of twins in Highland Park, New Jersey, observed, "And it's immensely valuable to the many non-Negroes who just don't know any Negroes, or don't know that all people mostly behave like people."

Perhaps these viewers denied the "otherness" of black people in an attempt to reduce white anxiety about racial difference. By affirming that blacks were "just people" and just like everyone else, these viewers defined "everyone else" as white.

"White" served as the norm from which the "other" deviated. In their sincere attempts to negotiate changing representations of race within a rapidly shifting social environment, these viewers denied that blacks historically had not fit the constructed norm of middle-class whiteness.

The program certainly assisted and encouraged viewers in this interpretative move. *Julia's* theme music was a generic sitcom jingle lacking any nod to the rich tradition of African American musical forms. Unlike the soul-oriented theme song for *Good Times* or the gospel-inflected music for *The Jeffersons*, black family sitcoms that would follow *Julia* in a few years, there was nothing in *Julia's* theme music to let viewers know that race was at all an issue in the series. That the *Julia* jingle had no lyrics to cue viewers about the show's premise, contributed to this shyness about the show's racial themes and concerns. Julia's apartment, while nicely appointed, and with a framed photo of her dead hero husband prominently displayed, also did nothing to suggest African American cultural roots. Consider Julia's generic abode to that of the Huxtable family in *The Cosby Show* (NBC, 1984–92). Strategically displayed African American artwork decorated their lavish townhouse, while Julia's apartment could just as easily have belonged to Doris Day. Julia and Corey's speech was also completely uninflected. On the one hand this differentiated them from their prime-time predecessors such as Amos, Andy, the Kingfish, and, to a much lesser extent, Beulah, but on the other hand it evacuated as much ethnic and cultural specificity as possible so that only skin color served as a signifier of difference. For viewers picking up on the interpretive clues provided by the show, black people were "just people" to the extent that they conformed to an unexamined norm of whiteness.

Although a significant number of viewers adopted this denial of difference strategy, it was by no means the dominant interpretive approach evident in the viewer mail. In fact, many viewers clearly struggled with the problem of representation, both of black characters and of white ones. The criticism leveled by many viewers—that the show was unrealistic and was not "telling it like it is"—reveals a fraught struggle over how reality should be defined.

The refrain "tell it like it is" became a recurring theme in debates about *Julia*, both in the popular press and among letter writers. In a scathing review, *Time* magazine criticized the show for not portraying how black people really lived: "She [Julia] would not recognize a ghetto if she stumbled into it, and she is, in every respect save color, a figure in a white milieu."[18] Robert Lewis Shayon, influential TV–radio critic for *Saturday Review*, also fulminated over *Julia's* deficiencies in representing this notion of a black reality. In the first of three articles on the series, he castigated the program for turning a blind eye to the realities of black life in the ghettos. For Shayon, the reality of the black experience was what the Kerner Commission had documented in its report: "Negro youth 'hustling in the jungle' of their 'crime-ridden, violence-prone, and poverty-stricken world'—that's the real problem, according to the commission report."[19] The world of *Julia*, on the other hand, was a fantasy because it did not focus on the problems of black youth (which for Shayon meant young black males) and because it did not take place in a ghetto. Popular press accounts seemed blind to the unconsciously racist assumption that "the black experience" which they constructed as unitary and singular was essentially a ghetto experience.

This attempt to define a singular "Negro reality" became a point of dispute in Shayon's follow-up columns. He received a letter in response to his first column from M. S. Rukeyser Jr., NBC's vice president for press and publicity, along with a letter from Dan Jenkins, an executive at the public relations firm handling television programming for General Foods, one of *Julia*'s main sponsors. Shayon juxtaposed the responses of these men with comments by Hal Kanter that the show would tell the truth and show it like it is. Shayon pounced on what appeared to be a contradiction: "Jenkins, the publicity agent, wrote: 'It is not and never has been the function of a commercial series to "show it as it is, baby." On those rare occasions when the medium has taken a stab at limning the unhappy reality of what goes on in much of the world (e.g., *East Side/West Side*), the public has quickly tuned out.'"[20] Shayon then quoted from Rukeyser's letter: "We have no real quarrel with your [Shayon's] subjective judgment on the degree of lavishness of Julia's apartment, wardrobe, and way of life. There has been controversy within our own group about this."[21] Shayon also quoted from another interview with Kanter, who seemed to step back from his earlier pronouncement: by "showing 'it like it is,' [Kanter] was talking not of ghetto life, but of 'humorous aspects of discriminiation . . . properly handled . . . without rancor, without inflammation, and withal telling their attempts to enjoy the American dream.'"[22] In his second follow-up article, Shayon added Diahann Carroll's response about the controversy generated by Shayon's initial article: "We're dealing with an entertainment medium. . . . *Julia* is a drama-comedy; it isn't politically oriented. Because I am black that doesn't mean I have to deal with problems of all black people."[23]

By bringing together the sentiments of the show's creator and its network, sponsor, and star, Shayon's pieces reveal the depth of conflict in *Julia*'s production process. There was no consensus on what "telling it like it is" meant. Rukeyser's letter openly admitted to controversy over how Julia and her world should be depicted. Shayon's articles opened up for public examination the problem of representation. If black identity had become a shifting field in the wake of the civil rights movement and black power politics, then "telling it like it is" would be impossible. Shayon, perhaps foolishly, thought he knew how *Julia* should tell it, but his articles indicated that in 1968 the program's creators were far less certain.

Unlike the critics, viewers generally did not want to relocate Julia and Corey to a ghetto. Instead, viewers who criticized the show for not "telling it like it is" zeroed in on the presentation of black characters rather than the upscale setting. A male viewer in Chicago wrote:

On another point which bears remarks is the unwillingness to allow the program to be "black." I do not object to white people being in the cast. What I do object to is selecting the black cast from people (black people) who are so white oriented that everybody has a white mentality, that is, their expressions are all that of white people. Choose some people whose expressions and manners are unquestionably black. The baby-sitter was, for example, so white cultured that you would have thought she was Caucasian except for the color of her skin.

Hal Kanter grumbled in reply: "We all make mistakes, don't we, Mr. Banks? Please try to forgive me for mine in the spirit of universality and brotherhood we are attempting to foster."

Mr. Banks's letter suggests an uncertainty over how to portray black people. Kanter's testy retort indicates that despite his rhetoric of brotherhood (and sameness), this problem plagued the show's creators. How would or could one represent "unquestionably black" expressions and manner? As we saw in the episode where Julia interviews potential babysitters, the choices available seemed to be the traditionally stereotyped and, in the case of the successful candidate, a set of expressions and manners that audiences read as "white." For Mr. Banks, the representation of "black" gets defined negatively by what it is not: it is not white. Left open to question is what "black" could mean outside a signifying system in which "white" is the undefined, if newly marked, norm.

Other viewers, also uncomfortable with the unrealistic quality of the program, pointed out more problems in the representation of blacks. A woman in Berkeley, California, observed:

Your show is in a position to dispell [sic] so *many* misconceptions about Black people & their relationships to whites. I am just one of many who are so *very* disappointed in the outcome of such a promising show.

Please, help to destroy the misconceptions—not reinforce them! Stop making Miss Carroll super-Negro and stop having blacks call themselves "colored" and make your characters less self-conscious and tell that "babysitter" to quit overacting.

This concern with portraying blacks as "Super Negro" was not uncommon through this period. In Hollywood cinema, Sidney Poitier, *the* black movie star, had by 1967 solidified his persona as the "ebony saint" who selflessly and heroically assisted white nuns (*Lilies of the Field*, 1963), a blind white girl (*A Patch of Blue*, 1965), and disadvantaged high school kids (*To Sir, with Love*, 1967). His "Super Negro" status as the black figure white America could most comfortably welcome into the family reached its apotheosis in 1967 when, as Dr. John Prentice, a stellar graduate of Johns Hopkins medical school and lauded for setting up health programs in Africa, he is deemed good enough to marry Spencer Tracy and Katharine Hepburn's daughter in the 1967 megahit *Guess Who's Coming to Dinner*. Poitier's character was both praised and damned for being so superior to all the whites around him. Similarly, on television Bill Cosby's Alexander Scott in *I Spy* was a university graduate, Rhodes scholar, linguistic genius fluent in eleven languages, and able to effortlessly navigate the international world of intrigue, spies, and Communists. Like Poitier, Scott was almost hyperbolically better, smarter, and more accomplished than any white around him.

Julia, coming on the heels of these two representations of eminently assimilable blacks, seemed to fit right in. But by the later 1960s, she also served as a site of increasing anxiety about this strategy of representing blacks as paragons of achievement and virtue. This "civil rights subject" earlier in the decade included exemplary black Mississippians denied the franchise and, at the March on Washington, dignified and formally dressed black participants congregating effortlessly and amiably with whites. By decade's end this was no longer an untroubled representation among more liberal whites.

These anxieties about what the signifiers "black" and "white" now meant also suggest that the previously successful theme of "black and white together," which circulated so optimistically on television screens earlier in the decade in network news programming and which appeared to reach its pinnacle in the entertainment branch with *I Spy,* could no longer circulate unproblematically. *Julia* attempted to present the same color-blind ideal to viewers with a protagonist who, like Alexander Scott, integrated effortlessly into a white world bringing no baggage signifying difference with her. Many white viewers and critics still wished to embrace this racial utopia, but by the late 1960s that utopian promise kept slamming up against newer, decidedly dystopian narratives and imagery of racial turmoil, anger, despair, and violence.

Hating *Julia*

The viewer letters we have looked at to this point suggest audience members who, either by denying difference or by trying to engage with it, actively worked with the show to rethink race relations. Many displayed unexamined racist discourses, but the racism seems unintended and unconscious, a manifestation of the shifting ground. *Julia* worked hard to evacuate politically charged images and potentially disturbing discourses of racial oppression and so hardly seems a likely target for overtly racist attacks. However, a surprisingly large number of letters to Kanter reveal an enormous amount of anxiety some viewers felt about the changes being wrought in the wake of the civil rights and black oppositional movements.

Many of these letter writers were intensely uncomfortable with the increasing numbers of Negroes on television. Others exhibited fears about traditional racial hierarchies being overturned. And some voiced anxieties about interracial sexuality. *Julia* never dealt with issues of miscegenation or intermarriage, of course, but numerous viewers read such themes into the program anyway. They may have been encouraged in these readings because Julia conformed to white standards of beauty. Diahann Carroll was quite far from the traditional mammy figure that Beulah embodied or the equally de-sexed shrew, Sapphire, of *Amos 'n' Andy*. Julia's white male bosses certainly recognizing her sexuality in the show's opening episodes. Other sequences in later episodes may have assisted in further exciting anti-miscegenation responses.

In one episode, for instance, we encounter Dr. Chegley in a fancy French restaurant.[24] He approaches the maître d', who exclaims his delight in seeing the doctor. Chegley asks for a table for two. Right behind Chegley, we (and the maître d') see a middle aged, white woman. The mise-en-scène would suggest she is Chegley's date. As the maître d' looks down at his table list, the white woman exits the frame and Julia enters and comes to Chegley's side. When the maître d' looks up and sees the interracial couple before him, he suddenly gets flustered and becomes rather less than welcoming.

> MAÎTRE D': Table for two? Do you have a reservation?
> CHEGLEY: I do.
> MAÎTRE D': Who made the reservation?
> CHEGLEY: Abraham Lincoln.

The still cool maître d' officiously guides the couple to a very cozy booth where Julia and Chegley sit side by side, very close to each other. Julia, equally coolly, responds "merci" as the maître d' adjusts the table toward them. In French, he replies arrogantly, "Oh, vous parlez français, mademoiselle?" Frostily, Julia, responds, "Madam, s'il vous plaît." She goes on to inform him, still entirely in beautifully accented and articulated French that she spent time in France where the people were tolerant and open-minded. Chegley then grumbles, "Stick that in your snails and broil 'em."

Everything in the visual construction of the sequence suggests that Chegley and Julia are on a romantic date, even though the scene is set up this way to spotlight the racism of the maître d'. Regular viewers of the show would, of course, know that there is no romance between the two, and Julia's insistence that she is a "madam" not a "mademoiselle" provides more verbal ammunition to counter the visual signifiers of romance. Nevertheless, the French bistro setting and the physical closeness between the two may have been all the cues that some viewers needed to construct scenarios such as this one provided by an anonymous viewer from Los Angeles: "What are you trying to do by making 'Julia.' No racial problems—she is playing opposite a white, she is suppose [*sic*] to live in an all white apt house. It's racial because you will have it so Nolan [Dr. Chegley] will fall in love with her and have to make her over—repulsive—You had better write a part for a big black boy so he can mess with a white girl or they will get mad."

For this viewer, the only way to make sense of social change in race relations and of integration was to connect them to interracial sexuality. This particular anxiety had a long-standing history in segregationist politics. In the school integration debates, segregationists would invariably argue that the "mixing and mingling" of black and white school kids would lead to interracial coupling and the "mongrelization" of the white race. Here we see that discourse mobilized again: if the white man can have the black woman, then in the equal rights politics of the period, it can only mean, also, that the black man has to have a white female "or they will get mad." "They" are black civil rights activists who, ultimately, do not really want voting rights and equal opportunity; they want white women.

Other viewers, less obsessed with miscegenation, exhibited their fears of integration by venting anger at television as an institution. They blamed TV for creating social strife and for encouraging blacks to forget their proper place. One anonymous viewer from Houston, who signed off as "the silent majority," wrote: "Living in Texas all my life I have always lived around the negroes and they used to be really fine people until the T.V. set came out & ruined the whole world! Not only have you poor white trash taken advantage of them & ruined their chances now you have ruined the college set. You are good at getting people when they are most vulnerable and changing their entire thinking!"

These letters indicate how besieged some people were feeling in the midst of the turmoil of the late 1960s. In Julia, some viewers may have seen the "new Negro" as one who threatened their racially hierarchical universe. All the anxiety-reducing mechanisms employed by the program's creators to defuse notions of difference merely exacerbated anxiety for these viewers.

Hostile viewers were also bothered by the mere presence of blacks on television. As we have seen, network news cut its teeth on the black freedom movement as television's first major, ongoing domestic news story. As television news matured through the mid-1960s, viewers would have gotten accustomed to a steady diet of stories about Negroes, at first mostly in the South and connected to civil rights activism, but after Watts increasingly in the North and increasingly connected to riots, disorder, violence, and crime. On prime-time entertainment television, blacks slowly became more visible, first on *East Side/West Side* and other "New Frontier" dramas, as specially featured "problems" to be solved by socially engaged white professionals. Subsequently, from 1965 on, blacks began appearing regularly in many new series as supporting players in shows like *Star Trek* (NBC, 1966–69), *Hogan's Heroes* (CBS, 1965–71), *Daktari* (CBS, 1966–69), *Mission: Impossible* (CBS, 1966–73), *Ironside* (NBC, 1967–75), and *The Mod Squad* (ABC, 1968–73). Beginning in 1967, viewers also saw blacks occasionally in TV commercials. But in the summer of 1968 the networks, at the urging of the Kerner Commission, outdid themselves by offering an unprecedented number of news documentaries on the state of black America. Most notable was CBS's seven-part series, *Of Black America*, a high-profile offering that treated audiences to a range of complicated issues around the history, misconceptions, and status of African Americans in the United States.[25]

For some viewers this was just too much: "We have had so much color shoved down our throats on special programs this summer its [*sic*] enough to make a person sick," wrote a viewer from Toronto. An anonymous viewer from Eufaula, Oklahoma, warned, "After the riots and [the] network filled 'Black America' shows all summer, white people aren't feeling to [*sic*] kindly toward colored people shows. You are ahead of the time on this one." Yet another anonymous viewer from Red Bluff, California, asserted, "I will not buy the product sponsoring this show or any show with a nigger in it. I believe I can speak for millions of real americans [*sic*]. I will write the sponsors of these shows. I am tired of niggers in my living room." A third anonymous viewer from Bethpage, Long Island, asked, "Is this what you mean by color T.V.? Ugh. *Click!!*" Many of these people made no distinction between documentary representations of civil strife and the fictional world of *Julia*. Since both in some way concerned black people, *Julia* was really no different from the news specials about ghetto riots.

Julia had received heavy criticism for constructing a "white Negro," for playing it safe in order not to scare off white viewers, and for sugarcoating its racial messages. That all may be true, but the show's "whiteness," "middle-classness," and inoffensiveness did not defuse its threat to a particular set of viewers with entrenched racist positions. The fact that many of the hostile letters carried no return address suggests just how much these letter writers felt themselves under attack. Unlike other viewers who wrote letters, both favorable and unfavorable, these hostile letter writers were not interested in opening up a dialogue with the show's producers. Anonymity both shielded their besieged positions and revealed that such positions were no longer easily defensible. By remaining anonymous, these letter writers tacitly admitted to moral and political bankruptcy.

Black Viewers Respond

Although the majority of Hal Kanter's letters appear to be from whites, a significant number of letters came from viewers who identified themselves as black.[26] Some of the letters share minor similarities with some of the responses from white viewers. For the most part, however, the reading strategies differ markedly.

Jacqueline Bobo, drawing on the work of David Morley and Stuart Hall, has discussed the importance of "cultural competencies," or cultural codes, in order to make sense of how black women made their own meanings of Steven Spielberg's film version of *The Color Purple*.[27] David Morley argues that different interpretations need to link back "into the socio-economic structure of society," showing how members of different groups and classes sharing different "cultural codes" will interpret a given message differently, not just at the personal idiosyncratic level, but in a way "systematically related" to their socioeconomic position.[28] Bobo shifts the emphasis from social and economic structures to those of race in order to determine the codes black women used in interpreting the film. Her approach is helpful toward understanding the unique ways black viewers of *Julia* made sense of the program.

One crucial distinction between black and white viewers involves black view-ers' level of engagement with the show. Many black letter writers, but none of the white ones, displayed a participatory quality in their relationship to the program. They tended to erase boundaries between themselves and the text. Many black letter writers asked if they could write episodes or play parts on the show. For instance, an eleven-year-old boy from the Bronx wrote: "I am a Negro and I am almost in the same position as Corey. . . . Your show really tells how an average black or Negro person lives. I like your show so much that if you ever have a part to fill I would be glad to fill it for you."[29] A teenage girl from Buffalo wanted to create a new character for the show: Julia's teenage sister. Describing the sister's characteristics, the letter writer indicated that she would like to play the part. A female teacher from Los Angeles wrote: "The thought occurred to me that *Julia* may be in need of a close friend on your television show—and/or Corey Baker may need a *good* first grade teacher (me). . . . I am not a militant but a *very proud Negro.*[30] This teacher felt that her lived experience could be an asset to the show. Interestingly, she positions herself politically as a supporter of black pride, but not black militancy, presumably to align herself with the show's race politics.

Although white viewers offered criticism of the show, only the black viewers took it upon themselves to offer their assistance in improving it. Their participa-tory relationship to the series indicated a far more active attempt at making the show meaningful and useful, both personally for the letter writer as well as for the broader viewing audience, both black and white. Black viewers struggled with the actual program created by white producers and desired a more au-thentic one to be created by the black viewers. By acting in and writing for the show, these viewers, imaginatively at least, became producers of meaning rather than mere recipients of meanings constructed by whites. Asserting the values of their cultural codes, they attempted to bring their socially situated knowledge about "blackness" to *Julia.*

Ebony magazine also tried to find race-affirming possibilities in *Julia.* Unlike other popular press accounts, *Ebony* took pains to emphasize the show's posi-tive aspects while acknowledging its shortcomings. Pointing to *Julia's* four black scriptwriters, the article suggested that the show would provide new opportunities for African Americans in the television industry.[31] *Ebony* appeared to support the program specifically because the magazine saw that blacks were assisting (even if in a limited way) in its production.

Black viewers voiced significant concerns about the show, particularly around the question of whether the show's representation of blacks was realistic or whether it portrayed a white world for white viewers. While many white viewers applauded the "denial of difference" stance they saw in *Julia,* many, although not all, black viewers were much more critical. A black woman from Los Angeles observed:

Your show is geared to the white audience with no knowledge of the realness of normal Negro people.

Your work is good for an all white program—but something is much missing from your character—Julia is unreal.

To repeat again—Julia is no Negro woman I know & I'm Negro with many friends in situations such as hers.

Kanter replied somewhat sarcastically: "I'm glad you think our work is 'good for an all white program.' I'll pass your praise along to our black writer and black actors."

Although some of the white viewers who had self-consciously identified themselves by race seemed to think *Julia* addressed itself primarily to black audiences, this black viewer thought the opposite. The black audience was ignored by a text that denied the "realness" of black identity and experience. The mass-media student we already heard from made a similar observation: "The show does not portray the life of the typical probing Black woman, it is rather a story of a white widow with a Black face. Even though she does possess the physical appearance of a Black woman (minus expensive clothing, plush apartment, etc.), she lacks that certain touch of reality." The problem of realism provided a manifestation of the crisis in representation: how to define black identity and who would be authorized to do so. In his reply, Kanter acknowledged the problem, admitting, "I have considered [your letter's] content and have come to the conclusion you may be right."

White viewers who agreed that the show was unrealistic and that Julia was a "white Negro" were more likely to do reality checks with other white characters with whom they could identify, such as Julia's neighbor, Marie Waggedorn, or Dr. Chegley. Black viewers who found the show unrealistic and who found Julia to be a "white Negro" had difficulty identifying with any of the characters. The woman with many friends in Julia's situation searched the text in vain for confirmation of her identity as a black woman. Unlike the black women Jacqueline Bobo studied who found positive, progressive, and affirming meanings about black womanhood in *The Color Purple,* this woman found nothing in *Julia.* The show did not speak to her experiences. It did not offer her a reading position from which she could use her cultural codes and find useful meanings. On the contrary, her experience as a black woman, along with that of her friends, blocked any possibility of finding a place for herself in the text. For other black viewers, breaking down textual boundaries and inserting themselves into the program by offering to write episodes or play a character based on their own experiences helped to avert the problem. This strategy gave some black viewers a way to assert their own identities as African Americans and assert the possibilities of "blackness" for *Julia.*

This struggle over "authenticity" indicates the limits of "simulacral realism" and the strategy of constructing aspirational figures of blacks with the assumption that such representations would provide suitable role models of middle-class respectability and achievement, inevitably resulting in positive social change in "real" African American social environments. By the late 1960s, numerous African Americans appeared to chafe under the assumptions of this representation (as did some whites). Increasingly, black viewers appeared to want what Phillip Brian Harper has termed "mimetic realism": socially "relevant" representations that "would 'reflect' the social reality on which it was implicitly modeled."[32] *Good Times* and the cycle of "ghetto sitcoms" would be network television's response to this call for "relevance" and "authentically black" images.

Black Women, Matriarchy, and the Portrayal of the Black Family

The other major concern for black viewers, as well as for some white critics, was the depiction of the black family. Of the black viewers (all were women) who offered comments about the representation of family in the show, all but one criticized the show for lacking a strong male head of the household. The one woman who did not take *Julia*'s creators to task for omitting a strong patriarch was herself reacting to *Saturday Review* critic Shayon's remarks that *Julia* perpetuated the "castration theme in the history of the American Negro male."[33] Offering her services as a writer of short stories and plays, this viewer noted: "No one ever lets the Negro woman have her say even the middle-class one. No one really knows how hard it is for the Negro woman when her man walks out on her leaving her with four or five babies." However, another black woman from Chicago offered an analysis more representative of black viewers on this subject:

> I don't think any more of you for excluding the black man from this series than I think of the "original" slave owners who first broke up the black family!
>   You white men have never given the black man anything but a hard time.
>   If you really want to do some good you'll marry "Julia" to a strong black man before the coming TV season is over and take her from that white doctor's office and put her in the home as a housewife where she belongs!
>   Otherwise a lot of black women—like me, who love, respect, and honor their black husbands—will exclude "Julia" from our TV viewing just as you have excluded our black male from your show!

A married "Ex-Black Viewer" from Brooklyn wrote, "After viewing the season premiere of 'Julia,' I, as a black woman find myself outraged. Is this program what you call a portrayal of a typical Negro family (which is, incidentally, fatherless?). If so, you are only using another means to brainwash the black people who, unfortunately, may view your program weekly."

Black academic circles also took up the problems associated with *Julia*'s portrayal of black family life. A 1974 article on blacks in American television in *The*

Black Scholar attacked *Julia* for ignoring black men. By making the central character a widowed black woman, the program sidestepped the critical issue of black
men and their position within African American culture, as well as their position
within American society: "Traditionally the black female has accommodated more
to the white power structure. The real social problems of blacks have always turned
around the black man's inability to have dignity, and the power and respect of his
family. 'Julia' disregards all this by turning the only black male roles into potential
suitors, not actual male figures involved in the overall series."[34] The article suggested that the focus on a female lead made the series safer, less likely to grapple
with issues of black masculinity that might upset white viewers.

How can we explain the responses from black women criticizing the lack of a
patriarchal family structure in *Julia*? White feminist approaches would certainly
be uneasy about the insistence on the desirability of patriarchy evidenced here.
From an African American perspective, however, feminist critiques of patriarchy tend to ignore questions of racism that are seen by many African American
women as crucial for understanding the situation of black women. Indeed, a more
historically grounded examination of the unique experience of black women
within family structures can help explain the responses of these women to *Julia*.

Angela Davis and Jacqueline Jones have pointed out in their histories of black
women that the life of the housewife within a patriarchal familial structure was
quite uncommon for black women. Work generally meant exploitative labor *for*
whites that took black women away from their own families and communities.[35]
Unlike middle-class white women who may have seen work outside the home as
potentially liberating, the history of work for black women had no such liberating connotations. The viewer who wanted Julia taken out of the white doctor's
office was making sense of Julia's labor from within this larger history of black
women's work. That Julia resorted to leaving Corey locked up alone in their
apartment while she went off to her job interview may have churned up painful
collective memories for black women who historically had been forced to leave
their children to fend for themselves while they cared for the children of either
white owners or white employers.

Another way to examine the perspectives of these black women is to situate
them in relation to dominant ideas about the black family in circulation at this
time. These ideas would likely have been familiar to educated, professional,
middle-class members of the African American community. Many of the black
letter writers identified themselves by profession—teachers, nurses, students—
and tended to write grammatically and stylistically sophisticated letters. We
can reasonably assume they were members of the black middle class. And the
dominant perspective on the black family these viewers were likely to be familiar
with was the misogynistic view of a destructive "black matriarchy."

Influential African American sociologist E. Franklin Frazier first put forth this
thesis in his writings about black familial structure in the 1930s. He attributed

a matriarchal character to black family structure and found its source in the dislocation and stresses of slavery and discrimination. Although this familial structure remained dominant within the black community after emancipation, Frazier contended that matriarchal formations were most common in lower-class, impoverished urban and rural families. Rather than give credit to the strength and resiliency of black women, Frazier saw their power within the family as a sign of dysfunction. Families that managed to achieve middle-class or upper-class status assumed patriarchal characteristics mirroring white families and thereby assimilated more successfully into the American norm. Frazier contended that blacks had been unable to retain their African cultural heritage when ripped away from their homeland by slave traders. He felt that blacks, therefore, needed to adopt the familial arrangements dominant in their new homeland in order to survive as a people. Thus, the two-parent, nuclear family with a strong male head, a structure Frazier saw in upwardly mobile black families, was desirable.[36]

Frazier, like many of the white viewers of *Julia* who attempted to deny difference, did not see any problems with this norm. Patriarchy seemed to work in constructing successful families if we view the white, middle-class model as the ideal. But Frazier, like most theorists of the black family, concerned himself mostly with the black male and was largely blind to the position of the female in familial structure, whether white or black.

Frazier's perspective can help us understand why many black viewers found the familial structure in *Julia* so problematic, as did numerous white critics who may have also been familiar with this thesis. On the one hand, the Baker family seemed the epitome of an upwardly mobile black family. Julia, as a nurse, was a professional who had joined the middle class. She and Corey, living in an integrated apartment building with white neighbors, appeared completely assimilated into white society. On the other hand, this assimilated, middle-class black family had no male head. Like lower-class and ghettoized black families, a woman took sole responsibility for running the family and raising a male child. The black family depicted in *Julia* threatened the dichotomized model Frazier had described. The Baker family collapsed the distinctions between the upwardly mobile, middle-class family predicated on patriarchy and the impoverished and dysfunctional lower-class family predicated on matriarchy.

The Moynihan Report was even more influential in distributing ideas about the black family in the 1960s.[37] Produced by the Department of Labor in 1965, around the time of the Watts riots, the report described black families caught within a "tangle of pathology." One characteristic of this "pathology" was a preponderance of female-headed black households in comparison to white households. Echoing Frazier, Moynihan felt this situation had grave consequences for African Americans as a people: "In essence, the Negro community has been forced into a matriarchal structure which, because it is so out of line with the rest of the American society, seriously retards the progress of the group as a whole, and imposes a crushing burden on the Negro male and, in consequence, on a great many Negro women as well."[38]

Many critics in the black community denounced the report for putting as much, if not more, blame on black family structure rather than on white racism and discrimination in order to explain the dire situation faced by many blacks in American society.[39] While some scholars attempted to trace matriarchal or matrilineal familial structure back to black cultural ancestry in West Africa, few in the 1960s were championing female-dominated families within scholarly or popular discourses.

Within this cultural climate, with so much attention focused on the apparently pathological and destructive quality of female-headed black households, *Julia* served as a likely target for criticism from black viewers. As an unattached, independent woman, Julia could be seen as a threatening figure, yet another strong matriarch perpetuating in the realm of popular culture a familial model menacing African American social life.

Julia left the air in the midst of the so-called "season of social relevance," when all three networks aggressively began to revamp their prime-time schedules to include more programming addressing the social problems of the day.[40] Its happy, integrationist world, already out of step with the directions American race relations were headed in 1968, was thoroughly anachronistic by 1971. Diahann Carroll's public critiques of the show and its representations of African Americans became harsher and angrier.[41] The show's producers tried to respond to criticism about the show's lack of a strong black male figure by pairing Julia with a steady boyfriend in later seasons. In the end, the show's "relevance" derived more from the debates, controversies, and struggles over meaning in the reception arena among viewers and critics. These agonized aspects also ended up paving the way for network television's "answer" to *Julia* in 1974, when CBS debuted *Good Times*, to which we turn in the next chapter.

CHAPTER 8

Prime Time, *Good Times*

On September 12, 1974, the first day of school for the Boston public school system, yellow buses rolled out from the black ghetto Roxbury, ferrying poor black students to white, working-class South Boston in order to integrate the stubbornly segregated schools of the "cradle of liberty." According to the court order handed down over the summer, students, both black and white, were to be forcibly bused all over the city in order to comply with the now twenty-year-old *Brown vs. Topeka Board of Education* Supreme Court ruling mandating school integration "with all deliberate speed." As one bus drove to "Southie's" previously all-white high school, the twenty black riders were greeted with signs reading "Niggers Go Home," then with thrown bottles, and with young whites yelling, "Die, niggers, die!" Massed police had to intervene to protect the schoolkids. Thus began the violent and ugly Boston busing crisis.[1]

Three weeks later, on October 1, ten-year-old Michael Evans, an academically talented and politically militant poor black youngster living in the Chicago projects with his parents and teenage siblings, just happened to grapple with the busing dilemma on the CBS hit family sitcom, *Good Times* (1974–79). The coincidence was probably serendipitous, the final draft script having been written in July.[2] School desegregation in the North was increasingly a focal point of civil rights attention, but certainly *Good Times* producers could not have imagined that their episode would coincide with news imagery of yellow school buses surrounded by hordes of angry whites. Wittingly or not, the show found itself in direct dialogue with a raging, anguished, convulsive crisis in urban, Northern race relations at the close of the civil rights era.

Chicago, rather than Boston, had been the setting for the civil rights movement's first venture north, as Martin Luther King and the SCLC turned their sights on the Windy City shortly after the 1965 victories in Selma. As in Birmingham, black Chicagoans were largely restricted to clearly demarcated areas and faced violence if they tried to move into white-designated neighborhoods. Eighty-four percent of Chicago's black schoolchildren attended substandard, overcrowded, segregated schools, a situation similar to Boston. Unlike Birming-ham, however, Chicago did not maintain its segregation through Jim Crow laws but rather through discriminatory real estate practices and gerrymandering of school districts.[3] The movement had, to a significant extent, managed to shake the conscience of the nation while focused on de jure desegregation and black disenfranchisement in the South, but the racial situation proved more com-plicated when attention shifted north. King and the SCLC did not find black Chicagoans willing and energized foot soldiers for a nonviolent army to protest discriminatory housing and real estate practices. Rather, they found an apathetic, cynical, and at times downright hostile black population. King and the SCLC also confronted an enraged and galvanized population of white ethnics fearful of ghetto blacks moving into their suburban enclaves. A few years later with the Boston busing crisis, a similar situation unfolded as working-class Irish com-munities rose up in anger at black kids coming into their schools.

When the movement headed north, it lost hold of its narrative of moral clarity, its racial melodrama of clearly delineated good vs. evil forces. As one civil rights historian has noted, "Unlike the campaigns in Birmingham and Selma, the one in Chicago brought no dramatic villains to the nation's television screens. The occasional news footage of police violence showed angry whites as victims."[4] The SCLC's campaign for "open housing" quickly fell apart but revealed fissures and racial tensions that Republican presidential candidate Richard Nixon would successfully appeal to in 1968. As he courted the votes and allegiance of these increasingly aggrieved and angered whites, the civil rights revolution encountered a swelling white backlash. In 1974, media images of South Boston whites cursing at school buses provided the latest manifestation of white rage.

Good Times waded into these troubled waters. As a comedy reaching a diverse audience, the show had to negotiate its representations with care in order, on the one hand, to circulate empowering messages about African Americans while, on the other hand, not to unduly discomfort more conservative white viewers, including those who might have seen the ethnic whites of Chicago and Boston as victims in the era's racial turmoil. The busing episode provides an instructive example of both the possibilities of prime-time programming as a venue for pursuing genuinely progressive racial politics, as well as the inevitable limitations of popular culture providing anything but the most compromised and defused images of such politics. *Good Times* quickly developed into an important site of contestation and struggle over questions of "blackness," the black family, "authenticity," and black-versus-white control in the immediate aftermath of the civil rights movement.

Was *Good Times* a victory for African Americans in the struggle for "positive images," or was it a particularly galling defeat—or both? What did it mean for post–civil rights race politics that the series, in such clear distinction from NBC's *Julia*, provided viewers with the first black family with a strong male patriarch? Also in contrast to *Julia*, what did it mean that they were poor and that the Chicago projects setting was an important aspect of the production? If urban black poverty was almost too hot to handle, as was the case for *East Side/West Side,* what happened when this subject matter shifts from very gritty drama to occasionally gritty comedy? In this chapter we will look at the frequently heated and very public debates about the image politics of *Good Times* as they circulated in both the mainstream press and the African American press, as well as how fans of the show participated in these debates. We will also examine the textual mechanisms employed by the show both to pursue divisive or difficult subject matter and to undercut that material. Of all the black-starred, "urban ethnic" comedies on network prime time in the 1970s, such as *The Bill Cosby Show* (NBC, 1969–71), *Sanford and Son* (NBC, 1972–77), *That's My Mama* (ABC, 1974–75), *The Jeffersons* (CBS, 1975–85), and *What's Happening!!* (ABC, 1976–79), *Good Times* provided viewers with the most consistent and insistent "socially relevant" material mixed in with the more mindless laughs.

Good Times' negotiation of the racial minefield is particularly noteworthy in the busing episode. After we hear from Michael, who establishes that the schools in the Evans's ghetto neighborhood are the worst in the city—"Our hardest math problem was how to divide forty students into twenty books"—he is given the opportunity to be *voluntarily* bused to a school in an upscale white area with the city's best schools. The narrative emphasizes a number of times that this particular busing scheme is not forced. In the controversy that convulsed Boston, as well as other school districts, the mandatory aspect of the situation served as one of the key flashpoints of anger for whites. The busing controversy also revealed the limits of white Americans' (especially Northern white Americans') tolerance for desegregation. In arenas of casual contact like restaurants and waiting rooms, integration was acceptable, but in more intimate surroundings such as housing and schooling, the situation was quite different. John Lewis, former head of the Student Nonviolent Coordinating Committee (SNCC), observed in 1974, "When it got to hard things, and when the problem started to touch the North, the whites turned around."[5] By emphasizing the voluntary nature of this busing scheme, the *Good Times* episode skirts the more painful questions around the need for mandatory programs to counter deeply entrenched patterns of racial segregation—whether in the South or the North. White viewers watching the episode would be more likely to feel good about their racial magnanimity if they could imagine themselves voluntarily welcoming little Michael into their schools rather than having Michael thrust upon them.

Although the vast majority of opposition to busing came from whites, in the episode it is Michael who speaks out against busing. If it is a voluntary program—he does not volunteer! This strategy also deflects attention away from the implications of white communities' opposition to busing and what that suggests about the possibilities of true integration in the urban North in 1974. The episode defuses that particular theme by insisting on Michael's refusal to go along with the program. From the series' first episode, Michael was established as the family's "militant midget," mouthing black power sentiments that might be too threatening coming from an adult male character. Michael pens slogans such as "Busing ain't nothing but a bunch of honky four-wheel jive" and "Black ain't beautiful on a yellow bus," slogans played solely for laughs rather than as serious Afrocentric critiques of school integration.

Nevertheless, despite these attempts to temper and lighten the threat associated with portraying the busing controversy, the episode, in a number of scenes played in a more serious tone, grapples forthrightly with the need for busing. In one, Michael argues the politics of busing with parents Florida and James. Notably absent is J.J., the skinny, rubber-faced teen son who typically functioned to goose up the laughs and divert attention from more thought-provoking themes. The phenomenal popularity of this character became a major flashpoint of controversy over the politics of "good role models" and "authenticity." With J.J. absent, the scene provides viewers with a few minutes to reflect meaningfully about the issue and its social context, with only a minimum of humor that arises directly from the situation. Standing in between Florida and James, who tells him it would be a shame to waste his talent in a bad school, Michael, asserting a black-power politics, proclaims, "If God gave me talent, it was meant to be used in my own neighborhood with my own people!" After asserting, "Mama, busing is just a way of buying us off," he asks James why he supports busing.

MICHAEL: You were never bused.
JAMES: Yes, I was, too. When I was a kid in Mississippi, I was bused—by foot.
    Passed three beautiful white schools to one crummy black one.

James's dialogue speaks to a number of issues. First of all, throughout the series, the fact that James never went beyond the sixth grade is narratively significant.

The "militant midget" confronts his parents about busing.

Always striving to find better work to raise his family out of poverty, James is often shown crippled by his lack of education. His dialogue links his lack of opportunity to the history of Jim Crow schooling and contextualizes busing to this history. His words also indict white power and privilege. Throughout the episode, characters point to racism and white power as oppressive agents against which they must struggle. The school district to which Michael will be bused is nicknamed the "Detergent District" by Florida, who quips, "Everything there is whiter than white." Responding to sister Thelma's comment that she's never heard of any racial trouble there, J.J. responds, "That's 'cause they ain't got no racials there. Only color problem they have there is matching the carpet to the drapes." The most significant indictment of white racism, however, is again given to James, whose stance throughout the show is privileged. In response to Florida and Thelma's sudden qualms about sending Michael so far away from home and separating him from his friends, James explodes: "Y'all talking just like white people do about busing. The only reason they talk that way is to cover up for the fact that they don't want to go to school with us." Throughout this episode and numerous ones throughout the run of the series, white people and white power are the "other" against which the Evans family struggles. But unlike the case with *Julia,* this white "other" is not merely a misguided, prejudiced individual. In *Good Times* the "other" is the white power structure.[6]

Inevitably, the show had to temper this material with straight comedy. Although the busing issue was the show's major theme, a big chunk of its twenty-two minutes of screen time focused on material that could in no way be potentially uncomfortable to white viewers. In order to defuse the more serious subject matter, the episode had sprinkled in it generous helpings of J.J. and Thelma trading jokes about how ugly and dumb the other was or served up J.J. doing comic routines and prancing about in red long johns. Viewers disinclined to grapple with the real-world issues of busing never had to wait long for the episode to fall back on more familiar black comic turns.

As we can see from this early episode of *Good Times,* the series negotiated a minefield of dilemmas in handling racial politics, socially engaged subject matter versus traditional sitcom fare, and the problem of black representation. In order to understand how and why *Good Times* operated as it did, we need to see the series in dialogue with a long history of concerns about African American representations on American television, especially in the wake of the civil rights movement. We need to situate the show back into its production and reception context. We also need to interrogate the trope of "authenticity" that bedeviled this example of media culture, as it did most representations of blackness in the wake of the black freedom movements of the 1960s.

We saw this preoccupation in relation to *Julia* and the dilemma of the show's white producers employing what Phillip Brian Harper dubs "simulacral realism" in providing an aspirational image of black success that supposedly could

J.J. in red long johns
diverts viewers away
from the tougher
real world issues
the series tried to
grapple with.

have palpable, real-world effects within black communities. We saw a certain amount of backlash against that figure and an emergent shift toward a "mimetic realism" to represent a more recognizable and presumably "relatable" image of black poverty and struggle that could have a different sort of liberatory impact for black viewers.

This concern with mimetic realism or "authenticity" has historically been a central theme in popular discussion about the portrayal of blacks on American television. From the 1960s, with fully assimilated "white Negroes" like Bill Cosby in *I Spy* to Diahann Carroll in *Julia,* to the 1970s and ghetto blacks in *Sanford and Son* and *What's Happening!!* and then later to upper-crust black profession-als in *The Jeffersons* and *The Cosby Show* (NBC, 1984–92), popular press critics and audience members have almost obsessively questioned to what degree these images were "realistic."

Both Herman Gray and Stuart Hall have interrogated this preoccupation with "authenticity" and the "realistic." Gray asserts, "No longer can our analyses be bur-dened unnecessarily by the weight of an eternal search for either 'authentic' media representations of 'blackness' or accurate reflections of African American social and cultural life."[7] Hall also problematizes the quest for an authentic black popular culture, arguing that black representations are dialogic, hybridized; black life and black experience are themselves imbricated in representation. "It's in how blacks represent and imagine themselves that they are constituted. 'Real life' is not a test against which cultural strategies or texts can be measured."[8] Calls for the "authentic" smack of essentialism and a singular vision of blackness. But if black popular culture (if we can speak of such a thing) is a contradictory space, inevitably contaminated with previous representations that are themselves built on representations and that are always in dialogue with generations of imagery produced in a racist environment, how can we interrogate more or less useful and empowering representations? Hall suggests: "However deformed, incorporated, and inauthentic are the forms in which black people and black communities and traditions appear and are represented in popular culture, we continue to see, in the figure and the repertoire on which popular culture draws, the experience that stands behind them. . . . [B]lack popular culture has enabled the surfacing, inside the mixed and contradictory modes even of mainstream popular culture, of elements of a discourse that is different—other forms of life, other traditions of representations."[9]

Producing "A Discourse That Is Different"

As a family sitcom, one of network television's most familiar and longstanding genres, *Good Times* provides a useful example of how black experience and traditions get incorporated by the genre, and how they change it. Of all the examples of network television's engagement with blacks and race relations, *Good Times* was the first to be created by nonwhites. Two African Americans, actor Mike Evans, best known as Lionel Jefferson in Norman Lear's phenomenally successful show, *All in the Family* (CBS, 1971–79), and writer Eric Monte, created the sitcom. In early publicity Evans and Monte garnered more attention than Norman Lear, the series' high profile executive producer. *Ebony* touted the two and proclaimed, "The 'soul' in *Good Times* is authentic."[10] The black weekly *Jet* emphasized the importance of Eric Monte's lived experience. He was a "bonified [*sic*] ex-hobo, cab driver, dish washer and tenant of Chicago's Cabrini-Green housing project. His name is no tip-off to his racial identity. 'But you know good and well there's no way a white cat could survive Cabrini-Green,' chuckles Monte."[11] *Newsweek* noted, "There are many who will see racial stereotyping in 'Good Times,' but they won't be able to quibble with the ancestry of its creators."[12]

This talk of authenticity obviously engaged with discourses of inauthenticity that swirled around *Julia*. If *Julia* was a white man's vision of black family, then *Good Times* was a vision of black family by soul brothers. If *Julia* gave TV viewers a fantasy "white Negro," thoroughly and effortlessly integrated into white, middle-class life, then *Good Times* countered by giving viewers a poor family struggling to survive in a largely segregated, grimy housing project. As the first network TV series created by African Americans, *Good Times* attempted to intervene in the history of black representations in popular culture and present something new, something presumably based on "reality."

The most important way that the show's creators attempted to negotiate black images was through James Evans Sr. During development meetings with Norman Lear's company, Monte was told over and over again to get rid of the father: "A strong black man is not funny in a sitcom."[13] Esther Rolle, for whom the series was created, adamantly refused to do the show if she did not have a strong husband for her character's three children. This struggle by the show's black talent to insist on the presence of a black father served as a counter to white hegemonic representations of black family.

Herman Gray has argued: "Television representations of blackness work largely to legitimate and secure the terms of the dominant cultural and social order by circulating within and remaining structured by them. . . . Just as often, however, there are alternative (and occasional oppositional) moments in American commercial television representations of race, especially in its fragmented and contradictory character. In some cases, television representations of blackness explode and reveal the deeply rooted terms of this hierarchy."[14]

In the early 1970s the dominant cultural image of the poor black family was that of a "black matriarchy." The term had been coined in the much-publicized 1965 Moynihan Report on the state of the black family. The federal government report blamed a "tangle of pathologies" for the deterioration of black families, including overly independent and dominant women, drop-out and delinquent youth, and socially alienated black men who withdrew from family life.[15] Female-headed households in the ghettos were both the cause of perpetual cycles of poverty and the effect. By the early 1970s, this controversial report achieved dominance in debates about the problems of the ghetto, alleviating pressure on policymakers to address a problem that appeared to arise from blacks' own lifestyle choices. In 1970 Daniel Patrick Moynihan, now working for the Nixon administration, advocated a policy of "benign neglect." Within this context, Monte and Rolle's demand for a strong black patriarch functioned as a powerful oppositional strategy to counter the black matriarchy image. It also countered popular culture images of fatherless black families such as the Baker family in *Julia*.

In this strategy, Monte and Rolle employed the politics of "good role models" or "simulacral realism," trying to use popular culture to circulate alternative

Countering the "black matriarchy": James Evans Sr. as strong patriarch.

images of poor black families that could hopefully have "extra-special effects" for black audiences in particular. But this mobilization of "good role models" had less to do with social reality and more to do with an oppositional politics of representation. *Julia* gave American viewers an anomalous, middle-class family headed by a single (actually widowed) black mother and became a target of censure by white liberals and many African American critics. *Good Times* gave an equally anomalous ghetto family with a male head. This representation won many kudus from black and white commentators when the show began airing, yet this image of black family quickly found itself in tension with governmental and social science reports suggesting a growing crisis among black families in the inner cities.

The 1970s saw a huge increase both in black families living in poverty and black families headed by single mothers as the post–World War II economic boom finally went bust. Even as civil rights movement victories helped foster a new category of black middle-class professionals, increasing numbers of poorer blacks entered a frightening downward spiral of unemployment and misery. Welfare rolls exploded, but Aid to Families with Dependent Children (AFDC) discriminated against families with husbands present, often forcing black women to become heads of families as few jobs for black men existed in the ghetto. By the early 1970s, the phrases "culture of poverty" and "feminization of poverty" became familiar. Historian William Chafe has noted, "For its victims, the social changes of the 1960s meant nothing. Instead, they found themselves more buffeted than ever by the triple whammy of race, class, and gender oppression."[16] The number of female-headed households ballooned in the 1960s and 1970s. By 1972 females headed two-thirds of all black families in poverty.[17] So while families like the Evanses did exist in the inner city, their numbers appeared to be diminishing at alarming rates, focusing a moral panic on female-headed ghetto families.

In this period, "culture of poverty" and "permanent underclass" became ominous new terms describing the urban black phenomenon. These labels were frightening to many whites, such as the working-class ethnics of the Boston busing controversy. *Good Times* had to negotiate this new post–civil rights terrain that had none of the optimism and hope of early to mid-1960s racial politics.

For many African American viewers, the representation of the black father would have particular political salience; for whites, an intact sitcom family, rather than being a political statement, might merely be another in a long line of comfortable, familiar images of the family unit. In significant ways, the Evanses fit the traditional sitcom family where warmth, humor, and good moral lessons prevail, where children are cute and cheeky but ultimately submit to parental wisdom, and where wives are domestic and recognize that Father Knows Best. *Good Times* did not violate any of these conventions. In order to negotiate its "authentic" image of inner-city poverty and the attending white racism, the series had to soften the representation, making it more palatable to white, middle-class viewers by giving them a familiar family image. For African American commentators, always aware of the disproportionate importance of black media imagery to the cause of black political and social advancement, this negotiation was useful: the familiar patriarchal family was novel in the repertoire of black media images and thus played into the "good role model" approach to black representation.

Good Times emphasized over and over again the importance of the patriarchal family. In one episode, sixteen-year-old Thelma is dating a graduate student, Eddie, who has written a thesis entitled "Sexual Behavior in the Ghetto."[18] The unexplained appearance of the report on the Evanses' couch causes consternation for Florida and James, but especially James who, not having read it, rails about its "filth." When the nerdy-looking, twenty-one-year-old presents himself to James and Florida and tells them that he wrote the thesis, James erupts and has to be placated by Florida. He gets particularly exercised when Eddie reveals that he interviewed Thelma in his research. The conflict resolves itself when Eddie further explains that Thelma's interview on page 25 supported the argument he was pursuing:

> EDDIE: In broken homes with just one parent, there's high percentage of loose attitudes towards sex.
> FLORIDA: (Reading from page 25 of the report) But in homes with a solid family foundation, especially a strong father figure, the incidence of unwanted pregnancy is almost nonexistent.
> JAMES: You mean page 25 is clean?
> FLORIDA: It sure is!
> EDDIE: And that's all Thelma's interview was about.
> FLORIDA: It makes real nice reading, too.

James asks Florida to repeat the part about the strong father figure as we cut to a close-up of James's self-satisfied grin as he listens again to the description of the importance of his strong parenting.

The sociopolitical ramifications of this form of representation are contradictory. On the one hand, it emphatically and even didactically presents viewers with the "good role model." A successful black family depends on a patriarchal structure, and *Good Times* attempts to model that structure for its presumably impressionable younger black viewers. Impressionable white viewers could also perhaps have some of their prejudice diminished by seeing an alternative image of black family. On the other hand, *Good Times* echoes the Moynihan Report. Nonpatriarchal families, female-headed families, nontraditional families are abnormal, deviant, and inevitably lead to out-of-control sexuality.

Along with portraying strong parents, *Good Times* is notable for the way it presented James and Florida's marriage. The two were frequently shown as strong romantic and sexual partners, and episodes often featured the two hugging and kissing, with James saying, "Gimme some sugar, baby." Viewers were often reminded that the two enjoyed an active sex life, despite the cramped quarters of their two-bedroom, one-bathroom apartment. In one episode with a "Women's Lib" theme, Florida feels that she is being taken for granted by her family.[19] She confronts James, asking whether he thinks of her merely as someone to sew on his buttons and asks when was the last time he made her feel like a woman. With a devilish look in his eye, he replies, "How 'bout night before last?" In answer to her question of whether he really loves her or whether she's only a habit, James sweeps her back in a big kiss. Whistling the children in from the bedroom where they've been banished for the scene, Florida, with her own devilish look, says they should call the children in for dinner—and get rid of them as fast as possible.

Respectful and affirming images of sexuality between African Americans have been historically rare in American popular culture. Julia may have been allowed a few black boyfriends, but through the series, her main love object remained son Corey. And if we go further back to *Beulah,* we saw how boyfriend Bill's effusive declarations of love and romance only served to render a sexual relationship between his elderly self and Beulah ludicrous. *Good Times* broke important ground here, but it remained the only television program to do so until *The Cosby Show*'s Claire and Cliff Huxtable a decade later.

Yet even in its portrayal of black sexuality, the series was not without contradiction. Balancing Florida and James's progressive images of sexuality was the clownish portrayal of J.J.'s sex life. A ludicrous "lady's man," J.J.'s sexuality was grotesque, laughable, and unbelievable. Preparing for dates, he would prance about the apartment in over-the-top outfits that only lampooned and ridiculed any notion of his attractiveness to the opposite sex. The clownishness of J.J.'s "sex appeal" also defused and calmed any underlying fears about black male phallic power. In attempting to circulate new, progressive, and "educational" representa-

"Gimme some sugar, baby!" *Good Times* breaks important ground by showing a loving black couple who clearly enjoy an active sex life.

tions of African Americans, *Good Times* constantly found itself negotiating the new and progressive with the old, familiar, and regressive.

Viewers Respond

Letters written by audience members suggest that, in the show's early years, questions of representation were as important as they had been for *Julia*'s viewers, although the areas of concern differed.[20] Self-identifying black and white viewers, encountering these images of black family, poverty, and ghetto life, attempted to make sense of them in various ways. Both blacks and whites often focused on the show's "educational" value, but whites and blacks differed somewhat in what they considered educational.

A self-described twenty-two-year-old white, suburban, Pentecostal Christian wrote to say that *Good Times* was "a show I can believe in. It is telling the truth about life in the projects, human nature, the social problems of our day, religion in the home, etc. . . . I don't think I've ever been very prejudiced but each week I think I get to understand black people better than I did before."[21] A self-described white schoolteacher asserted that the show was "absolutely *educational*. I recommend it to *all* my students and their parents (mind you, I'm in an upper-class white area.) I think we all have a lot to learn from the Evans family."[22] These white viewers emphasized not only their racial difference from the Evans family in making sense of the show's utility, but also their class difference. The white Christian in the suburbs of New York and the white teacher in a privileged enclave near San Francisco used the show's portrayal of black poverty as a marker of authenticity. Their racial and class distance from the Evanses worked together to mark the representation as truthful and real—perhaps largely *because* the distance was a dual one.

Good Times' white producer, Allan Manings, also talked about the educational nature of the series. In responding to a letter asking about the show's philosophy, Manings replied: "We believe that the presentation of a complete Black family on TV has done a great deal to educate people about Blacks. . . . Although the show is not a 'crusade' by nature, it is certainly hoped that understanding of minority people and their problems will result."[23] Manings assumed that white viewers would be the targets of this education, and also that seeing an intact black family was inherently educational.

While middle-class white viewers may have been the target of this "educational" mandate, a number of self-identifying black teachers also wrote Manings about the show. Most mentioned how much their students, who were predominantly black, enjoyed and discussed the series. One teacher in San Francisco noted: "It is certainly opening up a wholesome channel of communication between my students and I. Please keep it going. The positive self-image we need is coming through this program not just for blacks but for human beings."[24] Another black educator, a sociologist at New York University, also pointed out the importance of positive images: "As a teacher of a course called Black Life Styles . . . the program does capture an authentic strand of Black Life. For one thing, it is [the] first program on television that recognizes the Black 'family'—with a mother *and* a father. It also carries the spirit of Black life style; the desire for education; the take-off on the White power structure; the dignity; the tolerance; the love, of Black people."[25] Another viewer noted: "There is no 'Typical' black family, but this family has a mother and father struggling to make it economically, and doing pretty well at instilling into their children appreciation of education, morality and common decency. Many families can relate to it, or maybe learn something from it."[26] Although the documentation of ghetto life and the vicissitudes of poverty helped to authenticate the series for numerous whites, black supporters focused on family structure as the pedagogical aspect of the series for black viewers. Black, inner-city schoolchildren and their families presumably did not need *Good Times* to instruct them about being poor, but, according to these letter writers, the series was useful in instructing them about the nuclear family unit and the desirability of two-parent households.

The representation of a poor, ghetto family formed the heart of the show's presumptions to black "authenticity"; nevertheless, a small but significant number of letter writers were uncomfortable with this image of blackness. Responding to *Ebony*'s first profile of the new series in which the magazine described the show as "a slice of ghetto life as thick and juicy as a slab of salt pork simmering in a pot of collard greens," a number of letters subsequently published in the magazine questioned the image politics of depicting a poor black family.[27] Rather than embrace the "mimetic realism" exemplified by the series, these viewers wanted a return to the more "simulacral realism" exemplified by *Julia.* One letter writer suggested that *Good Times* presented a representation "quite encouraging to the white race and discouraging to the brothers and sisters." Another letter asked, "Why can't we have a program featuring a middle-class black family headed by a professional father? We know too well about lower-class living. . . . We need an ideal that we can strive toward rather than a show to cheer us up and make us content to laugh at the present predicament of our people."[28] These sentiments echoed a number of letters written to Allan Manings. One black viewer criticized the fact that the Evanses never seemed to rise above their current station. "Why must the father be out of a steady job no matter how willing he is to work? Why can't he have some semblance of education, be it self-taught or acquired from institutions of learning? Why is the mother constantly looking for the picture of Jesus Christ to have mercy instead of arming herself with the strength of her faith and getting up and dealing with the problems at hand?" The writer also criticized J.J.'s stealing and Thelma's preoccupation with her looks. The writer goes on to say, "The show does importantly portrait [sic] a black family that is pulling together. But that family is too stereotyped and more should be shown of them improving their situation."[29]

These viewers, unfortunately, would have a decade-long wait for the show they were calling for. In 1984, *The Cosby Show* did indeed give American viewers a black family that was middle class (actually upper class) with a professional father (and mother) and that was in no way "stereotyped." In the politics of "good role models," the representation of a poor black family that was not obviously "movin' on up" would have little political utility to black audiences who, according to these viewers, needed lessons on how to rise above their situations.

Here we see a tension between the show's impulses toward "realism" and its impulses toward "positive role models." It was far more "realistic" to show how institutional racism and the vicissitudes of poverty trap families into a prison box of disadvantage. On the other hand, such representations might not appear particularly empowering—at least not by black viewers with more middle-class sensibilities.

Six years earlier, with *Julia,* network television gave viewers a middle-class black family with an emphasis on "positive" and fully integrated black characters. But the show suffered a barrage of criticism for its lack of realism. TV critics like Robert Lewis Shayon made much of the fact that Julia and Corey Baker could not have been further from the ghetto if they tried. By 1974, in a postintegration-ist, post–racial optimism era, *Good Times,* along with the other "ghetto comedies," suggested how fraught televisual representations of blacks remained in the post–civil rights era. In the struggle over "realism" and "positive role models," the question of black images in popular culture assumed a higher profile than they had during the black freedom and equality movement. Neither *East Side/West Side* nor *Julia*—nor even the network news programming we examined in the first section—garnered the amount of commentary in the black press that *Amos 'n' Andy* and *Beulah* received in the immediate pre-movement period. And none received the amount of commentary that *Good Times* got in the immediate post-movement era. As activist politics ebbed, image politics reasserted their importance. A key battle over image politics centered on the representation of J.J. Evans, also known as "Kid Dyn-O-Mite!"

Kid Dyn-O-Mite: New Minstrelsy?

Good Times was originally developed as a vehicle for Esther Rolle, who had achieved great popularity as the tough-talking maid in Norman Lear's *All in the Family* spin-off hit, *Maude* (CBS, 1972–78). Having battled to secure a husband, Rolle's new series was supposed to focus on her character and John Amos as James Evans Sr. According to producer Allan Manings, if the show were to have a breakout star, he initially thought it would be Ralph Carter as Michael.[30] However, early in the first season, popular attention shifted to the eldest son, jokester, jive-talker, and aspiring artist J.J. Jimmie Walker, who took the role, was a stand-up comic, not an actor. His performance style thus differed markedly from the stage- and screen-trained Rolle, Amos, and Carter.[31] He used his impossibly skinny and pointy body in much of his comedy, frequently sauntering across the set, elbows at odd angles, and long fingers jutting out. His famous catchphrase was inserted in an almost obligatory manner into each episode. For instance, in a show where James completes a course in heavy equipment operation to qualify for higher-paying work, J.J. proclaims: "Hail to King James! A man of courage. A man of might. And the proud father of Kid [hand clap] DYN-O-MITE!"[32] The studio audience explodes. These moments were clearly privileged in the series and played to guaranteed audience response. Walker also used his face, with big, rubbery lips and bug eyes, to comic effect with regular extreme close-ups to accentuate the grinning, pop-eyed routines. No other cast member on the show engaged in this form of exaggerated physical comedy.

J. Fred MacDonald, in his history of blacks in American television, places J.J. firmly within "the age of new minstrelsy" of 1970s-era black comedies. Mac-Donald describes J.J. as "ultimately related to Mr. Tambo and Mr. Bones, those demeaning coons of another century."[33] Marlon Riggs, in his well-known documentary on the same subject, comes to similar conclusions. He superimposes images of nineteenth century minstrel figures over a slow-motion compilation of shots showing J.J. prancing. The remarkable similarity in bodily representation between the original minstrels and this latter-day version are undeniable.[34]

J.J. is a troubling figure because the show appeared to take seriously a mandate to present "good role models" and to be a force for racial amelioration and consciousness-raising among audiences. How could a project with such obviously liberal and race-conscious intentions circulate such a retrograde and demeaning image of blackness? John Fiske's theories of popular culture are useful here. He argues that television can be progressive, but not radical. He points out that "how-

The new minstrelsy: Kid Dyn-O-Mite and the undercutting of the "good role models" strategy.

ever we might wish to change the social meanings and textual representations of, say, women or nonwhite races, such change can only be slow and evolutionary, not radical and revolutionary, if the texts are to remain popular."[35] Popular texts cannot be free of the power structures and racial regimes that dominate the social order and that attempt to privilege particular meanings. *Good Times* took a progressive step forward in portraying an inner-city, intact, and functional black family, but the show needed to negotiate that progressiveness in racial imagery with a familiar sitcom family of warmth and good humor, but also a more reactionary "coonish" image traditionally associated in the white American imagination with "black humor." According to Fiske's argument, *Good Times* without J.J. might have been too radical, too different to achieve the popular relevancy and polysemy necessary to allow 1970s heterogeneous audiences to find narrative purchase in this text.

Within the reception context, J.J. provided a great deal of productive and contentious debate about the politics of racial imagery. Especially within the African American press, Esther Rolle and Jimmie Walker circulated contesting analyses about the social/political significance of their show.[36] In a major *Ebony* exposé at the beginning of the show's second season documenting trouble on the set and discontent among the cast about directions the series appeared to be taking, Rolle and Walker's differing attitudes about the politics of black representation were on display. Rolle complained: "He's 18 and he doesn't work. He can't read and write. He doesn't think. The show didn't start out to be that. Michael's role of a bright, thinking child has been subtly reduced. Little by little—with the help of the artist, I suppose, because they couldn't do that to me—they have made him [J.J.] more stupid and enlarged the role. [Negative images] have been quietly slipped in on us through the character of the oldest child. I resent the imagery that says to black kids that you can make it by standing on the corner saying 'Dyn-o-mite'!"[37]

Here and in her many other press interviews, Rolle speaks within the discourse of civil rights and, to some extent, black power and Afrocentricity. Rolle emphasizes over and over again the effect on black children of stereotyped black imagery. This concerned her far more than responses from white viewers. For Rolle, the struggle over black images was political and had significant repercussions for the African American community.

In another story in *Ebony* during the show's first season, Rolle said: "I've always been selective about my roles . . . still am . . . I couldn't like me if I depicted crap that made a black child hang its head. I feel an obligation to do something that will make him stick his little chest out and say, 'Did you see *that!?*' My goal is to give black women dignity."[38] Rolle connected her acting to the black community and its empowerment. Her series was a part of that community and needed to be responsive to it. *Good Times*, thus, had "extra-special effects."[39] It influenced the black community palpably and had either beneficial or deleterious material effects. As with *Julia* and *I Spy*, *Good Times* was not just a TV show with black characters; the show contributed directly to the social status of black people in relation to the white power structure.

Jimmie Walker, on the other hand, was almost wholly apolitical, reflecting no sense that black representations mattered, or that *Good Times* as a TV series in any way pursued a black empowerment agenda or had any effects on black material conditions at all. In the *Ebony* exposé, Walker responded to questions about positive black images, by declaring, "I don't think any TV show can put out an image to save people."[40] In *Jet* he argued, "It's a tough situation, having kids. . . . So parents sit them down in front of a TV and they want me to be a babysitter. That's not my job . . . Kids need parental guidance—they shouldn't look to me or the TV for that."[41]

Walker's public persona emphasized individuality over and over again. His focus was always on his own career, his hard work, and his drive to succeed. He never made any connection to the black community or its needs. For the twentysomething Walker, the struggles of the civil rights/black power movements seemed irrelevant. J.J. and his creator emphatically refused to participate in the "struggle for blackness": "All I do is deliver the lines the writers [by now mostly white] turn out for the series."[42]

Executive Producer Allan Manings also weighed in on the debate about J.J. Although very few letters in the producer's collected papers deal with the controversy, Manings' responses to the handful of letters that did raise questions about the character, are telling in their extreme defensiveness.[43] One gets the sense that Manings was very touchy about any suggestion that his series was less than exemplary in its approach to black images. His stock response to critical letters was to accuse the letter writer of racism. One viewer, echoing Esther Rolle's complaint about J.J. as a negative role model, wrote: "As you know racism is directed most virulently at black males in this age group and I dare say that most of the appeal of the character to white viewers lies in the fact that you have decided to portray J.J. as a poor student who is quite silly. Art ability as attached to the portrayal has some ameliorative effect but the stereotype of an anti-intellectual clown feeds white racism and is hurting efforts to develop black youth."[44] To this not unreasonable critique, Manings replied: "Forgive me if I detect a note of racism in your letter when you indicate the appeal of J.J. to white viewers is based on his being silly and a poor student. Rather than being silly, the character is that of a clown who sees things a little bit different than other members of his family and he is a very serious student of his art. I must point out to you that J.J. is not only liked by whites but our mail indicates that he is equally or more loved by black viewers and quite often for his artistic aspirations."[45]

While Rolle and this viewer emphasized J.J.'s detrimental image for black youth, Manings, perhaps suffering sublimated white liberal guilt, tried to convince his correspondent (and perhaps himself) that J.J. was actually a positive role model for black youths. Downplaying J.J.'s buffoonish aspects that were his main claim to fame, Manings insisted on overemphasizing J.J.'s artistic abilities. Proclaimed Manings: "We have in many episodes indicated J.J. referring to art books and art history books. He has been and will be involved in art shows. He will study in art school and work to support himself." J.J.'s art career was, of course, only a rather artificial add-on. Donald Bogle has noted, "Nothing about J.J. ever suggested he had any artistic impulse or temperament."[46]

For a liberal like Manings (and likely his white writers, too), obviously molded by the political ideals of the civil rights movement, the unexpected pop-culture phenomenon of J.J. could only have been a mixed blessing. In his letters to viewers, Manings embraced not only color-blind integrationism but also the discourse of good role models. In one letter Manings explains the problem of getting the right stories and "the added [problem] of being as positive as possible that nothing we do will be derogatory to Blacks . . . or to anyone."[47] Manings found himself with a minstrel coon on his hands, a representation that was utterly at odds with his talk of positive images. On the other hand, this minstrel coon had helped shoot Manings' series into the Nielsen's top ten.[48] Unlike Esther Rolle, Manings could not separate himself from the phenomenon of J.J. Manings thus had to negotiate the representation and find a race-positive strategy for making sense of the character. Over-privileging J.J.'s artistic aspirations and his presumed appeal to black viewers may have assuaged Manings' liberal guilt that a TV series premised on "authenticity" and "good role models" had, at its center, a figure that undercut all these representational ideals. Manings also attempted to find solace in the argument that J.J. was not, in fact, the creation of whites after all. Responding to the letter writer who criticized J.J. and who made a point about the ludicrous costuming of black performers, Manings fumed, "It is somewhat arrogant of you to assume that white writers and white directors and not a black actor put that hat on J.J." If a black performer created this representation, then it couldn't be detrimental: it was "authentically" black. And the white production personnel who amplified and profited from this creation were in no way culpable for its circulation.

The increasing centrality of J.J. did have some fans, however. A visiting scholar at the conservative American Enterprise Institute had this to say in the pages of the *Wall Street Journal*: "'Good Times' is now essentially a showcase for Jimmy [sic] Walker. . . . The new format puts J.J. at the center where he has room to operate. The action is fast-paced—some of the vignettes aren't much more than thirty seconds long. Basically the script tries not to fight the character, to allow J.J. to bring things to a halt every few minutes. No one is much interested in the plot anyhow, which is characteristic of good comedy."[49] This writer appears uncomfortable with socially and politically engaged approaches to comedy—the social relevance that was a trademark of the comedies associated with Norman Lear. Black and white supporters of *Good Times* in its early incarnation lauded the series precisely *because* it constructed its plots around African American social problems: for instance, hypertension in black men, the problems of youth gangs, the high cost of uninsured medical care, price gouging at ghetto grocery stores. Plots like these may have indeed been uncomfortable for conservative whites like the *Wall Street Journal* columnist. J.J.'s rise to centrality tended to shunt such narrative preoccupations off to the margins, and with them any pretense to a liberal, educational mandate. The rise of Kid Dyn-O-Mite indicates just how difficult it was to sustain narratives about African American poverty, "positive images," and empowering images of "blackness" in prime time. The *Wall Street Journal* piece gives some clue to the kind of white resistance such socially engaged representations could face.

The Return of a "Black Matriarchy": Killing Off James Evans Sr.

Along with the elevation of J.J. as star, the next major blow to the politics of authenticity for *Good Times* was the departure of John Amos after the series' third season. Press accounts quibbled over whether Amos had asked to be released from his contract or whether he had been fired. The African American press, privileging Amos and the people around him, got it right. Amos had been uncompromisingly critical of scripts and of J.J.'s elevation, and he had a generally abrasive relationship with Norman Lear. New York's black newspaper, the *Amsterdam News,* explained matters within a context of black/white power relations, suggesting a master/slave dynamic: "Here was ol' Norm giving all these spooks new sacks to pick cotton and there they were complainin' about the plantation."[50]

In 1974 the African American press touted *Good Times* as Michael Evans and Eric Monte's show and thus, implicitly, the property of black creators. Later, in 1976, it was Norman Lear's plantation. White power was now in control and blacks were back in their familiar, disempowered positions. Evans and Monte were no longer involved and the series had almost no black writers. All the markers of black "authenticity" were now gone. The *St. Louis Sentinel* mourned, "What started as a promising comedy series about a struggling black family in a Chicago slum has degenerated into a slap happy showcase of bellylaughs starring a 1976 adolescent version of Stepin Fetchit."[51]

The most tragic and ironic aspect of John Amos's ouster was that the first black TV family with a strong male head was now fatherless. Like Julia Baker before her, Esther Rolle's Florida would hereafter be in exactly the situation the actress has fought against so vehemently during the series' development. Allan Manings, who had proudly emphasized in letters to viewers the importance of portraying an intact black family, now declared, "There are other realities that deserve exploration—the fatherless family does exist in the ghetto."[52] It certainly would be more "realistic" to portray the Evans family as fatherless. However, only Amos's powerful presence as a counter to J.J. gave legitimacy to the claim that the series provided "good role models."

The National Black Media Coalition, a Washington, D.C.–based lobbying group, immediately sprang into action. The group clearly assumed the show's "extra-special effects" for the black community and the negative ramifications for African Americans' material circumstances with Amos's departure. The coalition launched a letter-writing campaign to the show's producers demanding an immediate replacement for John Amos.[53] Coalition chairman Pluria Marshall argued that black children, who watched a great deal of television, "desperately need positive black male images." He pointed to a recent Howard University study about the meanings black youngsters made of televised black images. According to the study's examination of *Good Times*, the children perceived James Sr. as a weak provider; however, "he was clearly seen as a strong father figure by black children viewing the show."[54] Killing off James would be akin to depriving these children of a virtual father, and the impact would be akin to the loss of a flesh-and-blood patriarch.

Mark Anthony Neal, in *Soul Babies*, his book about black popular culture, discusses at length the significance of both James's presence and his disappearance from the Evans family. He argues that the fictional death of James "has become a metaphor for the absence of black men in the black community, and that this absence represents a kind of trauma for the community."[55] He points to a number of more recent black popular-culture references to James's death in hip hop lyrics and in television programs produced by African Americans. Why are these members of the post–civil rights/black-power generation recovering this particular moment in popular culture over and over again? Neal suggests that it is "lodged in [the generation's] collective memory" as loss and trauma.[56]

The death of James also appeared to be intensely painful to the African American creative personnel who worked on the series. In a documentary about the making of *Good Times*, Judy Ann Mason, one of the show's very few black writers, speaks in rather anguished tones about the situation: "They killed that family when they killed that father. The show died when James Evans died." Ralph Carter recalls that the show was no longer the same and that he no longer enjoyed the work after Amos left.[57] A year later, Esther Rolle also left the series telling the *New York Daily News*, "They're not interested in the poor images that are being put across to the young viewers."[58] Irma Kalish, one of the show's principle writers, recalls Norman Lear coming to her and the other writers to ask if they could do a show without the mother or the father: "We said we could. We could deal with it."[59] In the struggle for "blackness," authenticity, and ownership, white power prevailed over black sociocultural needs. White creative personnel may have been able to "deal with" the amputation of the Evans family, treating it as merely another writing problem to solve on just another TV sitcom that was beginning to lose its vitality. For black creative personnel and for black audiences, the stakes appeared to be much, much higher.

Conclusion: The End of *Good Times*

After John Amos's departure, the series limped along for three more years, descending steadily in the ratings each season. The producers and writers tried unsuccessfully to give Florida a new man to fill James's empty space. J.J. began finally to "grow up," taking a job in an ad agency and becoming less overtly buffoonish—but also less funny. New characters were introduced in a vain attempt to revitalize the show. The series tried to reconnect with its socially relevant origins by having the Evanses' wise-cracking neighbor Willona adopt an abused child. After bowing out in the fifth season, Rolle agreed to return in the sixth—and ultimately final—season, telling the *Amsterdam News* that it wasn't "her right to withhold from the public anything that would help the imagery." In a final attempt to assert a measure of black cultural ownership over the show, Rolle proclaimed to the paper's black readership her ability to assert a higher quality in the scripts. She pointed out the problem of the writers allowing Willona to be out all the time, leaving little Penny, her adopted daughter, constantly with the Evans family: "This is a lack of supervision and it couldn't happen with me in the show. I'd refuse to do it. They can't be that loose in my house!"[60] From "ole Norm's plantation" the discourse of cultural ownership now tried to turn *Good Times* into "Mama Florida's house."

CBS cancelled the series during the 1978–79 season, but perhaps, in an attempt to appease those viewers who wanted the Evanses to transcend their situation, the final episode, in a *deus ex machina* fashion, finally moved the Evans family and neighbor Willona out of the projects. J.J. announces that he has sold his comic strip idea to a newspaper syndicate, Thelma's football playing husband announces that he's finally received a pro-ball contract, and Willona announces that she's been promoted to head buyer for her clothing store. After five years of toiling within the permanent underclass, the Evanses were to be vaunted into the black middle class. Viewers, of course, would never get to see them assume their upwardly mobile positions.

Although *Good Times* left prime time in August 1979, the show's cultural half life has continued in the recovery activity that Mark Anthony Neal discusses, and in its influence on latter-day black representations, such as the 1990s black family sitcom, *Family Matters* (ABC, 1989–98). That show's breakout star Jaleel White (as Steve Urkel), although more intellectually equipped than J.J. Evans, also recirculated the clownish, physically grotesque characteristics of Kid Dyn-O-Mite.

Unresolved questions remain about the cultural legacy of the show's racial imagery. What can we say about its effort to circulate "positive images," and for whom might those images be "positive?" Conflicting testimony from two of *Good*

Times' creative personnel suggest the complex and racially charged nature of the questions. The documentary on the making of the series places side by side the assessments of Judy Ann Mason, a black writer for the series, and Austin Kalish, a white writer-producer for the show. Mason, in an emotional and personally troubled tone states, "I left that show very ashamed of the fact that I had worked on the show . . . There was so much pain . . . in realizing that maybe we had done something wrong. The attempt to present realistic black life had failed." In a more emotionally neutral and impersonal tone, Kalish, observes, "[*Good Times* will] always be relevant because it's about a family, and it has to do with a family hanging together."[61]

Like Esther Rolle, Mason, as an African American, takes personal responsibility for the show and its representations. She emphasizes the ramifications to the black community of these "failed" images. To have failed in circulating "realistic" images of black life has costs. Kalish, on the other hand, evacuates any sign of blackness from his analysis. Appealing to universalisms about families hanging together, *Good Times* ultimately is not really about blackness or positive black representations; it's merely about positive families. By not assessing the show on its struggle over the sign of blackness, Kalish can deem the show a success for his colorless audiences. Mason, on the other hand, bogged down by an unrealizable quest for the authentic, could see the show as nothing but a tragic failure for black audiences and the wider black community.

Ultimately the show was both a success and a failure. Its groundbreaking attempts to circulate progressive and empowering images of African Americans along with socially relevant representations of poverty and racism inevitably and inextricably needed to be harnessed to older, regressive images so as not to alienate and alarm white audiences too much. The saga of *Good Times* reveals that prime time television could indeed provide a venue for the exploration of hitherto unrepresented aspects of African American life in the wake of the revolution in race relations of the 1960s. However, such representations could only be compromised ones. As a popular-culture institution, prime-time television could no more transcend power structures of white dominance and meaning construction than could other social, cultural, or political institutions. That prime-time television served as a venue for negotiating new and potentially empowering representations for African Americans during this period is a testament to the cultural power of the movement for black empowerment to assert itself in prime time. For a short period, black cultural producers with their liberal white allies (albeit soon-to-be adversaries) managed to circulate a discourse that was different, grounded in the particularities of inner-city black life, and did so from at least the semblance of a black point of view.

The Return of Civil Rights Television
The Obama Victory

On March 5, 2007, television cameras returned to Selma, Alabama. CNN's viewers saw footage of the day that looked similar to what viewers watching Selma coverage forty-two years ago saw night after night: shots of black people singing "We Shall Overcome"; individualized portraits of dignity, such as an elderly black man presented in a low-angle tilt, marching while holding an American flag; black and white crowds pouring over the Edmund Pettus Bridge. But this was not file footage hauled out of the archives. CNN and the other television news organizations were in Selma that day because Hillary Clinton, husband Bill, and Barack Obama were all in town in the early days of the Democratic primary season.[1] Yet all these decades later, CNN relied on a fixed semiotics for illustrating stories that touched on the civil rights movement.

CNN's correspondent Candy Crowley framed the story as a battle between Clinton and Obama, each "laying claim to the legacy of Selma in the search for black votes."[2] Clinton connected her run as a woman, Bill Richardson's as a Latino, and Obama's as an African American to Selma's "gift that keeps on giving." But it was Obama, shown speaking inside Brown Chapel and using cadences recalling those of Martin Luther King, who seemed to capture that legacy best for television cameras. Preaching from the pulpit, Obama declared to waves of applause, "Don't tell me I'm not coming home to Selma, Alabama! I'm here because somebody marched—for our freedom. I'm here because you all sacrificed—for me. I stand on the shoulders of giants."

Media coverage of Obama's historic run for the White House occasionally made use of a civil rights discourse. Obama's nomination as the Democrats' presidential candidate just happened to coincide with the anniversary of the March on Washington. Inauguration day just happened to fall the day after Martin Luther King Day. Both these scheduling coincidences helped the news media frame Obama's victories in connection to King, even as Obama himself appeared more interested in connecting himself to Abraham Lincoln. Yet on election night, cable and network news outlets fully embraced the civil rights discourse in making sense for their viewers the meaning of the Obama victory.

On CNN just after Wolf Blitzer announced that Barack Obama would be the next president of the United States, he turned to his panel of pundits for comments. Roland Martin was first, observing that Obama would be inaugurated in the one-hundredth-year anniversary of the NAACP. David Gergen connected Obama to King by quoting from his final speech about having been to the mountaintop and having seen the Promised Land. Gergen suggested that America was now closer to that Promised Land. At CBS, veteran newsman Bob Schieffer told anchor Katie Couric that he had attended segregated schools in the South and that no black had ever attended any school he had gone to: "Look where we have come to in less than my lifetime." On Fox News, Juan Williams, an African American commentator and historian of the civil rights movement, teared up on camera and linked Obama's victory to the history of voting for blacks and the importance of 1965. He proclaimed that this was "America at its finest." Over at NBC, Brian Williams announced the next occupant of the White House by saying the mansion would house young children for the first time since the Kennedy years and that "African Americans have broken a barrier as old as the republic." Williams turned to civil rights luminary John Lewis and observed, "You risked your life for this."[3]

In the minutes following the announcement that Barack Obama would be the next president, all these television news outlets made sense of the victory by connecting it insistently and repeatedly to King and Selma, while, in general, marking it as the culmination of the civil rights movement. In the narrative trajectory of civil rights for television news, at least, Obama's victory served as the denouement, the triumphant conclusion of the story, the happy ending that all Americans could now celebrate.

Network television had such an easy time folding Obama into this civil rights discourse in part because he, and just as significantly, wife Michelle and their two daughters, could so easily occupy the position of "civil rights subject," a trope we have encountered over and over again across these pages. While Obama cannot be reduced to this subject position, the fact that it was a position he could inhabit with such ease ensured that white Americans could be comfortable with him—and with his black wife and children who would all occupy the White House. Blogger and cultural critic Alisa Valdes Rodriguez's heavily discussed online article on the "Huxtable Effect" provides a useful bridge from Herman Grey's original concept of the "civil rights subject" to its more recent mobilization in the Age of Obama.

Rodriguez, assuming television's "extra-special effects" when it comes to images of blacks for the wider viewing community, suggests that television in the 1980s heralded Obama by ensuring that a new generation of Americans would be comfortable with a black president. "For those of us paying attention to shifts in popular culture and public consciousness," Rodriguez argued, "Obama came as no surprise; he was as predictable as a happy ending to a Cosby Show rerun."[4] Obama reaped the benefits in the realm of politics that positive, black, pop-cultural figures like Oprah Winfrey and Denzel Washington had sown in the realm of culture.

Herman Gray's work on black televisual representations in the Reagan years provides a more nuanced and complicated argument than Rodriguez's blogosphere thought piece, but the overall positions are similar. Gray points out the many ways that the Reagan administration and the New Right attempted to undermine the moral authority and claims to entitlement African Americans had achieved in the wake of the civil rights movement, along with the "culture of civility" that ground racial matters in the immediate post–civil rights years.[5] Gray shows how Republicans under the Reagan and first Bush administrations used representations of unworthy and frightening black bodies—rapist Willie Horton, "welfare queens," and black, unmarried teen mothers—to foment white resentment but, on the other hand, held up and celebrated black conservatives and representations of black middle class success, such as Bill Cosby, to avert charges of racism.[6]

But with respect to television and the cultural realm more generally, Gray asserts that African Americans provided a powerful counterforce pushing against the politics and representations of Reaganite racial resentment and fear: "Commercial media sites such as film, television, video, and music were among the most fertile social arenas in which African Americans engaged each other (and whites) over questions of African American presence in the United States."[7] Unlike most of what we have seen in televisual representations from the 1950s and 1960s, many of the images of "blackness" circulating in the 1980s and early 1990s were to some extent under the control of blacks themselves. And for Gray, what makes this period so significant is the heterogeneity and multiplicity of images on display.

So, as Gray ably points out, on TV screens in this era, viewers could start their day with figures like a suave Bryant Gumbel hosting a morning news and chat show and then move to the afternoon with an emotive and sisterly Oprah doing her talk show. During the news hour, viewers could tune in as black correspondents covered stories about black drug gangs or teenage welfare moms on the local and network news. In niche hour syndication, 1970s-era black sitcoms like *The Jeffersons* and *Good Times* ran in daily rerun while in prime time huge audiences tuned in weekly to *The Cosby Show*. Then, at the end of the broadcast day, late-night audiences had the debonair Arsenio Hall to entertain them before bedtime.[8]

Popular culture in the 1980s and 1990s may have been awash in a sea of often competing "signs of blackness," but certainly the most popular ones for heterogeneous audiences were those representations that did not trouble the social order too much and that could be embraced by a variety of differently situated audiences. This brings us back to *The Cosby Show* and to election night 2008.

On Fox News, the second George Bush's former advisor and political strategist, Karl Rove, made sense of the Obama victory by opining, "We've had an African American first family for many years in different forms. When 'The Cosby Show' was on, that was America's family. It wasn't a black family. It was America's family."[9] Rove's color-blind reading, his refusal to see difference, was certainly not unique. We have seen this reading strategy before as white Americans grappled, often painfully, fitfully, and with conflicted sense through the civil rights years with media representations of racial change. Just as some *Julia* fans embraced that show because Julia and Corey could be welcomed into white living rooms as people "just like everyone else," many white fans of *The Cosby Show* twenty years later would seek out the same comfort.

Sut Jhally and Justin Lewis in their audience study of *Cosby* viewers undertaken in the late 1980s and early 1990s found many white viewers insisting on the colorlessness of the Huxtable family. They would "forget" the family's blackness, or consider it unimportant because the family was so "typical" and "average."[10] *Julia* viewers could not "forget" the Baker family's blackness quite so effortlessly in large part because of the novelty of the imagery and also because the racial turmoil of the period forced whites to grapple with questions of race relations. By the 1980s and 1990s, these representations of professional, middle-class, respectable blacks who had "made it" by all the dominant markers of success and achievement, these "civil rights subjects," could have their blackness peeled off by white viewers who no longer felt they needed to grapple with issues of difference when encountering these images.

Jhally and Lewis were not encouraged by this color blindness, seeing it as a means for white viewers to avoid acknowledging the continued existence of systemic racism in American society. In fact, numerous viewers used the success of the Huxtables to argue that examples of civil rights legislation, such as affirmative action, were no longer needed. "Racism, in other words," writes Lewis, "is a disease that has been cured—no further medicine is required."[11] Not surprisingly, black viewers studied by Jhally and Lewis read the show very differently—insistent on seeing blackness and celebrating the Huxtables as "positive images."

So, to return to "the Huxtable Effect" and its assumed impact on the election of the first black president of the United States. Jhally and Lewis's findings should temper the hosannas about a "post-racial America" that has successfully worked its way through the challenges of the civil rights revolution and that has used television representations to build affinity between black and white. As with the Huxtables, many white Americans could "forget" the Obamas' blackness and focus on their "averageness" as an American family—where "average" equates with upper middle class.[12] Rove may have been correct in suggesting that the Obamas could become America's black First Family because the nation had already welcomed another "black first family": one that whites, like Rove, could render colorless.

While it is both reductive and simplistic to suggest that network television's circulation and audiences' embrace of certain types of black representation have led to the election of a black president, this book has traced the mobilization of a certain type of image that, when appropriately paired with figures of whiteness, were presumed to make whites less anxious about social change. From David Robertson, the black Cornell grad student and National Science Foundation member deemed illiterate by Mississippi voting registrars, to the dignified and crisply dressed marchers in the nation's capital petitioning with smiles for civil rights legislation or marching with flags and fortitude to Montgomery for voting rights, to Mr. and Mrs. Marsden, the eminently respectable couple trying to integrate a Long Island suburb, to Julia Baker effortlessly living and working with accommodating whites in Los Angeles, to, finally, the Huxtables and now the Obama First Family, we see a common link in these representations of a dignified blackness yoked to an accommodating and welcoming whiteness. If "black and white together" has been one of the recurring themes throughout these pages and across many of our case studies, it may not be too great a stretch to see that theme literally embodied in the figure of Barack Obama who, as he famously described himself, was "the son of a black man from Kenya and a white woman from Kansas."[13]

The story of "black and white together," the story of the "worthy black victim," and the story of the aspirational "civil rights subject": all these were narratives that network television liked to tell. The medium certainly did tell other stories of race relations, and with *Good Times* we saw an example of a different sort of discourse. But that representation may only have been possible at that particular moment in the aftermath of the civil rights and black power movements when television, for a brief period, was open to embracing some of the political positions associated with the social change movements of the era.[14] That *Good Times* remains a somewhat anomalous text with its focus on black poverty and sociopolitical issues suggests that despite this show's popularity, it did not provide a template for stories that television would want to continue telling. Similarly, *East Side/West Side* provided a different way to figure the "black and white together" theme, but it did not tell the feel-good story about that relationship that would comfort white audiences. Ultimately, it would be *I Spy* and *Julia* that provided television with its template for the kind of story about race that the medium felt most comfortable telling and which seemed to reach its apotheosis with the spectacular success of *The Cosby Show*.

So on election night 2008, when the broadcast and cable networks celebrated black and white voters coming together to put a biracial black man into the White House, they were returning to a familiar story.[15] For the news divisions, the election of a black president was a story of American triumph and moral clarity that seemed the culmination of the previous stories of triumph and moral clarity that we saw in the March on Washington and the Selma-to-Montgomery coverage.

All were stories packaged to make Americans feel good about their country and its race relations, all allowed news commentators to engage in a certain amount of utopian gushing. Celebratory coverage of civil rights media events in the 1960s gave viewers a "peek into utopia" that still lay in the future. Fictional shows of the civil rights era like *Julia* suggested what the "black and white together" future might look like. And then on election night 2008, news commentators told America the country was closer than ever to that racial utopia. CNN provided its viewers with shots of the exultant crowd of over two hundred thousand people in Chicago cheering their adopted son's victory. And just like the coverage of the March on Washington, the cable channel's cameras searched out images that framed blacks and whites together and that provided individual "portraits of dignity." And like the Selma-to-Montgomery coverage, cameras focused on the blizzard of American flags. Television news personnel probably had no idea that they were borrowing from an old script, but television's civil rights discourse was so deeply embedded in the medium's meaning-making regimes that the appearance of these themes and visual tropes may have been almost inevitable.

NOTES

Introduction

1. *CBS Evening News with Walter Cronkite,* CBS, March 17, 1965.

2. Garrow, *Protest at Selma,* 111.

3. "Playback: A Monthly Measure of Comment and Criticism About TV," *Television,* April 1965, 27.

4. Garrow, *Protest at Selma,* 226–27. Also Torres, 30.

5. Steinberg, 142.

6. The term comes from an NBC Washington bureau chief reflecting in 1965 on the relationship between television news and the civil rights movement. The term is used by television historian Mary Ann Watson (*The Expanding Vista*) in her chapter on the civil rights movement and television.

7. Theoretical and ethnographic work in media studies has long since undercut the notion of unified texts delivering singular messages to passive audiences structured to read the texts as producers dictate. However, historians of the twentieth century who take note of the importance of television tend to hold on to more simplistic notions of popular media and its audiences. Civil rights historian Brian Ward has noted, "Mainstream Movement historians have continued to pay relatively little attention to the various insights that scholars from elsewhere in the humanities—in film, media studies, cultural studies, literature, music, and fine art—might offer into a period whose changing race relations and protest politics they otherwise study so assiduously." See Ward, *Media,* 2. Ward's useful anthology includes articles about civil rights and black power relationships to print media, film, literature, radio, and music, but nothing about television.

8. See chapter 2 for more on how TV newsmen made sense of their civil rights movement coverage.

9. Torres, 23.

10. This argument is put forth in MacDonald.

11. Gray, "Remembering Civil Rights," 353–54.

12. See "Mississippi and the 15th Amendment," *CBS Reports,* discussed in chapter 2.

13. See "Color Line on Campus," *Eyewitness,* discussed in chapter 2.

14. We will see this particularly in coverage of the 1963 March on Washington and the 1965 Selma campaign in, respectively, chapters 4 and 5.

15. See, respectively, "No Hiding Place," *East Side/West Side,* discussed in chapter 6, and *Julia,* discussed in chapter 7.

16. See Harper.

17. See in particular chapters 3 and 5.

18. See in particular chapter 2.

19. Herbert Gans, in his seminal study of television news in the 1960s and 1970s, argues that one of the key values of the news is "moderatism": he asserts, "Insofar as the news has an ideology of its own, it is moderate" (52).

20. See in particular chapters 3 and 5.

21. Hale, 291.

22. Ibid.

23. Ibid., 128.

24. Ibid., 137.

25. Classen found, through his ethnographic work with black residents of Jackson, Mississippi, with regard to local television in the civil rights years, that his respondents when prompted to discuss television tended to want to discuss the medium "'of a piece' with larger civil rights struggles—past and present" (165). More generally, he notes that offensive television was of minor concern compared with survival and desegregation issues black Mississippians faced in these turbulent years (159).

26. See Haralovich, "*I Spy's* 'Living Postcards.'"

27. Nadel, 171.

28. Ibid., 119.

29. For more on the move to "socially relevant" programming in network prime time, see Bodroghkozy, 199–235.

30. Morley, 18.

31. See, for instance, Fiske, *Understanding Popular Culture,* for an exploration of audience pleasure; see Jenkins for a discussion of fans as a participatory community around their active engagement with specific television programs.

32. Staiger, *Media Reception Studies.*

33. Spigel, 2.

34. See Ginzburg, 5–36.

35. Spigel, 2–4.

36. Raymond Williams argued that it was in the documentary record of a people or civilization that we can uncover some sense of what it felt like to live in that period. See *The Long Revolution,* 47–50.

Chapter 1. Propaganda Tool for Racial Progress?

1. "Television: Negro Performers Win Better Roles in TV Than in Any Other Entertainment Medium," *EB,* June 1950, 22–23.

2. Ibid., 23.

3. "Talmadge Hits TV for Mixing Races," *NYT,* January 6, 1952.

4. Ibid.

5. Joseph D. Bibb, "Issues on TV: Television Will Be a Great Force in Racial Progress," *PC,* February 9, 1952.

6. Because "Negro" was an accepted and respectful term in this period, it will be used interchangeably with "black" and "African American."

7. MacDonald, 5.

8. See Hilmes, 87–96; Ely.

9. Pondillo, 107.

10. Ibid., 108.

11. MacDonald, 4.

12. Stumpf and Price, 171.

13. Toll, 195–96, 226–27.

14. *PC,* April 5, 1952, 16; April 25, 1953, 18. In the 1953 poll, *Amos 'n' Andy,* the radio show, was in sixth place. In the TV rankings, however, *Amos 'n' Andy* was more popular, sitting in fourth place, while *Beulah* came in tenth.

15. "Waiting for Beulah," *PC,* magazine section, November 18, 1950.

16. Ibid., 3.

17. Ibid.

18. Hilmes, 90–91.

19. "Waiting for Beulah," 3.

20. Ibid.

21. See *HK,* Boxes 5–9 for scripts produced between 1947–49.

22. "GI's Resent Racial Slur in Program," *CD,* January 27, 1951.

23. McCorkle, 60–72. See also Donald Bogle's recent biography of Waters, *Heat Wave.*

24. *BAA,* magazine section, October 7, 1950.

25. "Ethel Waters Named as 1 of 25 Leading Women," *PC,* May 26, 1951.

26. "'Keep Going Forward—' Ethel's Key to Fame," *CD,* October 21, 1950.

27. Joseph D. Bibb, "'Beulah' Flayed: Famed Radio and TV Critic Condemns Ethel Waters and TV Show," *PC,* May 19, 1951.

28. "Bud Harris Tells Chicago Defender Why He Quit 'Beulah': Says Scripts Placed Negroes in Bad Light," *CD,* November 25, 1950.

29. Joseph D. Bibb, "Quits 'Tom' Role," *PC,* December 2, 1950.

30. *OW,* February, 1951, quoted in Jackson, 23.

31. Ely, 213.

32. "Resolution Adopted by the Forty-Second Annual Convention of the NAACP at Atlanta, GA, June 30, 1951," *TC,* August/September 1951, 478.

33. Ely, 212.

34. Letter to NAACP Branches, Youth Councils, and College Chapters, quoted in Ely, 219.

35. The direct address is also a highly privileged situation and creates a relationship of intimacy with the audience. It emphasizes Beulah's subjectivity, encouraging us to see the narrative through her eyes. Thanks to Susan J. Douglas for this insight.

36. Collins, 8.

37. Giddings, 249–50.

38. Ely, 220–27.

39. Paul L. Jones, "Amos 'n' Andy Television Show Offends Some, Pleases Other," *PC,* August 4, 1951.

40. Joseph D. Bibb, "Flays Amos 'n' Andy," *PC,* August 4, 1951.

41. Ely, 226.

42. Bogle, *Prime Time Blues,* 25.

43. Few episodes of the series appear to have survived, some anecdotal sources suggesting only seven. A number of episodes were released on VHS by Shokus Video in the 1980s, and the UCLA Film Archive houses some of them. Another episode is archived at MRT. At least one additional episode is currently available on the Internet at the Internet Archive (www.archive.org). Unfortunately, I have managed to locate only one episode starring Ethel Waters and none featuring Bud Harris. Episodes starring Hattie McDaniel are the most well-represented in the material I have located, which is curious, since she

played the role for only a short period. It is, therefore, difficult to generalize too confidently about the show and its representations from the small sampling I have access to. This particular episode is included in a Shokus Video entitled "Vintage Television, no. 241. Comedy and Kidstuff V."

44. Screened at MRT.

45. This episode is available at the Internet Archive.

46. Jones, 130. Jones quotes from a "Negro nurse" describing her slavery-like life circa 1912.

47. Turner, 13–18.

48. Bogle, 25–26.

49. Ibid., 34–35.

50. Jones, 130–31.

51. See Haralovich, "Sit-coms and Suburbs," 111–41.

52. The Shokus Video for this Ethel Waters episode contains a number of ads for Proctor and Gamble products. None of the other episodes include ads.

53. Lipsitz, 71–108.

54. MacDonald, 74.

55. Nadel, 41.

56. Ibid., 112–56.

Chapter 2. The Chosen Instrument of the Revolution?

1. Peters, 81. William Peters was a producer of *CBS Reports.*

2. Monroe, 83–84.

3. Smith, 312.

4. See Tuchman.

5. Gitlin, *Whole World,* 7.

6. Donovan and Scherer, 4.

7. Ibid.

8. Roberts and Klibanoff, 160.

9. Curtin, 122.

10. Ibid., 24.

11. Torres, 13.

12. Ibid., 15.

13. "A Study of Two Cities," *See It Now,* May 25, 1954, LOC.

14. "Clinton and the Law," *See It Now,* January 6, 1957, Robertson Media Center, University of Virginia.

15. Kasper was head of the Seaboard White Citizens' Council, which worked to prevent the desegregation of Washington D.C.'s public schools.

16. In September 1962 a federal court ordered the University of Mississippi to allow African American military veteran James Meredith to attend the previously all-white flagship campus. Governor Ross Barnett, in an attempt to salvage his sinking popularity among voters, galvanized segregationists against the integration of Ole Miss. A few days after the airing of "Mississippi and the 15th Amendment," rioting broke out on campus, leading to two deaths, scores of injuries, and a major political crisis. Meredith did enroll.

17. "Mississippi and the 15th Amendment," *CBS Reports,* September 26, 1962, LOC.

18. In her extended textual analysis of the *NBC White Paper* report "Sit-In" (aired De-

cember 20, 1960), Torres finds similar visual techniques employed by this report to render segregationists unsympathetic and visually unappealing. "'Sit-In' shoots most such interview subjects in unforgiving tight close-ups, their faces filling the frame luridly, suggesting a lack of perspective and over-proximity both to the camera and to their own self-serving desires." See Torres, 41.

19. Gray, "Remembering Civil Rights," 353.

20. Fiske, *Television Culture*, 7.

21. "Ole Miss Coverage Courageous, Complete," *BC*, October 8, 1962.

22. "Video's Massive News Week: Riots, Rockets, and Baseball," *VA*, October 3, 1962.

23. For more on the climate of criticism toward network television in the early 1960s and around Newton Minow's famous "Vast Wasteland" speech, see chapter 4.

24. NBC ad, *VA*, October 3, 1962.

25. "U.S. vs. Mississippi," *Eyewitness*, September 28, 1962, LOC.

26. Full text of *Chet Huntley Reporting*, October 2, 1962, GG, box 306, folder 7. The script for the program, which aired 10:30 PM, does not contain any information about visual material included in the report.

27. Full text of *Chet Huntley Reporting*, August 3, 1962, RF, box 292, folder 26. The script for this program contains some information about visual material included in the report.

28. "The Other Face of Dixie," *CBS Reports*, October 24, 1962, LOC.

29. Gans, 50.

30. "Color Line on Campus," *Eyewitness*, January 25, 1963, LOC.

31. After graduating from Clemson, Gantt went on to become the first black mayor of Charlotte, North Carolina. In the 1990s, he challenged Jesse Helms twice for Helms's U.S. Senate seat. In the 1990 campaign, Helms famously ran a racist attack ad that helped sink Gantt's candidacy.

32. *Eyewitness*, "The Albany Movement," August 3, 1962, LOC.

33. Torres, 41.

34. Ibid., 45.

35. "The Children Were Watching" aired February 16, 1961; "Walk in My Shoes" aired one week later that year on September 19. Curtin has examined the latter in detail. He argues that the documentary, in order to emphasize the need for liberal reform, presents long takes of Malcolm X giving a speech about the need for black militancy. The film also gives voice to numerous black points of view in various black idioms and refuses to come to a comforting closure. However, Curtin concludes that the documentary ultimately employs black-nationalist discourse within the confines of a white institution for a white audience and frames the issues as problems for the white majority to solve. See Curtin, 175.

36. Winston, 180. Winston's comments are quoted also in Curtin, 175.

Chapter 3. Fighting for Equal Time

1. "Rep. Williams Hits Fairness Doctrine," *BC*, August 28, 1963.

2. Ibid., 45.

3. While viewers invoked the term "equal time" frequently, it should be noted that within the regulatory regime, the "Equal Time Rule" provision of the 1934 Communications Act referred only to the requirement that broadcasters provide political candidates equal access to the airways during a campaign.

4. Monroe, 94

5. Brechner, 103–4. Brechner was president of WFTV, Orlando, Florida.

6. Classen, 50–51. As Classen points out, the FCC directive led almost immediately to a petition by local Jackson citizens and the communications department of the United Church of Christ to deny local WLBT-TV and WJTV license renewal. Their suit finally succeeded in 1969.

7. For more information about the series, see Einstein.

8. NBC interdepartmental correspondence, October 3, 1960, IG, box 303, folder 12, SHSW.

9. James J. Kilpatrick to Robert Allison, November 7, 1960, IG, box 303, folder 12, SHSW.

10. James J. Kilpatrick to Robert Allison, November 30, 1960, IG, box 303, folder 12, SHSW.

11. Wyatt Tee Walker to Robert Allison, December 2, 1960, IG, box 303, folder 12, SHSW.

12. It is unclear to me whether a copy of this program exists anymore. The Irving Gitlin Papers include statements from both King and Kilpatrick outlining their general lines of argument. King emphasizes the morality of civil disobedience against immoral laws; Kilpatrick emphasizes individual property rights.

13. Alfred J. Marrow, New York, to Irving Gitlin, December 5, 1960, IG, box 303, folder 12, SHSW.

14. Robert Allison to James J. Kilpatrick, December 2, 1960, IG, box 303, folder 12, SHSW.

15. Robert Allison to Rev. Martin Luther King, December 5, 1960, IG, box 303, folder 12, SHSW.

16. Garrow, *Bearing the Cross,* 150.

17. Curtin, 31.

18. Ibid., 150.

19. Jack Gould, "Television: Controversial Viewpoint on Integration," *NYT*, Feb. 2, 1959.

20. Ruby Hurley, no address, NAACP, part 17 supplement, reel 11.

21. J. W. E. Bowen, bishop of Methodist Church, Atlanta, NAACP, part 17 supplement, reel 11.

22. Script, "The Second Agony of Atlanta," NBC, box 295, folder 6.

23. Elizabeth Tarlton, Fort Worth, CH, box 3, folder, 1.

24. Joseph Turner Jr., Albany, Ga., CH, box 3, folder 2.

25. Colonel Lester, East Point, Ga., CH, box 3, folder 1.

26. Marjorie Morsell, Brooklyn, N.Y., CH, box 3, folder 1.

27. Guy R. Brewer, Jamaica, N.Y., and Betty J. Stebman, New York City, CH, box 3, folder 2.

28. Glenn E. Smiley, Nyack, NY, NAACP, part 17 supplement, reel 11.

29. See Hurley.

30. Classen, 37.

31. Classen, 37–38.

32. See Lipsitz.

33. Torres, 23.

34. Henry Lee Moon to Roy Wilkins, NAACP, part 17 supplement, reel 11.

35. Frank, 143.

36. Samuel M. Sharkey, Jr., NBC Editor of News, to Richard E. Carey, NAACP, part 17 supplement, reel 11.

37. Quoted in letter by Channing H. Tobias, Chairman, Board of Directors, NAACP, to Robert E. Kintner, President, NBC, NAACP, part 17 supplement, reel 11.

38. Roy Wilkins to unnamed letter writer, Larchmont, N.Y., NAACP, part 17 supplement, reel 12.

39. Roy Wilkins to David J. Sullivan, Marketing and Public Relations Counsel. Wilkins explains to Sullivan, "We had—literally—to measure every sentence, even every word, for image-arousal, related associations, color, accuracy, impact, collateral connotation, etc." NAACP, part 17 supplement, reel 12.

40. Ibid.

41. Dan Rather noted King's "well-honed ability to size up an audience." Late in his career as he turned his attention North, King grappled with the difficulties of appealing to black and white constituencies: "You just can't communicate with the ghetto dweller and at the same time not frighten many whites to death. I don't know what the answer is to that. My role perhaps is to interpret to the white world. There must be somebody to communicate to two worlds." Sundquist, 19.

42. Dubois, 3.

43. Gertrude M. Moore, Detroit, to Wilkins, NAACP, part 17 supplement, reel 12.

44. J. H. Calhoun [head of Atlanta NAACP], Atlanta, to Roy Wilkins, NAACP, part 17 supplement, reel 11.

45. Rev. J. N. Spellman, LaGrange, N.C., to Wilkins, NAACP, part 17 supplement, reel 12.

46. Wyatt Tee Walker, Petersburg, Va., to Wilkins, NAACP, part 17 supplement, reel 11.

47. Wyatt Tee Walker to Chet Huntley, NAACP, part 17 supplement, reel 11.

48. Harrison Salisbury, "Fear and Hatred Grip Birmingham," *NYT*, April 12, 1960. Quoted in McWhorter, 158. McWhorter's book provides an exhaustive account both of the Salisbury controversy and the making of *CBS Reports'* "Who Speaks for Birmingham."

49. See McWhorter, 199–209; Smith, 269–70. See also Halberstam, for an in-depth account of the Freedom Rides and the significance of television coverage.

50. McWhorter, 186–87.

51. John Temple Graves, "Alabama's Shame Now Is Compounded," *BPH*, May 18, 1961.

52. "Birmingham Goes on TV Tonight," *BPH*, May 18, 1961.

53. "Who Speaks for Birmingham?" *CBS Reports*, Airdate May 18, 1961, LOC.

54. When the state of Alabama outlawed the NAACP, the ACMHR took its place under the leadership of Reverend Fred Shuttlesworth.

55. Birmingham's two daily newspapers, the *News* and the *Post-Herald,* provided extensive coverage about the program, both before and after it aired. There were news articles, editorials, and numerous reader letters. The *Birmingham World,* the city's African American weekly newspaper, carried no coverage or comment about the program at all.

56. Classen, 45.

57. "CBS Schedules Program on City," *BN*, May 16, 1961. For more on the history of television in Birmingham see http://www.birminghamrewound.com/radio-tv.htm (accessed July 11, 2011).

58. "Voice of the People," *BN*, May 26, 1961. Letter from Marshall Pitts, M.D.

59. "What Did Birmingham Folk Think of Show? It Varies," *BPH*, May 19, 1961.

60. John Temple Graves, "Distorted Picture of City Given on TV Program," *BPH*, May 20, 1961.

61. "Hanes Says CBS Broadcast Unfair," *BN*, May 20, 1961.

62. "Voice of the People," *BN*, May 22, 1961. Letter from Margaret Mauter.

63. "Voice of the People," *BN*, May 22, 1961. Letter from William J. Short.

64. Hale, 67–68.

65. According to McWhorter, Locke was a Klan lawyer "suspected of underwriting the Dynamite Hill bombings" of houses in a middle-class area into which upwardly mobile blacks attempted to move. See McWhorter, 187.

66. "Voice of the People," *BN*, May 14, 1961. Letter from Robert E. Yarbrough.

67. See Graves, "Distorted Picture."

68. "On 'Who Speaks For Birmingham,'" *BN*, May 19, 1961.

69. "We Might Have Known," *BPH*, May 20, 1961.

70. "Morning Mail," *BPH*, May 23, 1961. Letter from R. W. Gross, MD.

71. "Voice of the People," *BPH*, May 23, 1961. Letter from Gordon Sibley.

72. McWhorter, 200–201.

73. In fact, the CBS camera equipment was in a station wagon and was purposefully not operating, as Smith did not want to call attention to their presence. CBS did not record any film of the beating. See Smith, 271.

74. "People Are Asking: 'Where were the Police?'" *BN*, May 15, 1961.

75. "Voice of the People," *BN*, May 22, 1961. Letter from Charles M. Thompson.

76. "Voice of the People," *BN*, May 20, 1961. Letter from Shirley A. Parker.

77. See Gitlin.

78. See, for instance, Cobb.

79. This was the same editorial that insinuated collusion between Smith and Lowe and the Freedom Riders.

80. Smith, 273.

81. Friendly, 128.

82. Smith, 275. Bull Connor would become more famous in 1963 for turning dogs and high-powered fire hoses on civil rights demonstrators. Earl Warren was the liberal chief justice of the Supreme Court.

83. Curtin, 147.

Chapter 4. *The March on Washington and a Peek into Racial Utopia*

1. *BC*, September 2, 1963.

2. Gentile, 42. Gentile quoted a Gallup poll that indicated 63 percent of Americans held an "unfavorable attitude" toward the proposed march.

3. The March on Washington has been discussed in much of the civil rights movement literature. Gentile's is the most comprehensive study focusing solely on the march. See also Eucher.

4. In 1961, Brinkley famously editorialized in opposition to the Freedom Rides, charging they "are accomplishing nothing whatsoever and, on the contrary, are doing positive harm." In this stance, he was in lockstep with the Kennedy administration, which not only wanted the rides to stop, but resisted providing federal protection as well. See Arsenault, 272–73.

5. My partial reconstruction of how the *Huntley-Brinkley Report* covered civil rights in the run-up to the March on Washington is drawn from David Brinkley's scripts, DB. The scripts for the nightly news programs contain only Brinkley's introductions to news stories and his reading of news items that did not involve cutting to a correspondent. Except for correspondent Herb Kaplow's coverage of the Cambridge, Maryland, story (referred to later in the chapter), Brinkley's scripts contain no indication of how correspondents covered the stories that Brinkley set up. In other cases, Brinkley narrated the story himself over silent film footage that is not described in the script. The scripts also do not provide a full run for the period. Therefore, while the scripts provide strong clues about how NBC News framed the civil rights story, particularly in June and July, it is in no way definitive. Unfortunately, the television networks did not, as a matter of course,

save film or tape copies of news broadcasts during this period, so historical work requires a conjectural approach.

6. DB, box 28, folder 2, script for broadcast May 29, 1963. Ellipses in original.

7. Ibid., script for broadcast June 19, 1963.

8. For a discussion of the Selma voting rights campaign that led directly to passage of the Voting Rights Act of 1965 and its coverage by television news, see chapter 5.

9. Brinkley reported from the nation's capital; Huntley did so from New York. The two were linked for the nightly program via coaxial cable. For a lively history of NBC News, see the memoir by former head of NBC News, Reuven Frank, *Out of Thin Air.*

10. DB, box 28, folder 2, script for broadcast May 30, 1963.

11. Carson, 90.

12. None of the standard and most significant civil rights texts give the Cambridge movement more than a few lines. There is only one book-length study of the struggle in Cambridge, which garnered so much media attention (and not just from NBC) at the time. See Levy. The Cambridge movement was notable for its fiercely local, grassroots character. The organizers, including Gloria Richardson, one of the civil rights movement's most significant female leaders, rebuffed offers from King and the SCLC for assistance. The Cambridge movement also focused far more on economic issues of black poverty and joblessness and less on issues of public accommodation and lunch-counter desegregation. Cambridge activists also heralded a turn away from King-style nonviolence and toward a more aggressive and confrontational form of protest.

13. DB, box 28, folder 2, script for broadcast June 19, 1963 [ellipses in original].

14. Ibid., script for broadcast June 21, 1963.

15. DB, box 28, folder 3, script for broadcast July 8, 1963.

16. Ibid., script for broadcast July 11, 1963.

17. Ibid., script for broadcast August 15, 1963.

18. Much of the news media—newsmagazines and newspapers—also initially opposed the march and focused on the violence frame. See for instance, Lentz. Gentile also discusses the negative response of the news media.

19. Gentile, 157. The author quotes from a transcript of the broadcast provided him by NBC.

20. See manual for marshals, NAACP, part 21, reel 18.

21. Branch, *Parting the Waters,* 872–73.

22. Unsigned and undated public statement, NAACP, part 21, reel 18.

23. John Morsell to all [NAACP] staff, August 21, 1963, NAACP, part 21, reel 18.

24. My analysis of the networks' live coverage is based on viewing both CBS's and ABC's broadcasts, available at LOC. The CBS material includes approximately three hours of continuous coverage beginning shortly before the main program of speeches at the Lincoln Memorial and ending with the final benediction following King's speech. ABC's coverage comprises a series of often lengthy news bulletins and live special reports beginning in the morning as marchers slowly congregated at the Washington Monument and ends later with reports of march organizers meeting with President Kennedy following the march. NBC's coverage is not included in the LOC collection.

25. Gray, "Remembering Civil Rights," 353.

26. Gentile, 206. Citing statistics from a Bureau of Social Science study of march participants, Gentile further notes that two thirds of black marchers held white collar jobs, tended to be highly educated, and resided mostly in Northern and urban areas.

27. The formal program included only Mahalia Jackson and Marian Anderson. White

performers like Bob Dylan and Peter, Paul, and Mary entertained marchers earlier in the day and were not featured in ABC's or CBS's coverage at LOC.

28. There were no female speakers; Mahalia Jackson and Marian Anderson commanded the podium as singers. The absence of women was another indication of the endemic sexism of movement leadership. The only acknowledgment of women's crucial role in civil rights organizing was provided by Daisy Bates, a leader of the Little Rock school integration struggle. At the beginning of the formal program as a "tribute to the women," she was permitted a brief moment to pledge support to the movement on behalf of her sisters in the struggle, such as Rosa Parks, Diane Nash, Septima Clark, Ella Baker, and Gloria Richardson.

29. Edward P. Morgan to Roy Wilkins, NAACP, part 21, reel 18.

30. See Hallin, 116–18.

31. Ibid., 116–17.

32. Dayan and Katz, ix.

33. Ibid., 8.

34. Ibid., 5.

35. Ibid., 6.

36. "Big March, Big Coverage," *BR*, September 2, 1963, 47.

37. Mike Mosettig, "TV's Unprecedented Alert as 150,000 Civil Rights Advocates March on D.C.," *VA*, August 28, 1963.

38. "Radio-TV Get Set for Aug. 28 Rights March," *BR*, August 19, 1963, 60.

39. "Big March, Big Coverage," *BR*, September 2, 1963, 47.

40. Dayan and Katz, 5.

41. In the New York area, daytime viewing was up 15 percent on August 28 compared to the previous Wednesday. Viewership was most concentrated around noontime: Nielsen calculated it to be 61 percent higher than a week earlier. See "Big March, Big Coverage," *BR*, September 2, 1963, 48. CBS's afternoon coverage, according to the New York overnight Nielsen ratings, showed the network with a 40.7 percent share of the viewing audience.

42. Bill Greeley, "TV's 'Great Coverage of Great Event' Citation on D.C. March," *VA*, September 6, 1963.

43. Ibid.

44. Dayan and Katz, 6.

45. Ibid., 20–21.

46. For instance, they point to the example of the 1985 "Live Aid" set of concerts broadcast via satellite around the world to provide famine relief for Ethiopia.

47. Ibid., 48–53. The authors use the example of Czech television and the coverage of the demonstrations in Wenceslas Square in Prague that signaled the downfall of the Communist regime. "The television cameras revealed the mammoth scale and the intensity—but yet the discipline—of the protest rallies. These were broadcasts of the many to the many; they showed the people demanding change." (51–52).

48. *Television* 20, no. 3 (March 1963): 68–69.

49. Bill Greeley, "TV's 'Great Coverage of Great Event' Citation on D.C. March," *VA*, September 6, 1963.

50. *CBS Special Report: The Great March*, CBS. All subsequent quotes and descriptions come from my viewing of this program, which appears to be a kinescope and contains commercial breaks for products such as denture toothpaste and Saran Wrap.

51. There is, of course, a long history of white Americans' wanting to adopt some of their imagined attributes: from pre- and antebellum white minstrels to Norman Mailer's "white

Negro" hipster, to more contemporary suburban white youths emulating the gestures and stances of black rap artists.

52. ABC carried live all of Lewis's speech before returning to regularly scheduled programming.

53. Gentile, 172.

54. The full speech is reprinted in Gentile, 178–81, and also in Hansen, 43–48.

55. Hansen, 48.

56. Ibid.

57. Wilkins's joking with the crowd makes sense if one watches all the speeches in their entirety and in sequence. Wilkins was preceded on the podium by a number of flat, uninspired speeches that made the crowd visibly restless. The NAACP leader clearly was attempting to liven up the proceedings and keep marchers from decamping too early.

58. ABC used the time during King's speech to let anchor Bate sum up the day. As Bate speaks, one can clearly hear King in the background speaking and the crowd cheering. When the news team returned to the air for the 4:30 special report, ABC gave viewers a videotaped version of the full speech—the only instance in which the news division relied on nonlive footage for its March on Washington coverage. Clearly, ABC News recognized the news value of the speech and its power.

59. Hansen traces the origins and uses of the "I have a dream" set piece to speeches in Albany, Georgia, and Birmingham, and also most recently at a June 1963 speech in Detroit. See Hansen 109–13.

60. Ibid., 135.

61. Ibid., 55. Hansen reprints the speech in its entirety, including comparisons between the prepared text and what was actually delivered.

62. Ibid., 151.

63. CBS was not alone in considering the first part of the speech to be the newsworthy section. The *Washington Post* managed in its coverage to ignore the "I have a dream" section as well (Hansen, 140). The *Chicago Defender,* one of the most significant and nationally distributed African American newspapers, made a similar gaffe. It reprinted the released version of the King speech, which, of course, did not include the "I have a dream" section. See *CD,* August 31, 1963. One week later, having heard from hundreds of readers, the *Defender* noted its error, informed readers that because of the stepped-up publishing schedule, it had printed an advanced press release. "Probably the most beautiful and certainly most eloquent parts of the speech were omitted in our printing simply because Rev. King spoke from the heart. He never had written these words down." The paper reprinted the speech in its entirety and urged readers to save it for their grandchildren. See *CD,* September 7, 1963.

64. Hanson, 99.

65. Ibid., 153.

66. Ibid., 156.

67. Ibid., 60.

68. Many historians and commentators now feel that King's more overtly political and especially his later more radical pronouncements on issues like poverty and the Vietnam War have been elided by the obsessive attention given to "I have a dream." This one speech may have the resonance it has, in part, because it does not remind Americans that King was fundamentally not a dreamer or visionary, but rather a radical social change activist and leader.

69. *1963 TV Album,* CBS, December 22, 1963.

70. "Growing in Stature," *PC,* September 14, 1963; ellipses in original.

71. Roy Wilkins from Marie J. Baker, NAACP Secretary, Decatur, IL, NAACP, part 21, reel 19.

72. Lloyd General, "I Rode the Freedom Train," *CD,* August 31, 1963.

73. Wallace S. Hayes, "What Afro Readers Say," *BAA,* September 7, 1963, 12.

74. Jack Gould, "Television and Civil Rights," *NYT,* September 8, 1963.

75. Ibid.

76. King and the SCLC launched a direct-action protest campaign in Birmingham in the spring of 1963 to spotlight the vicious nature of segregation in the "Magic City" and to demand the integration of downtown businesses and the hiring of black workers. The campaign really came alive when the SCLC agreed to allow schoolchildren to march and risk arrest, as it was proving difficult to find enough adults to fill the jails. Shortly after the searing images of high school students and even younger children being brutalized by Connor's dogs and fire hoses flashed around the world, Birmingham's business establishment agreed to King's demands. The Birmingham campaign showed that King's strategy of creating a crisis through nonviolent confrontational activism worked.

77. See Roberts and Klibanoff (esp. 316–24) for more on the role played by photojournalists during the Birmingham campaign, in particular the work of Claude Moore, a photographer for *Life* magazine.

Chapter 5. Selma in the "Glaring Light of Television"

1. Carter, 248. The viewer figure comes from Carter; however, the author does not provide any citation to indicate a source for that number. Carter also identifies Richard Valeriani as the reporter narrating ABC's footage. This seems unlikely, as Valeriani was NBC's correspondent in Selma.

2. See, for instance, Garrow, *Protest at Selma,* which discusses press coverage and its political impact extensively. See also the first major history of the Selma campaign, Fager, 98–99. See also King's primary biographer, Branch, *At Canaan's Edge,* 55–56. And see George Wallace's primary biographer, Carter, 248–50.

3. Garrow, *Protest at Selma,* 163.

4. DB, box 28, folder 2, script for broadcast June 19, 1963.

5. Garrow, *Protest at Selma,* 31.

6. Garrow, *Bearing the Cross,* 390.

7. Young, *An Easy Burden,* 336.

8. Fager, 49.

9. Ibid., 10.

10. The information here is drawn from an official CBS news log that lists all the news items that aired. CBS-L.

11. All discussion of the *CBS Evening News with Walter Cronkite* is drawn from my viewing of aired news reports from that newscast at the CBS News Archive. Unfortunately, CBS did not regularly kinescope the live news broadcast, nor did it tape the aired broadcast for archival purposes. In this period CBS kept and archived only the individual news reports inserted into the newscast. Thus Walter Cronkite's comments and introductions in the studio to correspondents' stories are not available. As a result, I have no way to know how the CBS anchor set up the Selma stories for his viewers. CBS began systematically archiving these "insert reels" in the aftermath of the Kennedy assassination, according to

Dan DiPierro, head of the archives, as the network began to realize the historical importance of its news broadcasts. Unfortunately, the CBS News Archive is not easily accessible to scholarly researchers, nor is the facility set up to accommodate them. I am very indebted to Dan DiPierro and his staff for graciously giving me access.

12. See chapter 3 for discussion of Hallin's "three spheres" schema of journalistic operation.

13. Clark had been aggressively shoving and manhandling people on the line and had shoved Cooper so hard she lost her balance. Muttering a curse, she slugged Clark. Cooper was well known in the Selma black community. She had been fired from her job at a white-owned funeral parlor for her civil rights organizing two years earlier. She and her fired co-workers had then reportedly been blacklisted from employment by any other white establishments. See Fager, 44–45.

14. Garrow, *Protest at Selma,* 45–46.

15. J. Williams, 260.

16. This report was probably broadcast February 2; however, unlike most of the tapes in the CBS News Archive of the Cronkite newscast, the one that includes this report has no log with broadcast dates.

17. Branch, *Pillar of Fire,* 578.

18. "The Hate That Hate Produced" was the title of a 1959 CBS News documentary narrated by Mike Wallace.

19. Fiske, *Television Culture,* 6–7.

20. Branch, *Pillar of Fire,* 579.

21. Donovan and Scherer, 19. See also interview with Valeriani in J. Williams, 270–71.

22. Torres, 34–35.

23. Ibid., 35.

24. Unfortunately, Cronkite's introduction to this report and any possible comments at its end are not available in the CBS News Archive. Most likely, Cronkite would have had something significant to say about the report and the violence against newsmen. In 1968, when he witnessed Chicago police clubbing Dan Rather while both covered the Democratic National Convention, he famously referred to the police as "thugs" for their violence. Youth activists gleefully interpreted Cronkite's reaction as indication of an alliance between CBS News and the antiwar protesters out on the street who were also feeling the brutality of Chicago's police. See Bodroghkozy, *Groove Tube,* 108.

25. Fager, 92.

26. Branch, *At Canaan's Edge,* 40–42; Carson, 158.

27. By Monday evening's news show, Benton's report was nowhere to be seen. *Evening News* viewers saw only reaction to Sunday's violence. Attorney General Katzenbach led the news with his distress at the situation in Selma. Cronkite highlighted other official government responses and also provided footage of blacks picketing the Justice Department. The CBS News Archive apparently no longer has a copy of this March 8, 1965, Cronkite news broadcast. See CBS news log, CBS-L.

28. This report is contained on a CBS beta tape titled "Battle on the Bridge," CBS. It contained both raw and assembled news footage. The full Kuralt morning news piece is on this tape; however, the audio has been disassembled from the video. I have attempted to reconstruct the two.

29. Raines, 386.

30. L. Williams, xiv.

31. See P. Brooks.

32. Emmett Till was a 14-year-old Chicago boy sent to spend the summer with relatives in Mississippi. He apparently whistled at or spoke to a white woman, unknowingly flouting a cardinal Jim Crow law against interactions between black males and white females. He was brutally lynched by the woman's husband and compatriots. Till's mother decided to publicize the vicious murder in order to throw a spotlight onto the continuation of lynch law in the South. Her dead son's face graced the cover of *Jet* magazine and became a cause célèbre at the dawn of the civil rights movement. Till's murderers were acquitted by an all-white jury.

33. Garrow, *Protest at Selma*, 146.

34. Ibid., 163.

35. Public opinion polling was and is tricky on racial matters, but a nationwide Harris poll conducted in mid-May 1965 asked respondents whether they sided more with civil rights groups or the state of Alabama in the aftermath of the "showdown" in Selma. Forty-eight percent sided with the former, 21 percent with the latter, and 31 percent were uncertain. When broken down by region, 61 percent of those in the East supported civil rights groups, while 54 percent of those in the South supported Alabama. Approximately one-third of respondents in all regional categories indicated they were uncertain. Garrow attributes the large percentage of uncertains to a "substantial body of opposition to any public protest tactics." Nevertheless, he points to much larger support by the public for the Selma campaign than for the Birmingham campaign. See Garrow, *Protest at Selma*, 158–59.

36. George B. Leonard, "Midnight Plane to Alabama," *The Nation*, May 10, 1965, 502.

37. Todd Gitlin discusses how the mainstream media did precisely the same thing to Students for a Democratic Society (SDS) and young antiwar demonstrators. See Gitlin, *Whole World*.

38. Branch, *At Canaan's Edge*, 12.

39. Ibid., 114–15.

40. John F. Kennedy also benefited from a degree of tele-literacy. See Watson.

41. Hazel Garland, "Video Vignettes," *PC*, March 27, 1965.

42. "Wallace 'Little Man' in 'Big Job,'" (editorial), *PC*, April 3, 1965.

43. Unfortunately, the CBS News archive is also missing coverage for March 25, 1965, and the entrance into Montgomery of twenty-five thousand marchers who congregated at the Capitol.

44. Simeon Booker, "50,000 March on Montgomery," *EB*, May 1965, 56

45. Sokol, 70.

46. As he registered at the Albert Hotel in Selma, King was punched in the head and kicked in the groin by James Robinson, a member of the virulently racist and anti-Semitic National States Rights Party. Wilson Baker promptly grabbed Robinson and hauled him off to jail. See Fager, 29–30.

47. Charles N. Breeding, "Citizen of Selma," *STJ*, January 24, 1965.

48. James A. MacDonald, President, Selma Jaycees, *STJ*, January 29, 1965.

49. Gertrude Maness, Marion, Ala., *STJ*, January 24, 1965.

50. "Dallas County Registrars Speak Out," *STJ*, February 1, 1965.

51. "Publicity Hoax," [reprinted from the *Dothan Eagle*], *STJ*, February 2, 1965.

52. "Exploitation," [reprinted from the *Troy Messenger*], *STJ*, February 12.

53. James D. Pounders, Florence, Ala., *BN*, March 18, 1965.

54. Pam Daniels, Orrville, Ala., *STJ*, March 2, 1965.

55. "Sanity and Realism Must Come to Selma" (special editorial), *STJ,* February 18, 1965.

56. Charles L. Feltus, *BN,* March 11, 1965.

57. Mrs. D. B. Richards, *BN,* March 16, 1965.

58. "Alabama—Look in the Mirror," *BN,* March 13, 1965. Unfortunately, four days later, the paper ran another editorial that remobilized the "qualified voter" discourse. Fulminating about those with "low intelligence," both black and white who would be unable to judge candidates and issues, this editorial affirmed, "More than just the fact of drawing breath should be prerequisite to participate in the decisions of a free, responsible society." See "Voting: A Right, But . . .," *BN,* March 17, 1965. However, this editorial did not run on page one with a banner headline. The waffling seems symptomatic of the shifting ground and the atmosphere of rapid and transformative social change.

59. Shirley Farris, *STJ,* March 15, 1965.

60. Bernice Daffron, *BN,* March 17, 1965.

61. G. S. Forsman, *BN,* March 16, 1965. With the race riot to come later that summer in Watts, the letter writer would no longer be able to make this particular argument.

62. Mrs. Alfred G. Phillips, *BN,* March 28, 1965.

63. "Who Speaks for the South" [editorial cartoon], *BN,* March 24, 1965, 7. The cartoon was reprinted from the *Atlanta Journal.*

64. [Front page], *STJ,* March 9, 1965.

65. [Front page], *STJ,* March 10, 1965.

66. James Free, "National Headlines Spotlight Selma," *BN,* March 8, 1965.

67. Bob Ingram, "Lingo Nearly Got Ax Over Selma Debacle," *MA,* March 14, 1965.

68. Fairclough, 228–29.

69. Fager, 95–96. In fact, civil rights organizers worked frantically to calm the rage of the local residents who had been bullied off the streets, teargassed, and otherwise manhandled merely for being black and outside around Brown Chapel.

70. M. H. Smith, *MA,* March 21, 1965.

71. Mrs. J. E. Menegatti and Mrs. H. W. Wilder, *MA,* March 25, 1965.

72. "Silence" [lead editorial], *MA,* March 25, 1965.

73. Mrs. J. E. Menegatti, *MA,* March 25, 1965.

74. See Sokol for more on the concept of "our Negroes."

75. "How Long Can State Afford Present Road?" [p. 1 editorial], *BN,* March 28, 1965.

76. *CBS News Special,* December 25, 1965, CBS.

77. Horne, 3.

78. Ibid., 325. Horne quotes from legal recommendations to McCone.

79. Ibid., 323.

Chapter 6. Bringing "Urgent Issues" to the Vast Wasteland: East Side/West Side

1. Baughman, 60.

2. See Boddy.

3. Baughman, 64.

4. Watson, 43. See also Brook, 24–39.

5. By the late 1950s the mode of television production began changing over from New York-based live programming to Hollywood-based filmed series, usually in episodic formats. See Vianello, 204–18; and Boddy.

6. Metz, 228.

7. Lawrence White, Director of Program Development, CBS, to Larry Arrick, Talent Associates–Paramount, July 10, 1963, DS, box 66, folder 18.

8. Lawrence White to Michael Dann, May 7, 1963, DS, box 66, folder 18.

9. As we will see in chapter 8, White's argument was validated with the ratings success of *Good Times* a decade later, a situation comedy about an impoverished black family living in the projects on Chicago's South Side.

10. Larry White from Larry Arrick, Talent Associates–Paramount, July 2, 1963, DS, box 66, folder 18.

11. Joe [no last name] to David Susskind, May 29, 1963, DS, box 66, folder 18.

12. CBS interoffice memo entitled "Preliminary Report on *East Side, West Side* (Program Analysis), April 9, 1963, DS, box 66, folder 18.

13. Talent Associates–Paramount press release, August 31, 1963, DS, Box 67, Folder 1.

14. Watson discusses this issue extensively.

15. Brook, 27.

16. Ibid., 26. Brook quotes Mark Goodson, an independent television producer best known for game shows.

17. Eugene Kaellis, DDS, PhD, Roosevelt, N.J., DS, box 67, folder 4. All other viewer letters discussed in this section come from this folder as well.

18. Such fears were not without some merit. As MacDonald has noted, when Southern stations finally were able to hook up to the broadcast networks, programmers became notably more conservative in their programming choices, not wanting to offend what they considered to be Southern sensibilities, especially around race issues.

19. Watson discusses both these episodes at some length in her book, as does Mac-Donald. Marlon Riggs's important documentary on the history of African Americans in television, *Color Adjustment,* also features excerpts from the programs.

20. This episode was included as part of the Trio cable network "Brilliant but Cancelled" series. It is also available at the Wisconsin Center for Film and Theater Research, SHSW.

21. Arnold Perl, September 2, 1963, DS, box 67, folder 1.

22. Clipping file, DS, box 66, folder 16. Cecil Smith, *Los Angeles Times.*

23. Clipping file, DS, box 66, folder 16. Kay Gardella, "'Who Do You Kill?' Drama Should Start With Author" [unknown paper].

24. Clipping file, DS, box 66, folder 16. Cecil Smith, "A Tenderly Told Harlem Tragedy" [unknown paper].

25. In a letter to Senator Javits, David Susskind wrote, "Jack, this show needs all the help it can get from people with important pulpits. . . . [T]hose people who finally allowed ["Who Do You Kill?"] to be scheduled should be praised to the skies on the floor of the Senate." Letter, October 29, 1963, DS, box 66, folder 16.

26. Arnold Perl to David Susskind, Dan Melnick, and George C. Scott, October 17, 1963, DS, box 66, folder 16.

27. Nielsen and Arbitron ratings information on every episode of the series is available in DS, box 68, folder 1. In general, *East Side/West Side* "won" the ratings race against the NBC and ABC offerings broadcast during the same time slot. Usually, the show's "share" hovered around the 30 percent range—a respectable, if not superior, performance. Other programs from this era with similar ratings did not necessarily get cancelled after one season.

28. Alan Patureau, "2 Dixie Stations Cancel Show," *New York Newsday,* November 5, 1963, DS, box 66, file 16.

29. Volume was heavy if the amount of mail in DS is any guide. There are 204 letters and postcards; all but five are laudatory.

30. All viewer letters in this section are located in DS, box 69, folder 10.

31. Clipping file, DS, box 66, folder 16. Dave Kaufman, "On All Channels," *VA*, December 11, 1963.

32. The episode's ratings were similar to the other program as well. According to the Nielsen numbers, "No Hiding Place" captured 37 percent of the viewing audience. See DS, box 68, folder 1.

33. There are seventy-three letters and postcards in DS. Eleven expressed disagreement with integrated housing. All letters in this section are in box 69, folder 12.

34. Hazel Garland, "Video Vignettes," *PC*, December 14, 1963.

35. DS, box 66, file 16. Clippings for 1963–64. "*East Side/West Side* Story," *Philadelphia Daily News*, February 5, 1964. Another unidentified newspaper clipping indicates that CBS disputed this contention, arguing that only one station dropped the show, but that the network experienced difficulty selling airtime to sponsors for the series.

36. For a history of *Amos 'n' Andy* including middle-class black protest campaigns against both the radio series and the television program, see Ely.

37. Unidentified newspaper clipping, DS, box 66, file 16.

Chapter 7. Is This What You Mean by Color TV?

1. See Rhodes.

2. Farber and Bailey, 45.

3. *Amos 'n' Andy* remained in syndication until heavy protest from civil rights organizers forced it off local stations by 1966.

4. Brown, 78–79.

5. In its first year on the air, *Julia* was the seventh most highly rated show of the year. It did not rank in the top twenty-five in its final two years. See Brooks and Marsh, 927–28.

6. Harper, 62.

7. Ibid.

8. Appropriating Baudrillard's postmodernist theorizing suggesting that the simulacrum usurps the primacy of the "real," Harper suggests that "simulacral realism" in television results in the assumption that images of black people as successful and fully integrated will then play out in the "real world" (84).

9. Acham, 116. See also Richard Warren Lewis, "The Importance of Being Julia," *TVG*, December 14, 1968, 24, for an account of Wilkins's speech and Kanter's response.

10. See HK, which contain primarily final-draft scripts for all the *Julia* episodes, Kanter's personal correspondence, production material for the series, ratings information, and a large selection of viewer letters.

11. HK, box 18.

12. This is from an episode in the author's personal collection. Unfortunately, *Julia* is not, at this writing, in DVD release or in syndication.

13. HK, box 19. "The Interview" aired September 24, 1968.

14. HK, box 18, September 17, 1968.

15. My analysis is based on a close analysis of 151 letters and postcards.

16. All the following viewer letters, unless marked otherwise, are in HK, box 18.

17. The writers of these letters are, respectively, a male viewer from DuBois, Pennsylvania; a female viewer from Colton, California; and a female viewer from New York City.

18. "Wonderful World of Color," *Time*, December 13, 1968, 70.

19. Robert Lewis Shayon, "'Julia': Breakthrough or Letdown," *SR*, April 20, 1968, 49.

20. Robert Lewis Shayon, "'Julia' Symposium: An Opportunity Lost," *SR*, May 25, 1968, 36.

21. Ibid., 36.

22. Ibid., 36.

23. Robert Lewis Shayon, "'Julia': A Political Relevance?" *SR*, July 20, 1968, 37.

24. Undated episode in author's personal collection.

25. MacDonald, 147–50.

26. Thirteen women, one man, and three children or young people identified themselves as black. Additionally, a group of thirteen letters came from an inner-city grade school writing class. From the tone of the letters, I suspect the class was made up predominantly of African American children.

27. Bobo, "*Color Purple,*" 90–109. See also Bobo, *Black Women.*

28. Morley, 14.

29. This letter is located in HK, box 1, among Kanter's general correspondence. A significant number of letters from self-identifying black viewers can be found among this general correspondence rather than in the fan-letter files. Perhaps this suggests special handling of mail from black viewers by Kanter and his staff.

30. Ibid.

31. *EB,* November 1968, 56–58.

32. Harper, 70.

33. *SR,* April 20, 1968, 49.

34. Fife, 13–14.

35. See Davis; also see Jones.

36. See Frazier, *The Family: Its Function and Destiny,* and his classic statement on black families, *The Negro Family in the United States.* For a good introduction to the various debates about the black family in the 1960s and 1970s, see Bracey, Meier, and Rudwick.

37. Moynihan, *Negro Family.*

38. Moynihan, qtd. in Bracey, Meier, and Rudwick, 140.

39. See, for instance, noted black sociologist Billingsley, 199–202.

40. For an examination of the season of social relevance, see Bodroghkozy, "Make it Relevant," in *Groove Tube*; and Gitlin, "The Turn Toward 'Relevance,'" in *Inside Prime Time.*

41. See, for instance, Carolyn See, "I'm a Black Woman with a White Image," *TVG,* March 14, 1970, 26–30. See also Acham's discussion of this interview with Carroll, 125.

Chapter 8. *Prime Time,* Good Times

1. Metcalf, 206.

2. See AM, final draft script, "Crosstown Buses Run All Day," by John Baskin and Roger Shulman, July 24, 1974, box 6.

3. See Fairclough (279–307) for an exploration of the "defeat in Chicago."

4. Weisbrot, 185.

5. Qtd. in Carroll, 110.

6. In a scholarly article written about *Good Times* during its first year, Eugenia Collier, contrasts *Good Times* with *Sanford and Son* and argues that the latter gives no indication that the difficulties of the black characters have anything to do with racism or white

power. In *Good Times,* however, "the characters constantly do battle. . . . [T]he struggle against oppression, which is so deeply human and so indigenous to black art, is never totally absent [from *Good Times*]." See Collier, 214.

7. Gray, *Watching Race,* 3.

8. Hall, 30.

9. Ibid., 27.

10. Bob Lucas, "A 'Salt Pork and Collard Greens' TV Show," *EB,* June 1974, 51.

11. Ronald E. Kisner, "New Comedy Brings Good Times to TV," *Jet,* May 23, 1974, 58–60.

12. Harry F. Waters, "Good Apples and Bad," *NW,* February 25, 1974, 67.

13. Eric Monte interview, *The Making of Good Times* (E! Entertainment, 2000).

14. Gray, *Watching Race,* 10.

15. Rainwater and Yancy, 5–6. See also Franklin.

16. Chafe, 439.

17. Carroll, 111.

18. "Sex and the Evans Family," March 15, 1974.

19. "Florida the Woman," Feb. 17, 1976.

20. Most of the letters discussed here are collected in AM. There are approximately seventy letters dated between February 1974 (when the series first aired) and February 1975. All the letters have replies signed by Mr. Manings. I have supplemented these with letters published in EB.

21. Charles Holster, Wantagh, N.Y., AM, box 1. All viewer mail is located in this box.

22. Louise D. Kleinsorge, Tiburon, Cal., AM.

23. Manings to Ms. Teresa Green, Gary, Minn., AM.

24. Diane Bennett, San Francisco, AM.

25. Ms. Aldena B. Runnels, Assistant Professor, NYU, AM.

26. L. Boyce, Bronx, N.Y., AM. A similarly worded letter by this writer also appeared in *Ebony.* See "Letters to the Editor," *EB,* November 1975, 10.

27. Bob Lucas, "A 'Salt Pork and Collard Greens' TV Show," *EB,* June 1974, 51.

28. "Letters to the Editor," *EB,* Aug. 1974, 16–17.

29. Norma Jean Ellis, St. Louis, AM. Manings agreed with many of Ms. Ellis's criticisms and points out that J.J. will no longer steal, Thelma will become a more rounded character, both Florida and James will be pursuing their high school equivalency diplomas, and Florida will spend less time with the portrait of Christ. "In the next 21 weeks I think we will be covering many topics that will, I believe, meet with your approval."

30. Manings interview, *The Making of Good Times.*

31. BernNadette Stanis as Thelma was also a newcomer to acting. Ja'net Dubois, as wisecracking neighbor Willona, had extensive theatrical acting experience.

32. "A Really Cool Job," Sept. 23, 1975.

33. MacDonald, 186. See also Bogle, *Prime Time Blues.*

34. Marlon T. Riggs, director, producer, writer, *Color Adjustment* (San Francisco: California Newsreel, 1991). Two of the scholars who provide commentary about *Good Times* in the documentary are Henry Louis Gates and Herman Gray.

35. Fiske, *Understanding Popular Culture,* 133.

36. Acham discusses how Esther Rolle (along with Diahann Carroll) used the popular press to circulate resistant and oppositional discourse about the show and its representation of blackness (127–33).

37. Louie Robinson, "Bad Times on the 'Good Times' Set," *EB,* Sept. 1975, 35.

38. Bob Lucas, "A 'Salt Pork and Collard Greens' TV Show," *EB,* June 1974, 53.

39. Harper, 62.

40. Louie Robinson, "Bad Times on the 'Good Times' Set," *EB,* Sept. 1975, 38.

41. "Television's New Season Unveils J.J. in New Role," *Jet,* Sept. 9, 1976, 62.

42. Bob Williams, "Jimmy [sic] Walker Defends J.J.," *NYP,* Nov. 1, 1977.

43. The letters are dated no later than February 1975. Public controversy about the series did not really hit until the beginning of the 1975–76 season, after the *Ebony* exposé was published in September 1975.

44. William F. Brazziel, Mansfield Center, Conn., AM.

45. There is no evidence in the letters in AM for the assertion that black viewers loved J.J. particularly for his artistic ambitions. While such letters may well have existed, they did not make it into this collection.

46. Bogle, *Prime Time Blues,* 203.

47. Alan Manings to Teresa Green, AM.

48. In its second season, 1974–75, *Good Times* was ranked seventh in the Nielsen ratings. See Brooks and Marsh, 929.

49. Ronald Berman, "J.J. and the Limits of Human Nature," *WSJ,* April 15, 1977. This commentary was written about the series after John Amos as James Evans Sr. had left the show. See following section for more on this.

50. Mel Tapley, "Is 'Good Times' a Fatherless Family?" *AS,* May 22, 1976.

51. "John Amos Tired of J.J., so He's Leaving 'Good Times,'" *St. Louis Sentinel,* May 13, 1976.

52. Brown, "'Good Times' Will Drop Male Parent; Black Media Coalition Protests Move," *NYT,* June 7, 1976.

53. Jacqueline Trescott, "Good Times and Hard Times," *WP,* Nov. 2, 1976.

54. Brown, 59.

55. Neal, 65.

56. Ibid.

57. Judy Ann Mason and Ralph Carter interviews, *The Making of Good Times.*

58. George Maksian, "Esther: 'Good Times' Going Bad," *New York Daily News,* Oct. 26, 1977.

59. Irma Kalish interview, *The Making of Good Times.*

60. Martie Evans, "Florida Will Tighten Some Loose Screws in the Evans Household," *AS,* June 10, 1978.

61. Interviews with Judy Ann Mason, Austin Kalish, *The Making of Good Times.*

Epilogue

1. Obama had announced his candidacy for president less than a month before the Selma trip on February 10, 2007.

2. CNN, March 7, 2007.

3. Clips from 2008 election night coverage were viewed on YouTube.com.

4. Rodriguez, "'The Huxtable Effect' and Obama." Numerous media outlets picked up on the thesis, including the *New York Times.* See Tim Arango, "Before Obama, There Was Bill Cosby," *NYT,* Nov. 7, 2008.

5. Gray, *Watching Race,* 17–18.

6. Ibid., 34.

7. Ibid., 36.

8. Ibid., 39.

9. Arango, "Before Obama, There Was Bill Cosby," *NYT,* Nov. 7, 2008.

10. Lewis, 174. See also Jhally and Lewis.

11. Lewis, 183.

12. The Obama campaign made political hay on this issue as the national economic crisis deepened. Republican opponent John McCain was castigated for being out of touch with average voters and families, for having numerous houses, and for being unable to identify how many he and his wife owned, while Obama touted his normality and relatability by proclaiming that, like most Americans, he had one house.

13. Barack Obama, "A More Perfect Union," speech delivered in Philadelphia, March 18, 2008. This was candidate Obama's first major address on race in the midst of a controversy about sermons delivered by his pastor, the Rev. Jeremiah Wright.

14. For more on how network television embraced "socially relevant" programming and the discourses associated primarily with the youth movements of the 1960s, see Bodroghkozy, *Groove Tube,* and Gitlin, *Inside Prime Time.*

15. That America is no longer a merely black and white nation was mostly not remarked upon in this coverage. The position of Latino and Asian American voters did not quite fit the narrative. Rodriguez, in a (less-often-mentioned) section of her article on "The Huxtable Effect," notes the dearth of "positive" televisual imagery of Latinos, despite the fact that they make up 15 percent of the U.S. population. She notes the rise in hate mongering among anti-immigrant groups and TV commentators targeting Latinos, and she questions the specious "end of race" arguments spawned by Obama's electoral success.

BIBLIOGRAPHY

Primary Sources

Abbreviations Used in Source Notes

AM	Allan Manings Collection American Heritage Center, University of Wyoming
AS	*Amsterdam News* (New York)
BAA	*Baltimore Afro-American*
BN	*Birmingham News*
BPH	*Birmingham Post-Herald*
BR	*Broadcasting*
CBS	CBS News Archive, New York, N.Y.
CBS-L	CBS News Library, New York, N.Y.
CD	*Chicago Defender*
CH	Chet Huntley papers (NBC) SHSW
DB	David Brinkley papers SHSW
DS	David Susskind papers SHSW
EB	*Ebony*
GG	Gerald Green papers (NBC) SHSW
HK	Hal Kanter papers SHSW
HKS	Howard K. Smith papers SHSW
IG	Irving Gitlin papers (NBC) SHSW
Jet	*Jet*
LOC	Library of Congress, Division of Motion Pictures, Broadcasting and Recorded Sound
MA	*Montgomery Advertiser*
MRT	Museum of Radio and Television, New York
NAACP	Papers of the NAACP (microfilm), Alderman Library, University of Virginia
NBC	NBC papers SHSW
NW	*Newsweek*
NYP	*New York Post*
NYT	*New York Times*
OW	*Our World*
PC	*Pittsburgh Courier*
RF	Reuven Frank papers (NBC) SHSW
SHSW	State Historical Society of Wisconsin, Madison
SR	*Saturday Review*
STJ	*Selma Times-Journal*
TC	*The Crisis*

Time   *Time*
TV   *Television*
TVG   *TV Guide*
VA   *Variety*
WP   *Washington Post*
WSJ   *Wall Street Journal*

Secondary Sources

Acham, Christine. *Revolution Televised: Prime Time and the Struggle for Black Power.* Minneapolis: University of Minnesota Press, 2004.

Arsenault, Raymond. *Freedom Riders: 1961 and the Struggle for Racial Justice.* Oxford: Oxford University Press, 2006.

Baughman, James. *Television's Guardians: The FCC and the Politics of Programming 1958–1967.* Knoxville: University of Tennessee Press, 1985.

Billingsley, Andrew. *Black Families in White America.* Englewood Cliffs: Prentice-Hall, 1968.

Bobo, Jacqueline. "*The Color Purple*: Black Women as Cultural Readers." In *Female Spectators: Looking at Film and Television,* edited by E. Deidre Pribram, 90–109. London: Verso, 1988.

———. *Black Women as Cultural Readers.* New York: Columbia University Press, 1995.

Boddy, William. *Fifties Television: The Industry and its Critics.* Urbana: University of Illinois Press, 1990.

Bodroghkozy, Aniko. *Groove Tube: Sixties Television and the Youth Rebellion.* Durham, N.C.: Duke University Press, 2001.

Bogle, Donald. *Prime Time Blues: African Americans on Network Television.* New York: Farrar, Straus, and Giroux, 2001.

———. *Heat Wave: The Life and Career of Ethel Waters.* New York: HarperCollins, 2011.

Bracey, John H., August Meier, and Elliott Rudwick. *Black Matriarchy: Myth or Reality.* Belmont: Wadsworth, 1971.

Branch, Taylor. *Parting the Waters: America in the King Years 1954–63.* New York: Simon and Schuster, 1988.

———. *Pillar of Fire: America in the King Years 1963–65.* New York: Simon and Schuster, 1998.

———. *At Canaan's Edge: America in the King Years 1965–68.* New York: Simon and Schuster, 2006.

Brechner, Joseph L. "Were Broadcasters Color Blind?" In *Race and the News Media,* edited by Paul L. Fischer and Ralph L. Lowenstein, 98–104. New York: Praeger, 1967.

Brook, Vincent. "Checks and Imbalances: Political Economy and the Rise and Fall of 'East Side/West Side.'" *Journal of Film and Video* 50, no. 3 (Fall 1998): 24–39.

Brooks, Peter. *The Melodramatic Imagination.* New York: Columbia University Press, 1985.

Brooks, Tim, and Earle Marsh. *The Complete Directory to Prime Time Network TV Shows 1946-Present.* New York: Ballantine, 1981.

Brown, Les. *Television: The Business Behind the Box.* New York: Harcourt Brace Jovanovich, 1971.

Carroll, Peter N. *It Seemed Like Nothing Happened: The Tragedy and Promise of America in the 1970s.* New York: Holt, Rinehart, and Winston, 1982.

Carson, Clayborne. *In Struggle: SNCC and the Black Awakening of the 1960s.* Cambridge, Mass.: Harvard University Press, 1981.

Carter, Dan T. *The Politics of Rage.* New York: Simon and Schuster, 1995.

Chafe, William. *The Unfinished Journey: America Since World War II.* New York: Oxford University Press, 1999.

Classen, Steven. *Watching Jim Crow: The Struggle Over Mississippi TV, 1955–1969.* Durham, N.C.: Duke University Press, 2004.

Cobb, James C. *Away Down South: A History of Southern Identity.* Oxford: University of Oxford Press, 2005.

Collier, Eugenia, "'Black' Shows For White Viewers." *Freedomways: A Quarterly Review of the Freedom Movement* 14, no. 3 (1974): 209–17.

Collins, Patricia Hill. *Black Feminist Thought.* New York: Routledge, 1990.

Curtin, Michael. *Redeeming the Wasteland: Television Documentary and Cold War Politics.* New Brunswick, N.J.: Rutgers University Press, 1995.

Davis, Angela Y. *Women, Race, and Class.* New York: Vintage, 1981.

Dayan, Daniel, and Elihu Katz. *Media Events: The Live Broadcasting of History.* Cambridge: Harvard University Press, 1992.

Donovan, Robert J., and Ray Scherer. *Unsilent Revolution: Television News and American Public Life 1948–1991.* New York: Cambridge University Press and Woodrow Wilson International Center for Scholars, 1992.

Du Bois, W. E. B. *The Souls of Black Folk.* New York: Bantam, 1989.

Echols, Alice. *Daring to Be Bad: Radical Feminism in America 1967–1975.* Minneapolis: University of Minnesota Press, 1989.

Einstein, Daniel. *Special Edition: A Guide to Network Television Documentary Series and Special News Reports, 1955–1979.* Metuchen: Scarecrow, 1987.

Ely, Melvin Patrick. *The Adventures of Amos 'n' Andy: A Social History of an American Phenomenon.* New York: Free Press, 1991.

Eucher, Charles. *Nobody Turn Me Around: A People's History of the 1963 March on Washington.* Boston: Beacon Press, 2010.

Fager, Charles E. *Selma 1965.* New York: Scribner's, 1974.

Fairclough, Adam. *To Redeem the Soul of America: The Southern Christian Leadership Conference and Martin Luther King, Jr.* Athens: University of Georgia Press, 1987.

Farber, David, and Beth Bailey. *The Columbia Guide to America in the 1960s.* New York: Columbia University Press, 2001.

Fife, Marilyn Diane. "Black Images in American TV: The First Two Decades." *Black Scholar* 6, no. 3 (November 1974): 7–15.

Fischer, Paul L., and Ralph L. Lowenstein. *Race and the News Media.* New York: Praeger, 1967.

Fiske, John. *Television Culture.* London: Methuen, 1987.

———. *Understanding Popular Culture.* Boston: Unwin Hyman, 1989.

Frank, Reuven. *Out of Thin Air: The Brief, Wonderful Life of Network News.* New York: Simon and Schuster, 1991.

Franklin, Donna L. *Ensuring Inequality: The Structural Transformation of the African-American Family.* New York: Oxford University Press, 1997.

Frazier, E. Frankin. *The Negro Family in the United States.* Chicago: University of Chicago Press, 1939.

———. *The Family: Its Function and Destiny.* New York: Harper and Row, 1959.

Friedan, Betty. *The Feminine Mystique.* New York: Dell, 1963.

Friendly, Fred. *Due to Circumstances Beyond Our Control*. New York: Vintage, 1967.

Gans, Herbert J. *Deciding What's News (25th Anniversary Edition)*. Evanston, Ill.: Northwestern University Press, 2004.

Garrow, David J. *Protest at Selma*. New Haven, Conn.: Yale University Press, 1978.

———. *Bearing the Cross: Martin Luther King, Jr. and the Southern Christian Leadership Conference*. New York: William Morrow, 1986.

Gentile, Thomas. *March on Washington: August 28, 1963*. Washington, D.C.: New Day, 1983.

Giddings, Paula. *Where and When I Enter: The Impact of Black Women on Race and Sex in America*. New York: Bantam, 1984.

Ginzburg, Carlo. "Morelli, Freud, and Sherlock Holmes: Clues and Scientific Method." *History Workshop* 9, no. 1 (Spring 1980): 9–36.

Gitlin, Todd. *The Whole World Is Watching: Mass Media in the Making and Unmaking of the New Left*. Berkeley: University of California Press, 1980.

———. *Inside Prime Time*. New York: Pantheon, 1983.

Gray, Herman. *Watching Race: Television and the Struggle for "Blackness."* Minneapolis: University of Minnesota Press, 1995.

———. "Remembering Civil Rights: Television, Memory, and the 1960s." In *The Revolution Wasn't Televised: Sixties Television and Social Conflict*, edited by Lynn Spigel and Michael Curtin, 349–58. New York: Routledge, 1997.

Halberstam, David. *The Children*. New York: Random House, 1998.

Hale, Grace Elizabeth. *Making Whiteness: The Culture of Segregation in the South, 1890–1940*. New York: Vintage, 1998.

Hall, Stuart. "What is This 'Black' in Black Popular Culture?" In *Black Popular Culture: A Project by Michele Wallace*, edited by Gina Dent, 21–36. Seattle: Bay, 1992.

Hallin, Daniel. *The "Uncensored War": The Media and Vietnam*. Berkeley: University of California Press, 1986.

Hansen, Drew D. *The Dream: Martin Luther King, Jr. and the Speech that Inspired a Nation*. New York: HarperCollins, 2003.

Haralovich, Mary Beth. "Sit-coms and Suburbs: Positioning the 1950s Homemaker." In Spigel and Mann, 111–142.

———. "*I Spy*'s 'Living Postcards': The Geo-Politics of Civil Rights." In *Television, History, and American Culture: Feminist Critical Essays*, edited by Mary Beth Haralovich and Lauren Rabinovitz, 98–119. Durham: Duke University Press, 1999.

Harper, Phillip Brian. "Extra-Special Effects: Televisual Representation and the Claims of 'The Black Experience.'" In *Living Color: Race and Television in the United States*, edited by Sasha Torres, 62–81. Durham: Duke University Press, 1998.

Hilmes, Michele. *Radio Voices: American Broadcasting 1922–1952*. Minneapolis: University of Minnesota Press, 1997.

Horne, Gerald. *Fire This Time: The Watts Uprising and the 1960s*. Charlottesville: University Press of Virginia, 1995.

Jackson, Harold. *From Amos 'n' Andy to I Spy: Chronology of Blacks in Prime Time Network Television Programming 1950–1964*. PhD diss., University of Michigan, 1982.

Jenkins, Henry. *Textual Poachers: Television Fans and Participatory Culture*. New York: Routledge, 1992.

Jhally, Sut, and Justin Lewis, *Enlightened Racism: The Cosby Show, Audiences, and the Myth of the American Dream*. Boulder: Westview, 1992.

Jones, Jacqueline. *Labor of Love, Labor of Sorrow: Black Women, Work, and the Family, From Slavery to the Present*. New York: Vintage, 1985.

Lentz, Richard. *Symbols, the News Magazines, and Martin Luther King.* Baton Rouge: Louisiana State University Press, 1990.

Levy, Peter. *Civil War on Race Street: The Civil Rights Movement in Cambridge, Maryland.* Gainesville: University Press of Florida, 2003.

Lewis, Justin. *The Ideological Octopus.* New York: Routledge, 1991.

Library of America. *Reporting Civil Rights.* New York: Library of Congress/Penguin Putnam, 2003.

Lipsitz, George. "The Meaning of Memory: Family, Class, and Ethnicity in Early Network Television Programs." In Spigel and Mann, 71–110.

MacDonald, J. Fred. *Blacks and White TV: African Americans in Television Since 1948.* Chicago: Nelson-Hall, 1992.

McCorkle, Susannah. "The Mother of Us All." *American Heritage* 45, no. 1 (February/ March, 1991).

McWhorter, Diane. *Carry Me Home: Birmingham, Alabama and the Climactic Battle of the Civil Rights Movement.* New York: Touchstone, 2001.

Metcalf, George R. *From Little Rock to Boston: The History of School Desegregation.* Westport: Greenwood, 1983.

Metz, Robert. *CBS: Reflections in a Bloodshot Eye* (Chicago: Playboy, 1975).

Monroe, William B. "Television: The Chosen Instrument of the Revolution." In Fischer and Lowenstein, 83–97.

Morley, David. *The Nationwide Audience.* London: BFI, 1980.

Moynihan, Daniel Patrick. *The Negro Family: The Case for National Action.* Washington, D.C.: U.S. Department of Labor, Office of Planning and Research, March 1965.

Pondillo, Bob. "Racial Discourse and Censorship on NBC-TV, 1948–1960." *Journal of Popular Film and Television* 33.2 (Summer 2005): 102–14.

Nadel, Alan. *Television in Black-and-White America: Race and National Identity.* Lawrence: University Press of Kansas, 2005.

Neal, Mark Anthony. *Soul Babies: Black Popular Culture and the Post-Soul Aesthetic.* New York: Routledge, 2002.

Peters, William. "The Visible and Invisible Images." In Fischer and Lowenstein, 81–82.

Raines, Howell. *My Soul is Rested: Movement Days in the Deep South Remembered.* New York: Putnam's, 1977.

Rainwater, Lee and William Y. Yancy. *The Moynihan Report and the Politics of Controversy.* Cambridge, Mass.: MIT Press, 1967.

Rhodes, Jane. *Framing the Black Panthers.* New York: New Press, 2007.

Roberts, Gene, and Hank Klibanoff. *The Race Beat: The Press, the Civil Rights Struggle, and the Awakening of a Nation.* New York: Knopf, 2006.

Rodriguez, Alisa Valdes. "'The Huxtable Effect' and Obama," *Alternet* (Nov. 2, 2008) http://www.alternet.org/blogs/video/105793/'the_huxtable_effect'_and_obama.

Smith, Howard K. *Events Leading Up to My Death: The Life of a Twentieth Century Reporter.* New York: St. Martin's, 1996.

Sokol, Jason. *There Goes My Everything: White Southerners in the Age of Civil Rights 1945–1975.* New York: Vintage, 2006.

Spigel, Lynn. *Make Room for TV: Television and the Family Ideal in Postwar America.* Chicago: University of Chicago Press, 1992.

Spigel, Lynn, and Denise Mann, eds. *Private Screenings: Television and the Female Consumer.* Minneapolis: University of Minnesota Press, 1992.

Staiger, Janet. *Media Reception Studies.* New York: NYU Press, 2005.

Steinberg, Cobbett S. *TV Facts.* New York: Facts on File, 1980.

Stumpf, Charles, and Tom Price. *Heavenly Days: The Story of* Fibber McGee and Molly. Waynesville, N.C.: World of Yesterday, 1987.

Sundquist, Eric J. *King's Dream.* New Haven: Yale University Press, 2009.

Toll, Robert C. *Blacking Up: The Minstrel Show in Nineteenth Century America.* New York: Oxford University Press, 1974.

Torres, Sasha. *Black, White, and in Color: Television and Black Civil Rights.* Princeton: Princeton University Press, 2003.

Tuchman, Gaye. *Making News: A Study in the Construction of Reality.* New York: Free Press, 1978.

Turner, Patricia A. *Ceramic Uncles and Celluloid Mammies.* New York: Anchor, 1994.

Vianello, Robert. "The Rise of the Telefilm and the Networks' Hegemony over the Motion Picture Industry." *Quarterly Review of Film Studies* 9, no. 3 (Summer 1984): 204–18.

Ward, Brian, ed. *Media, Culture, and the Modern African American Freedom Struggle.* Gainesville: University of Florida Press, 2001.

Watson, Mary Ann. *The Expanding Vista: American Television in the Kennedy Years.* New York: Oxford University Press, 1990.

Weisbrot, Robert. *Freedom Bound: A History of America's Civil Rights Movement.* New York: Penguin, 1991.

Williams, Juan. *Eyes on the Prize: America's Civil Rights Years, 1954–1965.* New York: Viking, 1987.

Williams, Linda. *Playing the Race Card: Melodramas of Black and White From Uncle Tom to O. J. Simpson.* Princeton: Princeton University Press, 2001.

Williams, Raymond. *The Long Revolution.* New York: Columbia University Press, 1961.

Winston, Michael R. "Racial Consciousness and the Evolution of Mass Communication in the United States." *Daedelus* 11, no. 3 (Fall 1982): 171–82.

Young, Andrew. *An Easy Burden: The Civil Rights Movement and the Transformation of America.* New York: HarperCollins, 1996.

INDEX

THE HISTORY OF COMMUNICATION

ANIKO BODROGHKOZY is an associate professor of media studies at the University of Virginia and the author of *Groove Tube: Sixties Television and the Youth Rebellion.*

The University of Illinois Press
is a founding member of the
Association of American University Presses.

University of Illinois Press
1325 South Oak Street
Champaign, IL 61820-6903
www.press.uillinois.edu